CRIME, DISSENT, AND
THE ATTORNEY GENERAL

The SAGE Series on
POLITICS AND THE LEGAL ORDER

Editor: **Joel B. Grossman,** University of Wisconsin

GEORGE F. COLE
Politics and the Administration of Justice

JOHN T. ELLIFF
Crime, Dissent, and the Attorney General:
   The Justice Department in the 1960's

GEORGE H. GADBOIS
The Supreme Court in the Indian Political System

SHELDON GOLDMAN
Politics and Policy-Making in the U.S. Court of Appeals

JOEL B. GROSSMAN
Judicial Policy-Making:
   The Supreme Court and the Sit-In Cases

DONALD P. KOMMERS
The Federal Constitutional Court of West Germany

FRED L. MORRISON
Courts and the Political Process in England

HARRY P. STUMPF
Lawyers and the Poor:
   An Exploratory Study in Local Bar Politics

CRIME, DISSENT, and the ATTORNEY GENERAL

The Justice Department in the 1960's

JOHN T. ELLIFF

Department of Politics
Brandeis University

 SAGE PUBLICATIONS Beverly Hills, London

For information address:
SAGE PUBLICATIONS, INC.
275 South Beverly Drive
Beverly Hills, California 90212

International Standard Book Number: 0-8039-0048-8

Library of Congress Catalog Card Number: 70 -127984

FIRST PRINTING

CONTENTS

EDITOR'S FOREWORD

This is the first volume in a series designed to explore the policy-making role and functions of courts and other agencies concerned with law in the political system. Forthcoming monographs will focus on both American and foreign court systems. The purpose of the series is twofold. First, the books will report on original research in such a way as to invite the attention of both scholars and students. Many could be used in political science courses on the judicial process, comparative politics, and related subjects. Second, it is hoped that the books will contribute to the development of enough data and information to justify a final volume on comparative judicial policy-making. Each of the authors was asked to focus on the *policy* dimensions of his subject, although each will necessarily also be concerned with the process by which policies are made.

It is appropriate that the first book in the series be concerned with an institution currently the object of great public controversy but also one that has lacked until now the treatment it deserves. Richard Harris' recently published journalistic account of the Department of Justice has focused attention on some aspects of its role and has provided an interesting, if one-sided, description of the contrasting policy goals of Attorneys General Ramsey Clark and John Mitchell.* Professor Elliff's book provides a more detached and analytic perspective which describes and compares Justice Department policy-making in several areas and over a longer period of time. Based on extensive interviews with past and present officials within the Department, and on access to some records, the book describes the interplay of forces which have led to the adoption of particular policies, particularly in the 1960's, to the Department assuming a much larger role in the criminal justice process than had ever before been the case. Unlike many professional studies Professor Elliff's book has a point of view. I do not mean that he merely expresses opinions; he marshalls his evidence and carefully—and persuasively—explains his concerns about the nationalization of the criminal justice process. Yet his views are clearly separable from his evidence and the value of his book is not limited to those who agree with him. No future writing or discussion of the Department of Justice can fail to come to terms with this volume.

—JOEL B. GROSSMAN
Madison, Wisconsin
April, 1971

*Richard Harris, *Justice* (New York: Avon Books, 1970).

About the Author

John T. Elliff is Assistant Professor in the Department of Politics, Brandeis University. He formerly taught in the Department of Political Science, Barnard College, Columbia University. He received his B.A. from DePauw University and his M.A. and Ph.D. from Harvard University where he taught in the Department of Government. He was a Research Fellow in Governmental Studies at the Brookings Institution during 1966-67. His study, "Aspects of Federal Civil Rights Enforcement: The Justice Department and the F.B.I., 1939-1964," appears in Volume V of *Perspectives in American History* published by the Charles Warren Center for Studies in American History, Harvard University.

ACKNOWLEDGMENTS

The students of Barnard and Columbia Colleges whom I have taught and met are responsible for the form and content of this study of the Justice Department's policies toward criminal justice, black militancy, and antiwar dissent. Their questions made it easier to concentrate on policy rather than on process. As much as a political scientist might like to make a more systematic and empirically verifiable contribution to his discipline's knowledge of basic political processes, his duty as a teacher impels him to come to grips with current political and legal controversies—to make some sense out of the flow of national events in the area of his purported expertise. While this book attempts to be objective, by the nature of its subject matter it inevitably engages the values and preferences of the writer. Fundamentally, I share my students' belief that the Justice Department must never be allowed to become an instrument for political repression. I hope this book points out viable ways to achieve that objective.

Many individuals have helped me to better understand the problems of civil liberties, the role of the Justice Department, and the politics of the legal system. The late Robert G. McCloskey, Jonathan Trumbull Professor of American History and Government at Harvard University, provided deep insights into the nature of the Supreme Court's position in American politics. He demonstrated by his example that scholarship and teaching are united by their concern for reason, common sense, and clarity of thought and expression. My father, Nathan T. Elliff, who served as an attorney in the Justice Department during 1940-46, shared with me some of his experience in dealing with problems of Selective Service enforcement and national security during World War II. Irving Dilliard, Stephen T. Early, Jr., Sidney Hook, Arthur E. Sutherland, and the late Daniel M. Berman each in his own way influenced my concern for individual rights and political liberty. My Columbia colleague Christopher Pyle offered useful information about current intelligence operations and valuable comments on portions of this manuscipt.

A Brookings Institution Research Fellowship enabled me to spend the 1966-67 academic year in Washington where I conducted interviews and examined Justice Department files for an earlier study of the history of civil rights enforcement. Others who contributed to my knowledge of the Department include Arthur B. Caldwell, Henry Putzel, Jr., Nathaniel Kossack, David Burnham, Cecil Poole, Hugh Nugent, James Flug, William Foley, Warren Olney, III, Archibald Cox, Charles Fahy, William P. Rogers, and the late Francis Biddle. The participants in the Legal Action Fund for Peace workshop on dissenters and demonstrators in June, 1970, widened my perspective. As editor of this series, Joel Grossman gave both encouragement and excellent critical suggestions. Responsibility for any misjudgements or inadequacies is of course my own. Finally, this book owes its existence to my wife, Mary, who knows better than I how formidable is the task of assuring dignity and fairness for every human being.

For my father

1

INTRODUCTION:

THE DEPARTMENT OF JUSTICE

During the decade of the 1960's the American legal system confronted difficult social and political problems challenging its capacity to maintain a stable, progressive framework of law. Public fears of crime and violence, vigorous protest against war and injustice made law enforcement policy a leading issue in American political life. Not since the 1930's, when courts and lawyers were blamed for defending constitutional doctrines that blocked New Deal reforms, had the legitimacy of legal institutions been so seriously questioned. Tensions reached a peak in 1968 as Congress enacted measures to punish political agitators and to reverse Supreme Court decisions, while Presidential candidate Richard Nixon made Court rulings and the Attorney General's policies a major campaign issue. Widespread civil unrest in the cities and massive demonstrations against the Vietnam war placed unique demands on the legal system to come up with ways to maintain order without sacrificing the standards of legality.

Standing at the center of the legal policy-making process was the United States Department of Justice. The Attorney General's decisions determined how federal executive power would be enlisted to cope with these stresses. Because his responsibilities span the full range of federal litigation in the courts, because he speaks directly to Congress and the White House and maintains close relationships with the leaders of the legal profession, the Attorney General is in a position to exercise crucial influence over the combination of executive, legislative, and judicial policies that comprise federal justice. Increasingly during the 1960's his words and deeds affected state and local governments as well. At the same time the Attorney General has become the focus of all the political pressures for change in law enforcement policy. There are insistent demands that legal institutions initiate reforms to bring an end to the inequities of poverty, racial discrimination, and military conscription. Alarmed by rising crime rates and perceiving a breakdown of public order, many others call for the preservation of stability and safety by punishing the disruptive and increasing police power. Some of the pressure comes from the police, who have a growing tendency "to see themselves as an independent, militant minority asserting itself in the political arena."[1]

To explore in greater depth how these forces have influenced the Attorney General and how the Justice Department has used its resources, the following chapters examine three broad subjects that often preoccupied the public and federal legal policy-making during the 1960's—criminal justice, black militancy, and antiwar dissent. Each chapter presents a narrative of Department policy development through 1969 in the context of unfolding events and changing executives. Since an outsider has little access to the internal deliberations of the Attorney General and his advisors, he can make only tentative suggestions as to why they acted in the way they did. He must concentrate on the content, impact, and consequences of Department policy, as revealed through careful examination of the public record. The task is to bring some coherence to the welter of speeches, reports, litigation, executive statements, legislative measures, judicial decisions, critical comments, and journalistic stories that are available to an informed citizen. The fifth chapter evaluates in somewhat more detail the policy implications of one specific change in the structure of law enforcement that took place in the late 1960's—the development of domestic intelligence surveillance of activist political organizations.

The Justice Department confronts problems of criminal justice and domestic unrest with an institutional apparatus that has evolved over a century since its creation in 1870. Although the Attorney General belonged to the first Presidential cabinet, the United States Attorneys initially had independent responsibility for government litigation in the federal judicial districts; and executive departments maintained their own legal officers to represent them in court. After the Civil War and Reconstruction had increased federal law enforcement activity, Congress established the Department of Justice, giving the Attorney General authority over the United States Attorneys and the law offices of the other departments. Previously a counselor to the President and a barrister before the Supreme Court, the Attorney General became "immersed in the details of departmental administration and litigation on a national scale."[2] His Department included several assistants and a Solicitor General to take charge of all government cases in the Supreme Court. Informal organization soon gave way to a series of Divisions each headed by an Assistant Attorney General. Creation of the office of Deputy Attorney General added a third Department-wide executive; and a Bureau of Prisons and a Bureau of Investigation were set up by the early twentieth century.

In the 1930's, during the years of John Dillinger, the Lindbergh kidnaping, and passage of numerous federal laws against interstate crime, Attorney General Homer Cummings reorganized the Department and gave it the form it retains today. He adopted "two general bases of organization—one according to subject matter, such as taxation, customs, lands; another according to the stages or functions in the process of law enforcement, such as investigations and trials, appeals, opinions, and administration."[3] Each of the six litigating Divisions at that time (Criminal, Antitrust, Tax, Claims, Customs, and Lands) had this dual framework. Cummings eased the workload of the Attorney General's office by creating the Office of Legal Counsel to prepare legal opinions and by assigning the Deputy Attorney General to take charge of administrative and personnel matters and legislation. President Roosevelt increased the Attorney General's burden in 1940, however, when he transferred the Immigration and Naturalization Service from the Labor Department to Justice for the purpose of centralizing law enforcement efforts related to national security.

Major structural changes since World War II have come in two stages, one in the mid-1950's under Attorney General Herbert Brownell and another a decade later. Brownell combined the Customs and Claims Divisions into a Civil Division, making room for establishment of a new Division without need of Congressional authorization. He used this opportunity to raise the Criminal Division's Internal Security Section, which by 1953 was staffed with sixty-five attorneys, to the status of an Internal Security Division. The Civil Rights Act of 1957 authorized an additional Assistant Attorney General's position, which was used to create a Civil Rights Division replacing the Criminal Division's small Civil Rights Section. Both new Divisions had civil as well as criminal law enforcement tasks and conducted litigation that was not normally left in the hands of the United States Attorneys.

Innovations during the 1960's brought entirely new functions to the Department. The Community Relations Service, originally placed in the Commerce Department by the 1964 Civil Rights Act and designed to conciliate racial conflicts in local communities, was transferred to Justice in 1966. Under the Law Enforcement Assistance Act of 1965, providing federal grants to state and local criminal justice systems, an Office of Law Enforcement Assistance was set up to administer the program. Title I of the 1968 Omnibus Crime Control Act enlarged the agency and renamed it the Law Enforcement Assistance Administration, empowered not only to make grants but to operate a National Institute of Law Enforcement and Criminal Justice to engage in research projects and serve as a center for the collection of crime statistics.

The Attorney General and the Deputy Attorney General share policy-making authority for the entire Department, although the Solicitor General and the F.B.I. Director have considerable autonomy and the United States Attorneys are given wide discretionary powers. The Attorney General's choice of subordinates and the signals he gives them provide direction for the entire federal legal establishment. Each Attorney General combines two roles, one political and the other quasi-judicial. In his political role he works closely with the President to serve the interests of the Administration and to minimize outside criticism. As the nation's chief law enforcement official, on the other hand, he must apply Congressional statutes impartially within constitutional bounds and take the lead in improving the administration of justice. Both roles may serve the Justice Department's interests. By presenting an image of unbiased professional expertise, he may prevent political attacks on his program, while an Attorney General who responds effectively to crucial demands for specific policies may not need to appear above politics.

Some commentators in and out of the legal community believe the Attorney General should always fulfill the quasi-judicial role of complete impartiality under the law and should abjure the political role of acceding to outside pressures. But such expectations are unrealistic in view of the way men are recruited for the job. Some, like J. Howard McGrath (1949-52), Herbert Brownell (1953-57), Robert Kennedy (1961-64), and John Mitchell (1969), take office after having been close campaign advisors to a victorious Presidential candidate who values their political counsel or wishes to reward their service to the party. Others make their way to the top by virtue of their useful political associations. For instance, Tom C. Clark (1945-49) had close associations with House Speaker Sam Rayburn and Senator Tom Connally, both fellow Texans, whose support President Truman needed to cement Congressional relations. His career as Governor of Michigan made Frank Murphy (1939-40) a symbol of concern for organized labor and civil liberties under President Roosevelt. Still other Attorneys General had extensive experience in the Justice Department. Robert Jackson (1940-41), Francis Biddle (1941-45), James McGranery (1952), William Rogers (1957-60), Nicholas Katzenbach (1964-66), and Ramsey Clark (1967-68) all served as subordinate executives in the Department. Jackson and Biddle were Solicitor General, and the others were Deputy Attorney General. They took office already familiar with the political context in which the Department operated.

An Attorney General who seems politically motivated may use his influence to improve the effectiveness of Department programs rather than to compromise that interest in favor of partisan advantage. Moreover, it may be unwise for an Attorney General to attempt political or professional tasks for which he is unsuited. Francis Biddle, who is often thought the ideal of professional objectivity, relied on his Deputies to act for him "in matters political." As a former chairman of the Democratic National Committee, J. Howard McGrath let his Deputies set the Department's law enforcement policies and devoted himself to "the general duties of the Attorney General, as a member of the President's Cabinet."[4] Each Attorney General combines as best as he can the political and technical-administrative roles, relying in part on his Deputy and other subordinates to fill in the gaps.

By tradition the Solicitor General's office has great autonomy in directing government cases before the Supreme Court. The quality of his legal arguments and his sensitivity to the Court's workload may gain the respect of the Justices. He decides carefully when to petition for certiorari if the government has lost in the lower courts; and he may even confess error, asking the Supreme Court to reverse a lower court decision in the government's favor. Since the Solicitor General's office recruits the best legal talent to prepare briefs, its prestige within the Justice Department is unmatched. As litigant and as *amicus curiae* in many leading cases, the Solicitor General is obliged not only to promote the policy of the executive branch, but also to give the Court his own considered opinion. The Nixon Administration acknowledged the neutrality of this position when it retained in office Solicitor General Erwin Griswold, former dean of the Harvard Law School, who had been appointed by President Johnson in 1967.

Despite his independence the Solicitor General must maintain good lawyer-client relations with the rest of the Justice

Department and occasionally approves petitions for certiorari that he may feel are unwise in order to preserve his power for more important cases. Infrequently the Attorney General may overrule a Solicitor General's decision to confess error and will assign the appropriate Assistant Attorney General to argue the case instead. But the Department seldom presuades the Supreme Court in such circumstances.[5] Since he does not become involved in a case until it reaches the appellate stage, the Solicitor General neither participates in the initial decisions to prosecute nor influences the trial record. Divorced from political controversy, he prescribes the government's ultimate legal position only after its implications have been defined in the lower courts.

The United States Attorneys in the federal judicial districts also have significant, though diminishing, independence because they "are locally based, trained professionals, not civil servants dispatched from Washington; they owe their appointments in part to their political standing and support in the area where they serve; they perform non-routine tasks that require discretion and defy standardization."[6] As late as 1952 a management study concluded that the Department failed almost completely to make any provision for supervising and coordinating the United States Attorneys' offices. In response to this criticism Attorney General Brownell prohibited them from engaging in outside law practice, set up an Executive Office for United States Attorneys under the Deputy Attorney General, and inaugurated a statistical reporting system.[7] United States Attorneys continue to be appointed in consultation with the state's Senators or party leaders of the President's party; and they still are influenced by local politics, the character of the federal judges before whom they practice, and their own sense of professional expertise.

The Divisions in Washington use their formal powers of supervision over the United States Attorneys in three ways: "by establishing general policies and rules of procedure; by direct supervision from Washington of the handling of specific cases; and by actually taking over cases itself."[8] A United States Attorneys Manual summarizes general rules and lays down guidelines for the exercise of prosecutor's discretion. For example, civil rights cases and internal security cases, among others, may not be prosecuted without approval from Washington. Nevertheless, in larger districts where they have staffs of specialized assistants, the United States Attorneys may consider themselves the equal of an Assistant Attorney General.

Recruitment of legal personnel for the litigating Divisions was reformed in the 1950's after a management study reported that methods of appointment and removal were "founded upon considerations other than competency and satisfactory performance." Attorney General Brownell instituted a recruitment program for Honor Law Graduates selected "solely on the basis of professional training and accomplishment and scholastic standing."[9] By the mid-1960's the annual class of Honor Graduate recruits reached one hundred, thus imposing a systematic selection procedure onto what had been a highly personalized pattern relying largely on political contacts and varying from Division to Division. The Department came to be staffed by highly competent attorneys, many of them young men who would later move on to private practice. Since the career staff is no longer tied politically to any Administration, only the top executives of the Divisions were replaced in 1961 and 1969. (No change occurred in the Internal Security Division where J. Walter Yeagley had remained Assistant Attorney General since the Eisenhower Administration.)

Because their experience and training encourage them to define problems according to the facts of specific cases, Department lawyers tend to conceive policy issues in terms of particular prosecutions and lawsuits. While this has the advantage of compelling executives to concentrate on the immediate effects of their decisions, it hampers their ability to develop larger policy goals. Legal and factual idiosyncracies of a single case may force high-level choices that either have little relevance to other matters or fail to anticipate the variety of later cases. When decisions are made case by case, with more reference to what is needed for the present than to what is desired for the future, it becomes difficult to achieve broad program objectives. The litigating Divisions' inadequacy as sources of policy innovation was one reason why Robert Kennedy established an Office of Criminal Justice in 1964 and why Ramsey Clark created a Civil Disturbance Group in 1967. Law enforcement policy meant not only patterns of litigation, but standards for the reform of criminal justice and the organization of resources to maintain public order in the face of riots or demonstrations. Thus Department executives needed the advice and skills of men with wider experience in the administration of justice who were recruited from universities and urban police departments to supplement the litigating Divisions.

Perhaps the most difficult policies to define and evaluate involve the Department's investigative powers. As one Attorney General observed, a prosecutor "can have citizens investigated and, if he is that kind of person, he can have this done to the tune of public statements and veiled or unveiled intimidations. Or the prosecutor may choose a more subtle course and simply have a citizen's friends interviewed."[10] Short of arrest and trial, these actions may escape judicial scrutiny. While the federal government has a number of separate investigative agencies (the Secret Service, the Alcohol and Tobacco Tax Unit of the Treasury Department, the Intelligence Division of the Internal Revenue Service, the Postal Inspection Service, and the Federal Narcotics Bureau, among others), the largest and most visible and controversial is the Federal Bureau of Investigation. In its information-gathering role the F.B.I. performs two functions for the Department—investigation and intelligence. Investigations are tied to specific criminal violations, while intelligence serves a variety of purposes. Unlike state and local police, the F.B.I. seldom makes arrests without prior approval by a federal prosecuting attorney who reviews the facts before authorizing the arrest.

Criminal investigations, involving interviews with potential witnesses and suspects, examination of documents, and observation of suspect behavior, may begin in several ways. The F.B.I. has broad authority to make investigations on its own initiative; but there are certain offenses where special considerations require approval of an investigation by a Division. Such matters may include newly enacted statutes and what one directive called subjects of "unusual importance to the Government and to the public, e.g., civil rights, internal security, and antitrust cases."[11] In some categories a distinction is made between preliminary investigations, which the F.B.I. may conduct on its own, and full or complete investigations requiring Division clearance. Certain investigative techniques, such as wiretapping and electronic eavesdropping, must be approved by the Attorney General. If an F.B.I. field office is reluctant to bear full responsibility for an investigative decision, it may seek prior approval from the United States Attorney's office, from F.B.I. headquarters in Washington, or from a Division, even if clearance is not mandatory.

The F.B.I. secures intelligence information primarily to protect national security and, more recently, to combat organized crime and to anticipate civil disorders. While criminal investigations may contribute data to its intelligence effort, the F.B.I. gathers intelligence reports and undertakes intelligence surveillance even if it expects no specific prosecution to result. It receives inside information from undercover informants (who are seldom F.B.I. agents), it conducts electronic surveillance, it collects published materials, and it receives data from local police and other members of the national intelligence community—the military, the State Department, the C.I.A., the Secret Service. If criminal offenses are discovered in the course of intelligence surveillance, informants may be released to testify for the government; but when the need to keep up an informant's coverage outweighs the desire for his testimony, the prosecution seeks other witnesses. Inevitably, the F.B.I.'s intelligence role is difficult to separate from its criminal investigative function.

F.B.I. Director J. Edgar Hoover's position has been politically secure since 1933 when he survived the change of Administrations. His champion then was Supreme Court Justice Harlan F. Stone, who as Attorney General had advanced Hoover to head the Bureau in 1924. Hearing rumors that Hoover might be replaced, Justice Stone wrote President Roosevelt's advisor Felix Frankfurter, "He removed from the Bureau every man as to whose character there was any ground for suspicion. He refused to yield to any kind of political pressure; he appointed to the Bureau men of intelligence and education; strove to build up a morale such as should control such an organization. He withdrew it wholly from its extra-legal activities and made it an efficient organization for the investigation of criminal offenses against the United States." Frankfurter passed this message on to the President, who replied favorably.[12]

J. Edgar Hoover has developed a staff system which is not only honest and devoted to the interests of the Bureau, but flexible enough to provide the Director with intensive support whenever he calls for it. In return Hoover gives his agents unqualified backing, defending their reputations against outside criticism. He knows how bureaucratic machinery operates, keeping his own lines of communication open to the White House and to other departments. The Director may adjust F.B.I. operations to fit the priorities of a new Attorney General: as Francis Biddle recalled, "He knew how to flatter his superior, and he had the means of making him comfortable."[13] His ability to get appropriations from Congress is based on his sure knowledge of the Bureau's activities and his keen sense of Congressional sentiment. In creating the popular image of the F.B.I., he combined skill in public relations with an instinct for inspiring Americans' admiration for courageous police work. By maintaining the general public's confidence in the effectiveness of federal law enforcement, Hoover's prestige has been a valuable resource for the Justice Department.

These are the basic outlines of the Justice Department, as headed by four Attorneys General from 1961 through 1969. Robert Kennedy, who advised his brother on a wide range of domestic and foreign policy matters, made the Department a center of action and glamor with highest priority given to measures against organized crime and racial discrimination. Before leaving office to run for the Senate in 1964, he made a commitment to a program of criminal justice reform that was to involve the Department more deeply than ever before in policy-making for state and local law enforcement. Nicholas Katzenbach came to the Department in 1961 as Assistant Attorney General in charge of the Office of Legal Counsel and in 1962 became Deputy Attorney General. He succeeded Kennedy in 1964 and held office until late in 1966 when President Johnson appointed him Under Secretary of State. Ramsey Clark, son of Supreme Court Justice and former Attorney General Tom C. Clark, also joined the Department in 1961 as Assistant Attorney General for the Lands Division. He served as Katzenbach's Deputy and as acting Attorney General before his appointment to head the Department in 1967.

Although Katzenbach's austere personality contrasted sharply with Clark's unassuming manner, both shared a conception of the values federal justice should serve that was determined largely by their experience under the Kennedy Administration with civil rights problems in the South. "Out of this period," Katzenbach has written, "it was possible to learn that law and justice could equate—roughly, and with much sweat and pain. It was also possible to learn—indeed, I learned it, too—that government could be cynical and corrupt, that law could in these United States be an instrument of wrong, and that it was terribly difficult to put that kind of a system right."[14]

Attorney General John Mitchell, who took office under the Nixon Administration in 1969, lacked that kind of direct experience with the practical side of law enforcement. As a New York lawyer specializing in state and municipal finance, he emerged from the obscurity of Richard Nixon's law firm to become a trusted political advisor and later campaign manager for the Presidential candidate. He was closer to the Chief Executive than any other Attorney General in recent years, except Robert Kennedy. Since Nixon had made Ramsey Clark the object of strong campaign criticism, Mitchell was bound to set himself apart from his predecessor. One of the most significant questions raised in the following chapters is how the change of Administrations in 1969 affected the Justice Department's policies.

Throughout the 1960's the Attorney General played an increasingly visible role in the development of national law enforcement policy. If there is a single theme for the decade, it is greater centralization of criminal justice policy-making in the hands of the national government. What pressures brought it about? What are the consequences of increased federal power in this area, both for the Justice Department itself and for the entire legal system? A survey of how decisions were made and the forces that affected them is necessary for an evaluation of the advantages and disadvantages of the Department's growing influence. Does concentration of leadership responsibility under national executives improve the coherence and effectiveness of law enforcement programs? Or do the intense demands of national politics restrict the Attorney General's ability to provide consistent and useful guidance for the administration of justice?

These questions about the trend toward nationalization of criminal law enforcement must be coupled with a concern for the effects of Justice Department actions on basic civil liberties. The Attorney General's decisions have an impact on the Supreme Court's capacity to protect constitutional rights and on Congressional attempts to limit the Court's powers. In its own operations and by its influence over state and local agencies, the Department helps determine the conditions for political liberty in the United States. How did pressures to maintain order in the face of domestic unrest influence the Department's policies? To what extent may centralization of law enforcement responsibility threaten the freedom to protest and dissent? Expansion of domestic intelligence gathering during recent years must be examined carefully in order to determine what restraints should be placed on the proliferation of surveillance over political activities. Only by reviewing in detail the measures taken against black militants and antiwar demonstrators can we understand adequately the scope of federal power and the barriers to potential political repression.

2

CRIMINAL

JUSTICE

Before the 1960's criminal justice in America was primarily a matter of state and local concern. Each state maintained its own legal code and judicial structure, each city its own police force and prosecutor's office. Except for informal cooperation between local and federal law enforcement agencies in the solution of interstate crimes and other federal offenses, policy-making for criminal justice was largely decentralized. The Justice Department's role was limited to developing standards for federal agencies and influencing Congress and the Supreme Court to adopt appropriate constitutional and legislative rules governing criminal procedures in federal courts. Neither Congress nor the Justice Department felt responsible for the great bulk of criminal law enforcement activity in cities and states.

Beginning in the 1930's the United States Supreme Court had attempted to develop rudimentary constitutional standards for criminal due process in the states. Perhaps awakened to the realities of arbitrary law enforcement practices by the 1931 report of the Wickersham Commission, appointed by President Hoover to make the first national crime study, and by the pioneering field research of scholars like Roscoe Pound and

Felix Frankfurter, the Supreme Court under Chief Justice Charles Evans Hughes began to define the elemental rights of criminal defendants under the due process clause of the Fourteenth Amendment.[1] Accused persons had the right to consult legal counsel before trial, the right to a trial undistorted by the pressure of community hysteria, and the right not to have a coerced confession introduced as evidence against them.[2] The Justice Department supported the Court's efforts through its Civil Rights Section, established in 1939 by Attorney General Frank Murphy. It brought occasional prosecutions against police brutality and lynching under a revived Reconstruction statute making it a federal crime willfully to deprive a person of his constitutional rights under color of law.[3]

The Supreme Court was reluctant, however, to apply the entire Bill of Rights to the states. During the 1940's and 1950's it adopted a cautious intermediate position. The Justice Department's enforcement of the civil rights statute was strictly limited when the Court ruled that specific intent to deprive a person of his constitutional rights must be shown.[4] Instead of requiring that all indigent defendants be supplied free legal counsel, the Court held that states had to assign counsel only in capital cases and where special circumstances demonstrated a defendant's inability to defend himself effectively.[5] Confessions were excluded as evidence in state trials only when the defense could show that police coercion had compelled involuntary admissions from the defendant.[6] Although the Court decided that local police could not engage in unreasonable search and seizure practices, it refused to bar introduction of illegally seized evidence in state trials unless the police used especially shocking methods.[7] The prevailing doctrine guiding the Court's interpretation of the due process clause was a "fundamental fairness" standard which meant that only the most essential of the procedural safeguards in the Bill of Rights would apply to the states as well as the federal government. Thus some provisions of the Bill of Rights, like the guarantee of grand jury indictment, were not required at the state level, while watered-down versions of other rights were applied to the states. The theory behind this doctrine, as explained by Justice Felix Frankfurter and others, was that states should have the opportunity to develop a variety of alternative means for protecting defendants' rights since the rules embodied in the Bill of Rights were not the only way to design a fair system of criminal justice.

Implicit in the Supreme Court's policy before 1960 was an estimate of the practical obstacles to implementation of strict Bill of Rights procedures in the states as well as a belief in the advantages of having states themselves undertake criminal justice reforms after the Court had given the initial impetus to change. The potential hostility that might have been aroused by more stringent judicial rules was indicated when the Supreme Court ruled in Mallory v. United States (1957) that a confession was inadmissible in a federal trial if obtained by police while failing to arraign the defentant promptly before a judicial officer.[8] The Mallory case arose in Washington, D.C., and since the issue involved interpretation of the Federal Rules of Criminal Procedure adopted by Congress, no constitutional principle was yet at stake. Upon the urgings of the District of Columbia police department, Congressional critics proposed to amend the federal rules to reverse the decision by providing that no confession could be declared inadmissible solely because of delay before arraignment. Although the House passed the measure along with a series of other anti-Court bills in 1958, it failed to win Senate approval.[9] Had the Supreme Court attempted to impose similarly strict constitutional standards on the states, the prospects for Congressional reaction and non-compliance might have increased, especially during the 1950's when the Court was encountering serious difficulty because of its racial desegregation rulings and its restrictions on anti-Communist measures.

In the 1960's the Supreme Court moved forward much more rapidly to change state criminal procedures, initiating a sweeping re-examination of law enforcement throughout the nation. Consequently, the Justice Department was called upon to develop federal programs that would improve the fairness and effectiveness of the administration of justice by offering greater expertise and resources. At the same time crime and violence became a national political issue, taxing the Department's capacity to exercise leadership in bringing coherence to the work of the Supreme Court and Congress, the legal profession, and state and local governments. Courts and lawyers began pulling in one direction, legislators and police in another. By the end of the decade these efforts became fragmented among competing groups with widely different conceptions of the problem of crime. Justice Department policies failed to prevent the disintegration of what began as a creative endeavor uniting lawyers, judges, Congressmen, and law enforcement experts in a movement toward progressive reform of criminal justice in America.

1. MAPP, GIDEON, AND THE REFORM OF FEDERAL CRIMINAL JUSTICE, 1961-63

The Supreme Court's caution in dealing with state criminal justice seemed to be partially vindicated, if judgment is based on the efforts of state legislatures to adopt certain procedural reforms. By 1960 a majority of the states had enacted exclusionary rules, going beyond the Court's requirements and excluding illegally seized evidence from introduction in criminal trials.[10] Moreover, all but a few states offered some form of legal assistance to indigent defendants even in cases where current constitutional standards did not compel provision of free legal counsel. While these reforms may have shown that improvement of criminal justice in the states was possible without Supreme Court pressure, they also encouraged a belief that the states would be receptive to new judicial initiatives designed to speed the process of change.

The first case in the 1960's to reflect this belief was Mapp v. Ohio (1961) where the Court applied the exclusionary rule to evidence obtained by unreasonable search and seizure methods and offered in state criminal trials. Justice Tom C. Clark's opinion for the Court noted the significant number of states which had recently adopted exclusionary rules because other remedies, such as criminal prosecution or official discipline of offending policemen, had proved "worthless and futile."[11] The Court concluded that the only effective deterrent to illegal search and seizure was to render useless in court the evidence secured by improper police practices. While Justice Clark's opinion recognized that some criminals would go free because clear evidence of their guilt might not be admissible in court, he was unwilling to assume "that, as a practical matter, adoption of the exclusionary rule fetters law enforcement," since the F.B.I. had no difficulty under the federal rule and the states themselves seemed to be moving inexorably toward it.[12] Three dissenters joining in an opinion by Justice John Marshall Harlan found, however, that the indications of state movement toward the exclusionary rule pointed "away from the need of replacing voluntary state action with federal compulsion [because] preservation of a proper balance between state and federal responsibility demands patience on the part of those who might like to see things move faster among the States." Justice Harlan thought the Court should continue "to forbear from fettering the States with an adamant rule which may embarrass them in coping with their own peculiar problems in criminal law enforcement."[13]

The dissenting Justices in Mapp v. Ohio questioned not only the merits of the decision, but the propriety of adopting such a sweeping rule in a case argued on other grounds where only one amicus curiae (the American Civil Liberties Union) raised the exclusionary issue and the parties did not address it. They would have preferred to set the case down for rehearing to give the Court the benefit of full briefing and oral argument on the issue. If the problems of police misconduct in securing evidence had been fully considered, the Court's attention might have been directed to the 1961 Report of the United States Commission on Civil Rights which addressed the subject of police brutality. The Civil Rights Commission confirmed the majority's view that unlawful police action was "a serious and continuing problem in many parts of the United States" and that present remedies were inadequate. "State and local officials—police commanders, prosecutors, and others in positions of authority—who have the immediate responsibility and most effective means for preventing such abuses sometimes do not use their powers," the commission observed. "Police commanders at times take a protective attitude toward miscreant officers, and local prosecutors rarely bring criminal actions against them." The federal civil rights statutes providing criminal sanctions and civil liability for police violations of constitutional rights were also found to be ineffective because of inherent difficulties of proof. Successful federal prosecutions and private damage suits against policemen were rare.[14]

Although the Civil Rights Commission reinforced the Mapp majority's perception of the failure of many local criminal justice systems to control illegal police conduct, the commission's report did not mention judicial reforms like the exclusionary rule as a solution. Instead it emphasized, "The most effective 'remedies' for illegal official violence are those that tend to prevent such misconduct rather than those which provide sanctions after the fact. The application of professional standards to the selection and training of policemen is one such preventive measure." The commission recommended, therefore, that the federal government provide financial assistance to state and local governments for the purpose of encouraging police departments to develop and maintain "such positive programs as good pay, high recruit selection standards, and training in scientific crime detection, in human relations, and in police administration." Fundamental improvement in the quality of police practices required more than legal rules; it demanded financial resources and incentives that could only come from combined executive and Congressional policies, not judicial decisions.

Attorney General Robert Kennedy was in a crucial position to help implement this proposal and, if necessary, to communicate the commission's views to the Supreme Court. The latter opportunity was foreclosed, however, by the Court's decision to consider the exclusionary issue early in 1961 before the new Attorney General could digest the commission's findings. Preoccupied with more pressing civil rights matters in the South and the development of an organized crime program, Kennedy and his aides did not follow up on the commission's report. Instead of focusing broadly on the problems of criminal justice throughout the nation, Attorney General Kennedy concentrated at first on the needs of the federal legal system. In 1962 he appointed a Committee on Poverty and the Administration of Federal Criminal Justice, chaired by Dean Francis A. Allen, to study and recommend improvements in the practices of federal courts for handling indigent defendants. In addition, Kennedy directed the Department to develop an effective and realistic legislative proposal for the regulation of wiretapping by federal agencies.

The wiretapping issue had posed difficult legal questions for the Supreme Court since it first considered the subject in Olmstead v. United States (1928), ruling that wiretapping was not covered by Fourth Amendment standards for reasonable search and seizure.[15] In the 1934 Federal Communications Act Congress had outlawed the interception and divulgence of telephone conversations, but federal and state police agencies continued to engage in wiretapping. The Justice Department took the position that the 1934 act did not prohibit wiretapping alone, only tapping followed by divulgence, and that it was not a divulgence when wiretap information was shared within the government.[16] Since wiretapping was illegal, even if not unconstitutional, the Supreme Court applied the federal exclusionary rule to the introduction of evidence obtained by wiretapping in federal courts.[17] Before Mapp v. Ohio, however, the Court permitted state courts to admit wiretap evidence in state trials.[18] The decision in Mapp extending the exclusionary rule to illegally seized evidence in state courts indicated that the Supreme Court might no longer allow the use of evidence obtained by wiretapping in state prosecutions.

Since Attorney General Kennedy's first wiretapping bill was prepared before the Mapp decision, it concentrated on the federal level; for there was no immediate need to authorize wiretapping by local police who could tap and use the resulting evidence with relative impunity, depending on the nature of state statutory regulations. The Justice Department's policy for enforcing the 1934 act's ban on wiretapping was not to prosecute state and local law enforcement agents who violated the act. In 1961 the Justice Department submitted to Congress a proposal to authorize federal wiretapping in organized crime cases and certain other serious offenses, i.e., kidnaping and narcotics violations, under specified conditions. Those conditions acknowledged the possibility that the Supreme Court might reverse Olmstead, and subject wiretapping to Fourth Amendment standards for reasonable search and seizure. Among the conditions the Department requested for a federal wiretap was a judicial warrant, issued for a maximum forty-five days upon a showing by law enforcement officials that the particular telephone was being or about to be used in the commission of a crime and that no other means existed to obtain the evidence. Because national security considerations appeared to demand complete secrecy, the Department asked that the Attorney General be able to authorize taps for national security purposes on his own, without a judicial warrant and with the resulting evidence admissible in court, if he believed that application to a federal judge "would be prejudicial to the national interest."[19]

After Mapp v. Ohio the Department reconsidered its position on local wiretapping, consulting outside attorneys and law enforcement officials before revising its proposal. Anticipating that the Supreme Court might rule illegal wiretap evidence inadmissible in state courts, the Department broadened its bill to authorize wiretapping by local police under conditions similar to those proposed earlier for federal wiretapping. The most stringent limitation was placed on the kinds of crimes for which states could tap. Under the Attorney General's 1962 bill, states would be permitted to wiretap only with a court warrant in the investigation of murder, kidnaping, extortion, bribery, or narcotics offenses. The measure also added a rigid system for reporting all wiretaps and a total prohibition on the use of unauthorized wiretap evidence in state or federal courts, agencies, and legislative hearings.[20] Its effect would have been, therefore, to curtail the previously ungoverned wire-tapping practices of state and local police, while permitting federal agencies to use in court the results of wiretapping hitherto used only within the executive branch. To limit the scope of local wiretapping, the bill attempted the novel step of laying down by federal statute an exclusionary rule for state criminal procedures.

Although this carefully drafted proposal seemed to offer a middle ground that would satisfy Congress and help clarify a tangled legal situation, it did not come to a vote. Several local police chiefs complained before the Senate Judiciary Com-mittee about the narrowness of the category of cases in which wiretapping would be allowed, while the American Civil Liberties Union charged that any wiretapping constituted "an unlimited and unlimitable general search. . .contrary to some of the most fundamental principles of a free society." New York district attorney Frank Hogan expressed what was probably Attorney General Kennedy's prime motive for backing the bill when he testified that wiretapping was "the single most valuable weapon in law enforcement's fight against organized crime."[21] But the advice of such professionals was not enough to convince Congress of the immediate need for new legislation, especially since there was little public pressure or concern about crime or privacy as national issues. In addition, according to former Solicitor General Archibald Cox, there was "some reason to believe that F.B.I. Director Hoover. . .placed such value upon uncontrolled discretion to use electronic devices in cases 'involving the national security'. . .that he opposed any new legislation."[22] The wiretap bill remained part of the Department's legislative program through 1965, but made little headway. In the meantime federal agencies continued to wiretap for internal intelligence purposes, supposedly with the Attorney General's specific approval for each tap; and the F.B.I. began to rely more heavily on other forms of electronic surveillance or "bugging" that did not intercept telephone lines and therefore did not require the Attorney General's specific permission.

The absence of general public concern about crime, reflected in the lack of pressure for a wiretap bill, permitted an atmosphere to develop in which all the institutions of the federal legal system could focus on improving the fairness of criminal justice. In 1963 the Attorney General, Congress, and the Supreme Court took major steps in this direction, concentrating first on the rights of indigent defendants to counsel. The Allen Report on Poverty and the Administration of Federal Criminal Justice, prepared at the request of Attorney General Kennedy, found that the integrity of the adversary system was "imperiled by the large numbers of accused persons unable to employ counsel or to meet even modest bail requirements and by the large, but indeterminate, number of persons, able to pay some part of the costs of defense, but unable to finance a full and proper defense. Persons suffering such disabilities are incapable of providing the challenges that are indispensible to satisfactory operation of the system. . . .Loss in vitality of the adversary system, thereby occasioned, significantly endangers the basic interests of a free community."[23] Even though the

Supreme Court had long required counsel for all indigent defendants at the federal level, the Allen report contended that existing provisions were inadequate and led Attorney General Kennedy to propose the Criminal Justice Act, introduced in the Senate with bipartisan support from such conservatives as James Eastland of Mississippi, Roman Hruska of Nebraska, and Sam J. Ervin of North Carolina. As passed in 1964, the measure guaranteed counsel at every stage of federal judicial proceedings, made available auxiliary investigative and expert services necessary to prepare the defendant's case, and covered all federal defendants financially unable to obtain an adequate defense, not just the destitute.[24]

Similar standards for defender services had earlier been recommended to the states by an American Bar Association committee and the National Legal Aid and Defender Association, although in 1963 only three states were completely covered at the felony court level by such a comprehensive defender system.[25] In the context of these federal and state reform efforts, the Supreme Court decided to abandon its earlier standard requiring counsel for indigent state defendants only in capital cases and where special circumstances indicated the defendant could not effectively defend himself. In Gideon v. Wainwright (1963) the Court ruled that all indigent defendants must be guaranteed the assistance of counsel.[26] Since twenty-two states had joined in an amicus curiae brief urging the result, the unanimous decision caused little adverse reaction. While it did not specify in detail the scope of constitutionally required defender services or the applicability of its principles to minor offenses, the Court gave impetus to state reform activities which were further encouraged by the A.B.A.'s special committee on defense of indigent persons.

Another result of the Allen Committee's report was increased attention to the unfairness of the bail system. Bail reform gained momentum in the early 1960's largely because of the success of the Vera Foundation's Manhattan Bail Project, which demonstrated the inequities of pretrial detention procedures and the effectiveness of a system permitting reliable suspects to be released on their own recognizance without having to post money bail. Other successful experiments with alternatives to bail took place in Detroit, San Francisco, St. Louis, Tulsa, and Illinois.[27] After the Allen report expressed concern about federal bail procedures, Attorney General Kennedy convened a National Conference on Bail and Criminal Justice in May, 1964. A working paper for the conference identified the fundamental problem: "In a system which grants pretrial liberty for money, those who can afford a bondsman go free; those who cannot, stay in jail."[28] Working closely with Senator Sam Ervin, the Justice Department subsequently drafted a federal Bail Reform Act modeled on the Manhattan Bail Project. Enacted in 1966, the measure provided for pretrial release of those federal criminal suspects charged with non-capital offenses whose community and family ties and past record indicated they would appear for trial. By eliminating most of the money bail system, the act was designed to insure that suspects would not needlessly be detained because of their financial status. Because pretrial detention was now based explicitly on the single ground that the defendant was likely to flee before trial, the Bail Reform Act prevented federal judges from detaining suspects in non-capital cases who might appear only "dangerous." According to prevailing legal doctrine, the sole legitimate purpose of the bail system was to assure the presence of the accused at his trial.[29] The act's sponsors did not expect the release of a significant number of dangerous suspects, nor did they anticipate that highly publicized arrests of newly released defendants in the District of Columbia might be used to discredit the measure.

Passage of the Criminal Justice Act and the start toward bail reform marked the highpoint of cooperation among Congress, the legal profession, and the courts, with the Justice Department serving as the agent to coordinate their efforts. Attorney General Kennedy had used the Allen Committee and the Bail Conference as vehicles for bringing expert opinion to the attention of Congressmen and keeping pace with the Supreme Court's growing concern for fairness in criminal procedures. Although Kennedy wanted at the same time to strengthen law enforcement through adoption of a carefully drafted wire-tapping statute, neither crime rates nor public pressures made Congress receptive to his request. By the end of 1964, however, new Supreme Court decisions and increased political sensitivity to crime problems would change the environment for Department policy-making.

2. ESCOBEDO AND CRIMINAL JUSTICE AS A NATIONAL ISSUE, 1964

By 1964 a broadly based movement toward the improvement of criminal justice through revision of procedural rules was underway and was probably given greater momentum because of the drive to end racial discrimination. As A. Kenneth Pye observed, "Concern with civil rights almost inevitably required attention to the rights of defendants in criminal cases. It is hard to conceive of a Court that would accept the challenge of guaranteeing the rights of Negroes to equality before the law and at the same time do nothing to ameliorate the invidious discrimination between rich and poor which existed in the criminal process. It would have been eqully anomalous for such a Court to ignore the clear evidence that members of disadvantaged groups bore the brunt of most unlawful police activity."[30] Since Congress and the Justice Department were taking up the burden of combatting racial discrimination under the Civil Rights Act of 1964, the Supreme Court was freed to look elsewhere for pressing social needs that might be satisfied by judicial intervention. Its apparently successful effort to inspire reapportionment of state legislatures may have reinforced the Court's confidence in its capacity to provide redress for basic grievances. The development of egalitarian constitutional doctrines received explicit support from Attorney General Kennedy, not only by his civil rights program and his endeavors to reform federal criminal justice, but also through the Justice Department's endorsement of the "one man, one vote" standard for legislative apportionment.[31] In this atmosphere the Supreme Court, having been rendered somewhat more activist by the appointment of Secretary of Labor Arthur Goldberg to replace Justice Felix Frankfurter, took major new initiatives to extend Bill of Rights guarantees to state criminal procedures and police practices.

One of the Court's leading decisions representative of its reluctance to incorporate procedural guarantees from the Bill of Rights into the Fourteenth Amendment had been Adamson v. California (1948), holding that the full scope of the Fifth

Amendment privilege against self-incrimination did not apply to the states.[32] Concurring and dissenting opinions by Justices Frankfurter, Black, and Murphy had explored in great depth the historical and practical arguments for and against an interpretation of the due process clause that would absorb the entire Bill of Rights; and four dissenting Justices had endorsed that position. Now in 1964 the Court was ready to reconsider whether the same constitutional protection for a defendant's right to remain silent should apply to both federal and state criminal justice. While only Justices Black and Douglas still defended complete incorporation of the entire Bill of Rights, Chief Justice Warren and Justice Goldberg joined an opinion by Justice William Brennan declaring that the Fifth Amendment's protection against compulsory self-incrimination applied with full force to the states. Justice Brennan's theory for interpreting the Fourteenth Amendment required that, if a specific guarantee in the Bill of Rights were to be incorporated into the due process clause, the right must not be a "watered-down, subjective version" of the federal standard. The Mapp and Gideon decisions had enforced the Fourth Amendment prohibition against unreasonable search and seizure and the Sixth Amendment right to counsel guarantee upon the states "according to the same standards that protect those rights against federal encroachment." To have different rules for determining an accused person's right to silence in state and federal proceedings "would be incongruous."[33]

Even more significant was the Court's assumption that its precedents dealing with the admissibility of confessions had already applied the federal standard for "free and voluntary" confessions to the states and, moreover, that the common standard was based on the privilege against self-incrimination. Justice Brennan's opinion noted that counsel for the state in Malloy v. Hogan shared his premise "that an accused is privileged against incriminating himself. . .in the police station." The state's brief argued that there should be a uniform rule governing compulsory self-incrimination "in the jail house, the grand jury room, or the witness stand in a public trial" because a single standard "would not only clarify the principles involved in confession cases, but would assist the States significantly in their efforts to comply with the limitations placed upon them by the Fourteenth Amendment."[34] Accepting the state's invitation to establish a general formulation of the Fifth Amendment privilege, Justice Brennan observed "that the American system of criminal prosecution is accusatorial, not inquisitorial, and that the Fifth Amendment privilege is its essential mainstay. . . .Governments, state and federal, are thus constitutionally compelled to establish guilt by evidence independently and freely secured, and may not by coercion prove a charge against an accused out of his own mouth." The constitution guaranteed "the right of a person to remain silent unless he chooses to speak in the unfettered exercise of his own will, and to suffer no penalty. . .for such silence.[35]

While the Court was considering the overall scope of the privilege against self-incrimination, it confronted another case that forced it to explain what the privilege meant in the police interrogation setting. The American Civil Liberties Union had chosen Escobedo v. Illinois as a vehicle for advising the Court as amicus curiae to hold that a confession obtained during police questioning of a suspect in custody following their denial of his request to consult counsel was inadmissible as evidence against him. Principally relying on the right to counsel guarantee in Gideon and the voluntariness standard followed in previous confession cases, the A.C.L.U. argued that since normal police interrogation practices described in published police manuals were "inherently coercive," the Court should restrict the power of the police to deny access to counsel to a suspect being questioned.

The state's brief replied that such a rule would logically mean requiring provision of free counsel to every indigent suspect from the moment of arrest. This policy would not only be unfeasible in light of existing capabilities and resources for the administration of criminal justice in the fifty states, but it would arouse hostility and meet with noncompliance. Police would not abandon their interrogation practices, "not because of any disrespect for this Court and its teachings, but simply because society will not let them, because society cannot let them. The 'deeply rooted feelings of the community' will demand that those who murder and rape and would escape unknown—but for the confession following arrest—be at least unmasked though they may go unwhipped of justice."[36]

Perhaps recognizing these practical obstacles, the Supreme Court adopted a narrow construction of the A.C.L.U.'s position in Escobedo. Confessions had to be excluded as evidence if obtained when "the investigation is no longer a general inquiry into an unsolved crime but has begun to focus on a particular suspect, the suspect has been taken into police custody, the police carry out a process of interrogation that lends itself to eliciting incriminating statements, the suspect has requested and been denied an opportunity to consult with his lawyer, and the police have not effectively warned him of his absolute constitutional right to remain silent." Standing alone, this rule did not make a great change in police conduct since few suspects ever asked to confer with their lawyers and the state was not compelled to provide counsel for indigent suspects. Justice Arthur Goldberg's opinion, however, more than hinted at future expansion of the Court's limits on the use of confessions. Citing the Allen report's concern for the integrity of the adversary system and the recommendations of a 1962 District of Columbia Commissioners' Committee on Police Arrests for Investigation, which had led to reform of police interrogation practices in Washington, Justice Goldberg declared,

"We have learned the lesson of history, ancient and modern, that a system of criminal law enforcement which comes to depend on the 'confession' will, in the long run, be less reliable and more subject to abuses than a system which depends on extrinsic evidence independently secured through skillful investigation. . . .We have also learned the companion lesson of history that no system of criminal justice can, or should, survive if it comes to depend for its continued effectiveness on the citizens' abdication through unawareness of their constitutional rights. No system worth preserving should have to *fear* that if an accused is permitted to consult with a lawyer, he will become aware of, and exercise, these rights. If the exercise of constitutional rights will thwart the effectiveness of a system of law enforcement, then there is something very wrong with that system."

Justice Byron White's dissent underscored this prospect of further restriction by charging that the majority opinion reflected "a deep-seated distrust of law enforcement officials everywhere" and that law enforcement "will be crippled and its task made a great deal more difficult" by the decision.[37] Since the Court qualified its sweeping language by emphasizing the particular circumstances in the case, legal experts could say only that Escobedo's meaning would depend "on how far and fast a majority of the Court is willing to use the opinion's potential for expansion" in later cases.[38]

The Justice Department's reaction to Escobedo, in which it had not participated as amicus curiae, was crucial to the Supreme Court's future course. Attorney General Kennedy knew by now that the Civil Rights Commission's 1961 recommendations represented growing concern that police needed assistance to meet their Constitutional responsibilities. The A.C.L.U.'s brief had asserted that if the decision hampered legitimate police work, "then it is the responsibility of the community to provide the police with the human and material resources needed to do a better job." If there was to be substantial improvement in the quality of law enforcement, the Justice Department would have to play an increasing role in providing professional advice and financial aid to state and local criminal justice.

Another problem identified by the A.C.L.U. was the absence of information about the need for and probable impact of decisions like Escobedo: "Given the complexity of the problem and the lack of reliable data, the courts are not in a position to make informed judgments about the effects of particular constitutional rules on police efficiency." Nevertheless, the A.C.L.U. did not believe this should prevent the courts from insuring "the basic constititional rights of prospective defend-ants to a fair trial."[39] Dissenting Justice White, who had served as Deputy Attorney General under Robert Kennedy in

1961-62, disagreed and found the assumption that the Escobedo rule was a necessary safeguard against the possibility of extorted confessions to be "unsupported by relevant data or current material based upon our own experience."[40] If the Supreme Court was to be able to make informed judgments about the nature of criminal justice in the states, someone needed to sponsor major research into law enforcement problems. Both Justice White and counsel for the state suggested an alternative to judicial implementation of criminal justice reforms. Since legislatures in many states had paved the way for Supreme Court decisions on the right to counsel at trial and on the exclusion of illegally seized evidence, it would be appropriate for legislatures to develop new rules for police interrogation before the Court proceeded further. To persuade the Escobedo majority that they should defer to state reform efforts for several years might require an organized attempt to focus state attention on the need for reform.

The Justice Department's decision to take on these tasks was influenced by the political environment in 1964 as well as by concern for the interests of the Supreme Court. When the Republican Party nominated Senator Barry Goldwater as its Presidential candidate, he blamed restrictive Court decisions for rising crime rates and made "law and order" a national issue. In his speech accepting the nomination, Goldwater declared, "The growing menace in our country tonight, to personal safety, to life, to limb and property, in homes, in churches, on the playgrounds and places of business, particularly in our great cities, is the mounting concern, or should be, of every thoughtful citizen in the United States. Security from domestic violence, no less than from foreign aggression, is the most elementary and fundamental purpose of any government, and a government that cannot fulfill this purpose is one that cannot long command the loyalty of its citizens." After rioting took place in Harlem a week later, the Republican nominee charged the Administration and Attorney General Kennedy with being too moderate and failing to "apply the law."[41] Criminal justice had become more than a technical law enforcement problem; it was a political issue with wide implications for the prestige and electoral success of the President.

Although Robert Kennedy was soon to leave office to run for the Senate in New York, he and Deputy Attorney General Nicholas Katzenbach (who succeeded him in August) began working with legal scholars and leaders of the bar to develop criminal justice reform programs that would not only provide a constructive response to the Supreme Court's new initiatives, but satisfy the Administration's political needs. Building on the contacts regularly maintained between Justice Department executives and the American Bar Association, as well as on their personal acquaintance with law professors concerned with criminal justice, Kennedy and Katzenbach used both informal influence and official authority to promote their objectives. Among other organizations sensing the need for greater attention to criminal justice was the American Law Institute, composed of judges and scholars devoted to the aim of drafting and persuading states to adopt uniform statutory laws. The A.L.I. decided to propose a uniform code of pre-arraignment procedure for state criminal law enforcement. Harvard Law Professor James Vorenberg, one of the men assigned to draft the A.L.I. code, became an advisor to the Attorney General. Justice Department executives also supported the American Bar Association in its decision to sponsor a sweeping research project to formulate standards for "improving the fairness, efficiency and effectiveness of criminal justice in state and federal courts." Advisory committees made up of judges, law enforcement officials, and lawyers would examine six areas—the police function, pretrial proceedings, the prosecution and defense functions, the criminal trial, sentencing and review, fair trial and free press.

While increasing crime rates were apparently the most urgent factor in the A.B.A.'s decision, almost as important was its recognition "that in some aspects of the administration of criminal justice there are now no standards at all, and that in other respects standards vary widely among the states." These procedures needed to be brought up to date to cope with modern crime conditions and to respond effectively to "changes in the law resulting from decisions of the United States Supreme Court and other courts"[42] In a widely publicized speech, A.B.A. President Lewis F. Powell, Jr., emphasized "the mounting crime problem...in which law abiding citizens are unsafe in their homes and are denied the privilege of using public streets and parks for fear of their personal safety." But Powell thought it "both unproductive and even destructive to criticize the Court" for decisions that had rendered law enforcement more difficult. Instead, he called for modernized and strengthened criminal laws, improved enforcement techniques, and higher educational standards, better compensation, equipment, and training for police. "Not the least of the benefits," Powell predicted, "would be the minimizing of lawless conduct by police themselves."[43]

At the time of the A.B.A.'s convention in the summer of 1964, when the criminal justice project was authorized, Kennedy announced the Justice Department's program. It involved, first, establishment of a new agency under the Deputy Attorney General to concentrate on nationwide problems of criminal justice. The Office of Criminal Justice, headed by Professor James Vorenberg, would provide "a voice inside the Department and a forum outside the Department" for dealing with "the whole spectrum of the criminal process, from arrest to rehabilitation" and with "social problems that affect the criminal process." The new agency would try to open communications "between law enforcement officials on the one side and other legal figures concerned with protecting the rights of the individual on the other." Observing that the debate over criminal justice standards was becoming "emotionally polarized," the Attorney General hoped the Office of Criminal Justice could "serve as a meeting ground for more profitable appraisal of...issues, so that each side may better understand the outlook and the practical problems faced by the other." Since lack of understanding rested in part on lack of information and little had been done to collect and evaluate data about crime and law enforcement, Kennedy believed that government resources should be used to go beyond what private research could do. Recalling the similar role of the 1931 Wickersham Commission, he proposed another national commission to conduct a "comprehensive survey designed to study and strengthen enforcement of and obedience to criminal law all over the country." The Attorney General also suggested creation of a permanent National Institute of Criminal Justice to sponsor continuing research.[44]

Upon leaving office Robert Kennedy had thus committed the Department to a deep involvement in the task of reforming criminal justice in states and cities as well as at the federal level. Under the leadership of his successor, Nicholas Katzenbach, the Department would apply its successful experience with the Allen Committee and the Bail Conference to the larger problems of crime control and the administration of justice throughout the nation. These initiatives meant that the federal government was assuming greater responsibility than ever before for the legal system's ability to deter crime. While Senator Goldwater's campaign made this commitment seem a short-run political advantage, it posed greater political risks for the future if crime rates increased and the Administration's critics could make its response appear ineffective.

3. MIRANDA AND THE PRESIDENT'S CRIME COMMISSION, 1965-66

After President Lyndon Johnson's election in 1964, Attorney General Katzenbach secured White House approval for the major elements in the Department's program. The President sent a message to Congress in March, 1965, stating his intention to appoint a Presidential commission to study crime and setting forth a new legislative proposal. The Law Enforcement Assistance Act, providing limited financial assistance to state and local law enforcement agencies, represented a federal commitment to more than just research. As adopted in September, 1965, the measure set up an Office of Law Enforcement Assistance to make grants to and contracts with public or private nonprofit organizations for training state and local police and for improving the capabilities, techniques, and practices directed at the prevention and control of crime.[45] Since its initial appropriation was a modest ten million dollars, however, the act did not significantly increase the financial resources available throughout the country for the administration of criminal justice. Neither Congress nor the executive was yet ready to devote massive federal funds to this task.

The President's crime commission was not appointed until July, 1965, partly because the Office of Criminal Justice was engaged in other activities focusing on the District of Columbia courts and national bail reform as well as Congressional passage of the Law Enforcement Assistance Act. The nineteen-member Commission on Law Enforcement and Administration of Justice, headed by Katzenbach with Professor Vorenberg as its staff director, began its work in the summer of 1965 by setting up citizen advisory committees and securing the services of social scientists and law enforcement experts. A parallel District of Columbia Commission on Crime and Law Enforcement was established at the same time.

The Justice Department's program constituted a highly professionalized attempt to bring the best expertise to bear on the complex technical and legal problems of criminal justice. President Johnson also sensed the political need to curtail what he called "the present wave of violence and the staggering property losses inflicted upon the nation by crime," and thus he made the war against crime part of his Great Society objectives. But the impact of Administration programs and bar association efforts on the structure and operation of local justice would not be felt in the short run. Meanwhile, crime rates continued to rise, and as federal Judge J. Edward Lumbard of the A.B.A. project put it, the average citizen had the impression "that the public interest is not receiving fair treatment and that undue emphasis has been placed on safeguarding individual rights."[46] F.B.I. Director J. Edgar Hoover stated that restrictive court decisions had resulted in an increase in acquittals and dismissals in criminal cases, while many prosecutors and police chiefs were publicly critical of the Escobedo decision.[47] When attorney Abe Fortas was nominated to replace Justice Goldberg on the Supreme Court in mid-1965, Senators interested in the Court's future course questioned him closely about his views on police interrogation during hearings on his confirmation.

A crucial political question, therefore, was whether the Supreme Court would continue to extend its restrictions on police practices and be held responsible by the public and many politicians for the increase in crime. The potential danger to the Administration should have been clear. As Judge J. Skelly Wright pointed out, the way to instant popularity for political candidates might soon be "to denounce crime in the streets and then accuse people in high places of being soft on criminals."[48] If the Attorney General wanted to protect the Court against serious attacks that might easily become assaults on the Administration, he could either attempt to persuade the Court to move more slowly or prepare Congress and the public to understand why the Court made its decisions and what their effects were on police effectiveness and criminal conduct. Even if the Justice Department chose to urge judicial caution, it needed to anticipate the Court's possible rejection of its advice. In either case it was in the Attorney General's interest to use resources like the crime commission to educate the public about police interrogation practices.

Attorney General Katzenbach's early statements emphasized "the urgency of the need for clear standards" to determine the balance between police interrogation requirements and the right to counsel and privilege against self-incrimination. Katzenbach believed the answer should be the product of "positive, constructive debate and. . .must thus necessarily represent some form of compromise."[49] Many advocates of reform hoped the Supreme Court would wait for a consensus to develop among the groups now studying criminal justice. Stanford Law Professor Herbert L. Packer, for example, wanted the Court to avoid speaking in "broad and unqualified terms" and instead to follow Escobedo with "a series of cases in which 'special circumstances' will determine the outcome." Yet Packer realized critics would then "complain about the lack of predictability in the Supreme Court's performance."[50] There was an unresolved contradiction in the desires both for clear general rules to guide police and for a fully considered policy reflecting a consensus that could only develop over a long period of time.

The intensity of debate over police interrogation standards was revealed in the summer of 1965 when Attorney General Katzenbach made his position public. The occasion was the American Law Institute's release of its first draft of a model code for pre-arraignment procedure, which had been written in part by the Attorney General's advisor James Vorenberg. It proposed that police be required to advise all arrested persons of their rights to remain silent and to have the advice of a lawyer, but that free legal counsel need not be provided to suspects who did not have access to a lawyer. Only those suspects with their own private counsel would be able to consult a lawyer before police interrogation. Vorenberg explained why he did not believe interrogation should always be conditioned on the presence of counsel:

In a vast number of cases this would completely prevent any questioning at all at the very time such questioning is most necessary—when the facts are fresh, when the authorities need a rapid 'picture' of the case in order to make judgments about preliminary disposition, and indeed when the safety of persons and property may require the swift obtaining of information. The very purpose of efficient screening would be lost if in every case the police had to postpone inquiry until a person's counsel had arrived at the stationhouse or until provision could be made for appointed counsel. And any such rule would greatly prolong the duration of custody of innocent people mistakenly (but not necessarily illegally) arrested who are now rapidly questioned and released."[51]

The Attorney General shared Vorenberg's views. Replying to a letter from federal Judge David L. Bazelon asking him to repudiate the A.L.I. draft because it failed "to provide equal protection to the poor and inexperience," Katzenbach asserted that the main purpose of police interrogation was not "to insure equal treatment" but rather "to discover those guilty of crime." Rules governing investigative procedures could not "remedy all the inequities which may exist in our society as a result of social and economic and intellectual differences."[52] Judge Bazelon renewed his attack on the A.L.I. rules several months later, charging the authors with having

"arrived at the unarticulated conclusion that our society cannot 'live with' the privilege against self-incrimination; that if every suspect were allowed a meaningful choice, based on legal advice and information, law enforcement would be unduly hampered. Instead of openly confronting this question by proposing that the privilege. . .be abolished, [they] seem to have taken the easy way out by devising a system under which most suspects would be denied the information to effectuate the privilege."[53]

Other influential legal scholars, including Professors Yale Kamisar of the University of Michigan and Anthony G. Amsterdam of the University of Pennyslvania leveled strong criticism at the Attorney General and the A.L.I. proposal.[54]

In his letter to Judge Bazelon, Katzenbach emphasized that law enforcement officials and trial judges were "increasingly unsure of the law with respect to arrest and post-arrest procedures" because judicial standards had been established "in the context of specific cases and unique factual situations, rather than after review of all the considerations which might be thought relevant in designing rules for the system as a whole." Perhaps unintentionally, this was an open invitation to the Supreme Court to take up again the issue of police interrogation and provide a comprehensive set of rules. The need to clear up post-Escobedo confusion was further made apparent when the federal Courts of Appeals for the Second and Third Circuits adopted conflicting standards. Bowing to these pressures for clarification, the Supreme Court decided in November, 1965, to hear five cases raising basic issues in the interpretation of Escobedo. Since one of these involved a federal prosecution, the Justice Department was able to present its views to the Court as a party to the litigation.

Once the Court had agreed to consider Miranda v. Arizona and its companion cases, Department executives needed to determine how to advise the Court and what steps to take to prepare the public for a decision that might move significantly beyond Escobedo. Possibly preoccupied with devising their argument in Court, they chose not to use the crime commission's resources for the latter purpose. Deputy Attorney General Ramsey Clark had commented earlier, "Court rules do not cause crime. People do not commit crime because they know they cannot be questioned by police before presentment, or even because they feel they will not be convicted." Clark doubted that crime could be reduced by "court rulings affirming convictions based on confessions secured after hours of questioning."[55] To substantiate Clark's assertions or at least to explore their validity, Katzenbach and Vorenberg could have focused a portion of the crime commission's research on the effects of various reforms in police interrogation practices. During 1965 courts in many states had ruled that police were required to advise all suspects of their right to counsel and privilege against self-incrimination before interrogation.[56] There was little evidence, moreover, to show how many criminal convictions were based primarily on confessions. In

Detroit and Philadelphia where police had instituted pre-interrogation warnings, they reportedly continued to secure
confessions and incriminating statements as suspects chose to
waive their right to counsel. Many prosecutors believed that
since confession rates had remained stable after police began
warning suspects of their rights, law enforcement would be
hampered only if the Supreme Court required that lawyers be
present during all interrogation.[57] Ignoring the immediate
need for accurate and persuasive data on interrogation, the
Attorney General allowed the crime commission to remain
aloof from the controversy. Instead, he announced that it
would concentrate on bringing "science and technology to the
law enforcement field."[58]

James Vorenberg later rationalized this policy by claiming
that the crime commission hoped to shift attention away from
the Supreme Court's decisions to more fundamental problems
of crime and criminal justice reform. He feared it would "be
difficult to get support for the process of change if discussion of
issues is confined to whether to be for or against the Supreme
Court, whether to be tough or soft on criminals, whether to
support or leash the police. The issues are complicated, and our
thinking must be equally complicated."[59] Another reason
why the commission side-stepped the confession issue may have
been that the nineteen members were deeply divided over it, a
division underscored in 1967 when seven members filed a
minority report criticizing the Supreme Court. Having failed to
conduct extensive research on police interrogation practices,
however, the commission's majority was unable to refute the
minority's arguments. Vorenberg apparently did not realize the
vital importance of protecting the Supreme Court, which had
led the movement toward criminal justice reform that he and
the Attorney General desired to extend. The practical effect of
the Court's ruling in Miranda was seriously misunderstood, not
only by the public but in Congress and among crime commission members, because of this decision to soft-pedal the issue.

The refusal to use commission resources to examine the impact of Escobedo and improve public knowledge of the role of confessions in law enforcement was a devastating political miscalculation. That it resulted from the highest professional motives and a desire to emphasize more fundamental problems in the administration of criminal justice suggests that technical expertise is not the sole quality needed for effective Justice Department leadership.

Katzenbach's position was viable only if the Supreme Court accepted the Department's advice in the Miranda case. Suspected of kidnaping and rape, Ernesto Miranda was arrested and taken to a police station where he was questioned for two hours. When he confessed, he signed a statement that his admissions were made voluntarily, without threats, and with full knowledge of his legal rights. The interrogating police officers admitted they had not advised Miranda that he had a right to remain silent and consult with an attorney. Unlike Escobedo, Miranda was not barred from conferring with his own attorney, nor was there any other evidence of police coercion. The Supreme Court now had to define what police should do before a confession they obtained could be used as evidence.

The A.C.L.U. proposed as amicus curiae that counsel be required during all interrogations. Since police custody was so inherently coercive that the suspect's privilege against self-incrimination could not be protected without a lawyer, the A.C.L.U. argued that mere warnings from police to a suspect would be inadequate. The poor and ignorant would waive their rights unless they could confer with legal advisors who were not their adversaries. Going to the opposite extreme, Solicitor General Thurgood Marshall's argument asked the Court virtually to abandon Escobedo and rule that there was "no general right to counsel under the Sixth Amendment prior to the institution of formal proceedings before a magistrate in court." Denial of access to counsel or failure to warn a suspect of his right to silence should only be factors in the "totality of circumstances surrounding the interrogation." The Solicitor General's proposed standard for the inadmissibility of confessions was "whether the official conduct, taken as a whole, had the effect on the arrested suspect of overriding his free choice to refuse to 'be a witness against himself' within the meaning of the Fifth Amendment." In line with the American Law Institute draft, Solicitor General Marshall contended that suspects should generally be allowed to confer with their own lawyers, but that counsel need not be furnished to indigent suspects before interrogation.[60]

Between these two extremes other participants in the Miranda argument suggested compromise alternatives. Counsel for the defendant in a companion New York case believe it would be sufficient for the Court to require police to warn a suspect of his right to counsel and offer to secure a lawyer for any suspect who could not obtain one. Recognizing "some of the realities of law enforcement," however, he argued that the suspect could waive his right to counsel in writing and police questioning could then proceed. A similar position was urged by counsel for the National District Attorneys Association as amicus curiae, who agreed that if a suspect asked for a lawyer and did not waive his right to counsel, he should have a lawyer appointed by the state if necessary. The latter argument differed from the former only to the extent that police would not be required to offer legal counsel *before* the suspect requested it.[61]

Both the Justice Department and the District Attorneys Association urged the Court to withhold decision on the issue until state legislatures and advisory bodies had an opportunity to develop solutions based on empirical data and comprehensive study. But the District Attorneys Association argued concurrently that if the Court chose to decide the cases, it should not revert to the "totality of circumstances" doctrine supported by the Solicitor General, but should lay down specific rules to guide law enforcement agencies who were uncertain of what to do. The only response the Court could make to satisfy the Justice Department and the District Attorneys, therefore, would be to refuse to decide Miranda and dismiss the writs of certiorari as improvidently granted. Yet Attorney General Katzenbach had emphasized the need for clear standards, and lower courts were in such confusion that the Supreme Court could not easily avoid its responsibility to make a decision.

Announcing its decision in June, 1966, the Court chose to adopt the device of a pre-interrogation warning to suspects of their rights to remain silent and to have counsel present during questioning; lawyers were to be provided to indigent suspects only if they requested counsel after having been informed by police of their rights. If police failed to warn a suspect, refused to halt questioning when he desired to remain silent, or failed to provide counsel when requested, a subsequent confession would be inadmissible as evidence. Although Chief Justice Earl Warren's opinion recognized that "a once stated warning, delivered by those who will conduct the investigation," was insufficient to "assure that the individual's right to choose between silence and speech remains unfettered throughout the interrogation," the Court did not extend this reasoning to the choice between asking for a lawyer and confronting the police alone. If a suspect affirmatively waived his right to counsel, a lawyer did not have to be present during the questioning. Any evidence of deceptive police tactics which might have "threatened, tricked, or cajoled" the suspect into a waiver would, however, "show that the defendant did not voluntarily waive his privilege."[62] In other words, the traditional standards for evaluating the "totality of circumstances" surrounding a confession were transformed into similar rules for determining whether a waiver of rights was voluntary. The main difference was that now the prosecution had the burden of proving at trial that the defendant had "knowingly and intelligently" waived his rights, while earlier the defendant had had to show that his confession was involuntary.

Few public officials realized how far the Supreme Court had compromised in Miranda, since the dissenters raised the spectre of an end to effective police interrogation and confessions. Judge J. Skelly Wright was one of a handful of people who explained the decision accurately. Addressing a conference of lawyers and law enforcement officials meeting to discuss Miranda, Judge Wright observed that unless the decision produced "lawyers in the stationhouse, instead of waivers," would turn out to be a "pious fraud." If the question of the voluntariness of the waiver became a "swearing contest" between the defendant and his police interrogators, just as it was before on the issue of the voluntariness of the confession itself, then there would be "very little change in police practices."[63] Yet Chief Justice Warren had specifically stated that his opinion did "not mean, as some have suggested, that each police station must have a 'station house lawyer' present at all times to advise prisoners."[64] All that was necessary to confirm Judge Wright's analysis was empirical data showing that most arrested persons waived their rights and submitted to interrogation, despite police adherence to the Miranda warnings.

The President's crime commission could have easily found such data, even in Washington, D.C., where the local anti-poverty legal services agency had been providing lawyers for poor suspects who requested counsel at police stations since February, 1966.[65] Cities like Detroit offered similar opportunities to validate the conclusion that Miranda would make little difference in normal police interrogation and the availability of confessions. Without this kind of evidence, the crime commission's minority members were able to assert that Miranda "could mean the virtual elimination of pretrial interrogation of suspects" and that it "in effect proscribes the use of all confessions."[66] The full commission report, endorsed by a majority and drafted under the supervision of James Vorenberg, replied only that it was "too early to assess the effect of the Miranda decision on law enforcement's ability to secure confessions and to solve crimes." Instead of explaining the limited scope of the Supreme Court's ruling, especially as contrasted with what the A.C.L.U. had urged, the commission merely suggested that legislators and police should "establish through empirical research what the needs of law enforcement are" in order to "affect the nature and result of court review" in the future. By observing that many court decisions "were made without the needs of law enforcement, and the police policies that are designed to meet those needs, being effectively presented to the court," the commission itself implied some misgivings about the ability of judges "to balance accurately law enforcement needs against human rights."[67]

Acting on the basis of their misperception of Miranda's impact, the commission minority proposed a constitutional amendment modifying the privilege against self-incrimination for the purpose of providing "an adequate opportunity. . .for interrogation at the scene of the crime, during investigation and at the station house, with appropriate safeguards to prevent abuse." The amendment would reestablish "the legitimate place of voluntary confessions in law enforcement" by making the admissibility of confessions "dependant upon meeting due process standards of voluntariness." Similar amendments had already been introduced in Congress, and a speaker at the American Bar Association's 1966 convention had urged the bar to begin a "great dialogue" over "our entire position with respect to the Fifth Amendment."[68] Illinois Supreme Court Justice Walter V. Schaefer and former New York Police Commissioner Vincent L. Broderick had recommended changing the Fifth Amendment to permit the prosecution to tell a jury that the defendant refused to answer questions during police interrogation.[69] The crime commission thus gave added force to the widespread critical reactions to Miranda, persuading even the editors of the New York Times that the argument for a constitutional amendment to permit the use of "freely given confessions" as evidence was impressive.[70]

The first sign of Congressional reaction came in the fall of 1966 when a District of Columbia crime bill was passed. Largely the product of the southern-dominated House District Committee, the measure included a provision designed to permit police to question suspects without counsel over a ten-hour period before having them arraigned in court. Although its original target was the 1957 Mallory decision requiring that federal courts exclude confessions obtained when police violated the procedural rule demanding arraignment of suspects "without unnecessary delay," the bill now raised serious constitutional questions since Miranda declared that suspects had a right to counsel during interrogation. Many Congressmen apparently voted for the bill, not out of any desire to attack the Supreme Court, but because, as Senator Joseph Tydings of Maryland explained, the House District Committee had "made agreement on a crime bill the sine qua non of mutual accommodation between the two Houses of Congress on other District matters."[71] Indeed, few legislators realized that the measure was in direct conflict with Miranda.

Near the time of the D.C. crime bill's passage, President Johnson appointed Attorney General Katzenbach to be Under Secretary of State, and Ramsey Clark became Acting Attorney General. It was up to Clark, therefore, to advise the President whether to veto the bill as Washington civil rights groups demanded or to sign it as urged by Washington police officials and business leaders. Since Congress had adjourned, the President could have allowed the bill to die quietly without his signature—a pocket veto. Instead, he used the opportunity of his veto to issue a message drafted by the Justice Department charging that the bill went "far beyond the necessities of interrogation in most cases" and that it failed to improve "the quality or quantity of law enforcement resources: more, better-trained, better-equipped and better-paid police and correction workers." The President's message did not, however, assert directly that the measure was unconstitutional under Miranda, nor did it explain clearly why a change in interrogation rules would not make a significant difference in police effectiveness. Its main conclusion was that the bill would "create problems instead of solving them" by provoking years of litigation and by adding "endless complications and confusion to an already complex situation."[72] The Justice Department had thus missed another chance to contribute to public and Congressional understanding of the meaning and consequences of Miranda. It could have publicized findings, soon to be released by the District of Columbia Crime Commission, which showed that the stringent Mallory rule limiting police interrogation had not substantially reduced the number of incriminating admissions and that many suspects confessed even after consulting lawyers or relatives. When the D.C. commission's report was issued six weeks later, the data about confessions were buried among a mass of findings and recommendations for criminal justice reforms.[73]

The dissenting views within the crime commission and the critical reaction to Miranda among segments of the legal profession should have warned the Administration that its ambiguous position on Miranda would allow the initiative to pass to the Supreme Court's opponents. The Justice Department was seriously hampered in its ability to offer strong policy guidance during the winter of 1966-67, however, because of a gap in executive leadership. For months after Katzenbach's shift to the State Department, Ramsey Clark served merely as Acting Attorney General, while Washington speculated about whether he or someone else would be appointed to head the Department. President Johnson's delay may have seemed necessary because Katzenbach still was crime commission chairman. Until after the commission completed its work, the President allowed policy-making responsibility to remain divided. Hence Ramsey Clark, who had once spoken out firmly in defense of Miranda, remained silent on the issue until Katzenbach finally completed his crime commission duties.

4. THE OMNIBUS CRIME
CONTROL ACT, 1967-68

The Johnson Administration began 1967 with the hope that it could deflect attention away from the Supreme Court. To avoid the political liability of being tagged with the label "soft on crime," it proposed new legislation to implement the national crime commission's recommendation for massive federal aid to state and local criminal justice. The Safe Streets and Crime Control Bill, submitted to Congress in February, offered federal grants to cities and states to improve their police, courts, and correctional systems under coordinated plans approved by the Justice Department. This greatly expanded version of the Law Enforcement Assistance Act would, the President stated, insure that law enforcement was "staffed and nourished by first-rate skills and modern equipment." President Johnson's message to Congress also endorsed the commission's view that crime prevention meant alleviating the conditions that stimulate criminal conduct—eliminating slums and ghettos, improving education, providing jobs. President Johnson declared, "To speak of controlling crime only in terms of the work of the police, the courts and the correctional apparatus alone, is to refuse to face the fact that widespread crime implies a widespread failure by society as a whole."[74]

Besides stressing the social bases of crime, the President's message raised a new controversy which undermined its effectiveness as a strong anti-crime statement. With considerable fanfare the President revived the issue of electronic surveillance. He recommended outlawing all wiretapping by federal and state law enforcement agencies, "except when the security of the nation itself is at stake—and only then with the strictest safeguards." In addition, he urged Congress to exercise the full reach of its constitutional power (apparently including its authority under the Fourteenth Amendment) to bar law enforcement officials from using electronic bugging devices. The President's stand on electronic surveillance created the conditions for sharp conflict with both the crime commission and Congress.

Lyndon Johnson apparently held strong personal views against electronic surveillance. One of his early decisions after becoming President had been to reassert the ban on all federal wiretapping except in national security cases. Then in June, 1965, he had issued a directive to all federal agencies curbing their use of other electronic surveillance techniques. Electronic surveillance which did not intercept telephone conversations was covered by a different set of legal rules than was wiretapping. If an electronic eavesdropping device physically invaded private premises, the Supreme Court had ruled that it was subject to Fourth Amendment search and seizure standards barring penetration of a "constitutionally protected area" without a judicial warrant.[75] Neither Supreme Court decisions nor the 1934 Communications Act applied to electronic surveillance which, like a parabolic microphone aimed through a window from across the street, did not physically enter such an area or intercept telephone lines. President Johnson's 1965 order provided the first administrative limits on all these non-wiretap forms of electronic surveillance.[76]

A hint of the President's decision to ask Congress to prohibit all electronic surveillance came in March, 1966, when Attorney General Katzenbach testified on the Kennedy bill to allow wiretapping with court permission in serious criminal cases. At that time Katzenbach suggested that if Congress could not agree on the terms of such a bill, it should bar all wiretapping.[77] After the Miranda decision limiting police interrogation, however, some experts including federal Judge J. Edward Lumbard who headed the A.B.A.'s criminal justice project, proposed that lawmakers consider approving the use of electronic surveillance. "If we take away the means of the possible solution of many crimes by confessions," Judge Lumbard asked, "is it not then logical that these other means be made available?"[78] The national crime commission, perhaps sharing this view as well as the Justice Department's evaluation of the issue under Robert Kennedy, made a preliminary decision to support federal legislation authorizing court-approved electronic surveillance in organized crime investigations. These developments set the stage for a direct clash between the President, who was determined to propose a ban on electronic surveillance, and a substantial commission majority.

When Acting Attorney General Ramsey Clark attended his first commission meeting in November, 1966, soon after Katzenbach was appointed Under Secretary of State (he still remained commission chairman), Clark advised avoiding the issue entirely so as not to distract from the commission's fundamental reform program. Staff director Vorenberg agreed that there was not enough information to resolve the question whether electronic surveillance was a waste of time, as Clark suggested, or was a source of valuable data about organized crime, political corruption, and gambling, as an F.B.I. official asserted.[79] The commission was most impressed, however, by a report prepared for its organized crime task force by Notre Dame Law Professor G. Robert Blakey, who had served in the Justice Department's Organized Crime and Racketeering Section from 1961 to 1964. Professor Blakey marshalled persuasive evidence, based largely on the experience of New York district attorney Frank Hogan's office, for the use of electronic surveillance against organized crime. Submitting a draft electronic surveillance statue similar to the Kennedy wiretap bill, Blakey argued that a carefully drawn law could provide safeguards for the right of privacy if it required a judicial warrant and placed severe restrictions on the scope of surveillance.[80]

When the commission seemed ready to endorse this proposal at a meeting in December, Texas lawyer Leon Jaworski, a close friend of President Johnson, threatened to file a strong dissent charging the majority with acting on ideological rather than factual grounds. Other members then warned that if the recommendation was deleted, they would dissent and charge political interference.[81] To resolve the conflict chairman Katzenbach devised a compromise which slightly modified the majority's stand in favor of electronic surveillance. Several weeks earlier the Supreme Court had agreed to hear the case of Berger v. New York, an appeal challenging the New York statute authorizing court-approved electronic eavesdropping. Since it was deemed inappropriate for the commission to make major recommendations in an area under Supreme Court scrutiny, the majority agreed to condition its stand on the outcome of that case. The commission thus stated its belief "that legislation should be enacted granting carefully circumscribed authority for electronic surveillance to law enforcement officers to the extent it may be consistent with the decision of the Supreme Court in People v. Berger."[82] Two weeks before the report was released, President Johnson sent his message to Congress urging a ban on all electronic surveillance.

After the commission made its report, a Senate Judiciary Subcommittee headed by Arkansas Senator John McClellan began hearings on anti-crime legislation. Adopting the commission minority's view of Miranda and the majority's position on electronic surveillance, Senator McClellan and Senator Sam J. Ervin drafted legislation to modify the Supreme Court's police interrogation rules and to authorize wiretapping. Instead of preparing a constitutional amendment to reverse Miranda, Senator McClellan offered a bill to admit voluntary confessions as evidence in federal courts, regardless of the absence of warnings or counsel, while Senator Ervin advanced a broader measure limiting the jurisdiction of the Supreme Court to review the admissibility of confessions in state criminal trials and curtailing the powers of federal District Courts to consider appeals from state criminal convictions. The subcommittee's wiretapping bill had a wider scope and fewer safeguards than either Attorney General Kennedy's 1962 proposal or Professor Blakey's draft for the commission.

In the spring of 1967, therefore, the political lines were clearly drawn between the Johnson Administration and its Congressional opponents over these two issues. In mid-March the President finally decided to appoint Ramsey Clark as Attorney General (he had only acting status for four months), and Johnson used the occasion of Clark's swearing-in ceremony to speak out strongly in support of Supreme Court decisions protecting the rights of criminal suspects. The following week Attorney General Clark told a House Judiciary Subcommittee he doubted "that anything approaching a case" had been made for changing the Miranda rules.[83]

The controversies over Miranda and electronic surveillance were far more politically significant now than when Robert Kennedy had submitted his wiretapping bill in 1962 and when the President had vetoed the District of Columbia crime bill in the fall of 1966. They were no longer technical law enforcement issues attracting the attention of a few interested groups. Public opinion polls and 1966 election results confirmed the impression of rapidly growing public concern about crime. In New York City a highly charged campaign led by the Patrolmen's Benevolent Association defeated Mayor Lindsay's Civilian Complaint Review Board in a referendum.[84] A survey for the crime commission disclosed that crime was second only to race relations as the domestic problem to which citizens were paying the most attention. Nevertheless, the same poll reported sixty-five percent of the public favored the Supreme Court's ruling that police could not question a suspect without his lawyer being present, unless the suspect agreed to be interrogated without counsel. Since fifty-two percent favored giving the police more power to question people, however, many respondents apparently did not yet associate the Miranda decision with reduced police interrogation powers.[85] For Congressmen and other officials who wanted to capitalize on the public's concern about crime, there was a great temptation to criticize the Supreme Court's rules as a symbolic way to demonstrate their anti-crime commitment. Even if the general public did not oppose the Miranda standards, policemen were extremely hostile to them, as their testimony before Senator McClellan's subcommittee revealed.[86]

When a National Conference on Crime Control met to discuss implementation of the crime commission's report in late March, James Vorenberg still rebuffed participants who wanted to talk about Miranda, explaining that the decision had already been much discussed elsewhere and that the meeting should focus on "the kinds of issues the states and cities can do the most about." Former Attorney General Katzenbach touched on the question briefly when he labeled complaints that crime had increased because of judicial decisions as "emotional nonsense." Although he argued that "able police forces and adequate communications systems will accomplish more than the reversal of Supreme Court decisions," Katzenbach admitted that the new standards did make police work more difficult.[87] Thus another crucial opportunity was lost to inform leading law enforcement officials from across the country about the limited effects of Miranda.

The crime control conference marked the end of Katzenbach and Vorenberg's role in Justice Department policy-making, as Attorney General Clark took over full control. Within six weeks Clark began to conduct the kind of analysis and education of Congress and the public his predecessor had failed to provide. Appearing on a nationally televised Law Day program, he reported surveys indicating "that confessions are coming in at about the same rate or perhaps even higher than they were before Miranda." At the same time the United States Attorney for the District of Columbia told a House subcommittee that Miranda had not made any noticeable difference in the number of cases Washington police had been able to solve.[88] These statements contributed important evidence but may have come too late to clarify the confused debate.

At a lawyers conference on crime control in May, Attorney General Clark stressed that crime was "the most critical problem in society today. Reducing crime is a matter of great urgency for our people. We must find better ways to secure their safety—to prevent crime as well as to punish it—to preserve public order without denying private rights." A week after this speech, however, Clark granted an interview which gave a completely different impression of his outlook. He was quoted (or misquoted) as saying, "The level of crime has risen a little bit, but there is no wave of crime in the country." Asked about statistics showing a rising crime rate, Clark replied, "We do ourselves a great disservice with statistics." He cited the murder rate, which had declined steadily since the 1930's, and emphasized "that murder is the crime most accurately reported, so we can make comparisons with the past." In the same interview the Attorney General defended the Administration's stand on electronic surveillance. Focusing on its use against organized crime, as had the crime commission, Clark stated that after President Johnson banned wiretapping by the Federal government (except for national security purposes) in 1965, Justice Department organized crime prosecutions had increased thirty percent the first year and were now "at an all time high." In these cases, he observed, "with the rarest exceptions we have found that electronic surveillance was unnecessary, either in obtaining direct evidence of crime or in developing leads." He concluded that wiretapping and bugging were "neither effective nor highly productive."[89] Since Clark's interview was far more widely publicized than his address to the lawyers conference, it may have contributed to his public image as an Attorney General who did not take crime seriously.

Clark's unwillingness to play up public apprehension about crime may have been due to his political ineptitude, as journalist Richard Harris has suggested.[90] But another plausible explanation would attribute his statements to thought-ful deliberation and political necessity. While the crime commission had found an increase in the volume and rate of crime, it expressed concern that exaggerated public fear of crime would disrupt the fabric of society and lead to unnecessary interfer-ence with individual liberties. The public feared most the crimes that occurred least often, crimes of violence, and there was a dangerous tendency to use violent crime as a stereotype for crimes in general. Yet not only was the homocide rate down, but most violent assaults were committed by and against persons who knew each other, and only a small proportion of violent crime was interracial. Crime statistics were unreliable because they measured only the increase in reported crime and police reporting systems were constantly changing.[91] On the basis of the commission's report, therefore, Clark was fully justified in his attempt to inform the public about the character of violent crime. When he coupled his analysis of crime statistics with adamant opposition to electronic surveillance, however, he contradicted the commission and detracted from his central message. Yet as the President's Attorney General he was bound to defend the Administration's stand. Whether or not Clark fully shared President Johnson's aversion to wiretapping and bugging, even against organized crime and with strict safeguards,

White House policy was unmistakably clear. Clark's position was the only politically viable one, given his recognition of the need both to prevent public fears from being exaggerated and to retain the President's confidence.

The Attorney General's response to the Supreme Court's decision in Berger v. New York indicated how far his adherence to Presidential policy on electronic surveillance could distort his technical-legal judgment. The Court declared unconstitutional New York's statute permitting court-approved electronic eavesdropping, applying strict Fourth Amendment standards to all electronic surveillance which penetrated protected areas such as homes, private offices, hotel rooms, and automobiles. The Court's requirements for a valid eavesdropping statute, including precise description of the conversations to be overhead and notice to the person under surveillance, seemed so rigorous as to create doubt that an effective law could be drafted; but the Court did not find electronic surveillance per se to be unconstitutional.[92] Nevertheless, four days after the decision Attorney General Clark issued a directive to all federal agencies asserting, "Eavesdropping in any form which is accomplished by means of a trespass into a constitutionally protected area is a violation of the Fourth Amendment."[93] He thus overlooked Berger's implication that electronic eavesdropping governed by stringent limits was constitutional.

Differing sharply with the Attorney General, crime commission consultant G. Robert Blakey told Senator McClellan's subcommittee the Supreme Court was signalling that electronic surveillance would win approval if Congress drew up a careful law keeping it under tight control. He saw Berger as an advisory opinion to guide legislatures, leaving the fundamental policy issue up to Congress. Since Blakey's draft for the commission had taken account of the need for precision and notice, he was convinced it was possible to strike a reasonable balance between privacy and law enforcement uses of electronic surveillance.[94] Soon thereafter Solicitor General Thurgood Marshall, whom the President had just appointed to the Supreme Court, supported Blakey's view when he testified at hearings on his confirmation. Marshall thought the Berger decision "left

open the opportunity" for Congress to pass electronic surveillance legislation that would satisfy the Supreme Court.[95]
Although he must have been aware of Solicitor General
Marshall's judgment, Clark had seriously overstated the constitutional obstacles to electronic surveillance in order to justify
the President's policy. The A.B.A.'s criminal justice project and
Columbia Professor Alan Westin's study of privacy sponsored
by the Association of the Bar of the City of New York agreed
with Blakey and Marshall that a proper electronic surveillance
statute would be constitutional.[96]

The Attorney General's position was made more vulnerable
by the President's approval of electronic surveillance directly
related to the protection of national security. Acknowledging
"special problems" which arose in such matters, Clark continued to authorize wiretapping and bugging in national security
investigations. The Administration's bill to prohibit electronic
surveillance permitted the President to authorize wiretapping
and eavesdropping without court order "to protect the Nation
against actual or potential attack or other hostile acts of a
foreign power or any other serious threat to the security of the
United States, or to protect national security information
against foreign intelligence activities." The Justice Department
had informed a House Judiciary subcommittee that this would
allow wiretapping to prove an individual was a Communist
Party member and to investigate domestic organizations
controlled by a foreign government. Citing these policies,
dissenting Justice Byron White had commented in Berger, "It
seems obvious from the Department of Justice bill that the
present Administration believes that there are some purposes
and uses of electronic surveillance which do not involve
violations of the Fourth Amendment by the Executive
Branch."[97] Critics of the Attorney General pointed out he
had "never explained why wiretaps and bugs are essential in
national security cases but useless against organized crime."
Clark's stand on electronic surveillance almost invited his
opponents to charge that the Administration's "war on crime is
a phony war."[98]

By the summer of 1967, therefore, the Justice Department was already in a weak position to influence Congressional action on the anti-Miranda and electronic surveillance bills being drafted by Senator McClellan's subcommittee. Although neither measure appeared in the crime control bill passed by the House in August, authorizing federal grants to state and local criminal justice, the Senate subcommittee wrote a new provision to reverse another Supreme Court decision, Wade v. United States, which ruled that suspects had a right to counsel at police line-ups.[99] To counter Wade the subcommittee proposed that all eye-witness testimony be admitted in federal trials no matter how pretrial line-up identification had been conducted. Senators McClellan and Ervin chose not to rush their omnibus crime bill through the full Judiciary Committee in the fall, however, partly because the Supreme Court was considering another electronic surveillance case, Katz v. United States, and because the committee members were evenly divided on the Miranda and Wade bills. The summer's riots in Newark, Detroit, and elsewhere combined with the growing force of antiwar protest culminating in the October demonstration at the Pentagon to distract Justice Department executives from crime legislation. The urban disorders had a decisive effect on the environment for federal policy-making on criminal justice since they intensified public fear of violence and made it more likely that "law and order" would be a major issue in the 1968 elections. Opinion polls soon revealed that anger over crime and riots overshadowed all other domestic issues and that sixty-three percent of the public believed the courts did not deal harshly enough with criminals—an increase from forty-eight percent in 1965.[100]

The Supreme Court decided Katz v. United States in December, 1967, clarifying its standards for electronic surveillance. The case involved an F.B.I. listening device placed on the outside of a public telephone booth, thus differing from Berger where a "constitutionally protected area" had been physically invaded. Abandoning this distinction, the Court now ruled that "the Fourth Amendment protects people, not places." Justice

Potter Stewart's opinion for a near-unanimous Court made clear, however, that all forms of electronic surveillance, including wiretapping, were constitutionally permissible as long as they met Fourth Amendment requirements. The Court removed any impression left by Berger that electronic surveillance would be impossible. It did not demand, for instance, that prior notice be given to the person under surveillance, although it still required a judicial warrant on a showing of probable cause, specifying the scope and duration of the surveillance and providing for a return on the warrant informing the judge of all that was overheard. In short, the Court virtually invited Congress and the states to enact laws consistent with these standards.[101] Senate Judiciary Committee members moved quickly to revise their electronic surveillance bill so they could claim to follow the Court's guidelines.

Anxious for a crime bill to be passed so that federal grants could reach local police to help control or prevent civil disorders and anticipating that crime would be a crucial issue in the 1968 campaign, the White House let it be known President Johnson would accept an electronic surveillance measure even though he continued publicly to endorse a ban on all wiretapping and bugging except in national security cases. If the bill passed, the President intended not to implement it while he remained in office. The White House shift placed the Attorney General in a difficult predicament. Although he dispatched Department officials to consult with the Senate Judiciary Committee on the final draft of its electronic surveillance section (Title III), they did not have sufficient influence to eliminate several portions of questionable constitutionality and wisdom. One objectionable element permitted law enforcement officers to undertake electronic surveillance in "emergency situations" for forty-eight hours before securing a judicial warrant. In addition, the length of time allowed for surveillance and the breadth of criminal offenses for which surveillance could be used, especially by state authorities, appeared excessive.[102] Since the Justice Department was not in a position to endorse any bill, it was unable to persuade the Senators to modify these sections. If the Attorney General had been able to propose his own measure instead of leaving the initiative to the Senate committee, it might have served as the basis for more carefully circumscribed legislation than Title III.

When the Judiciary Committee turned to the anti-Miranda and Wade sections (Title II), the Justice Department paid the full price for its failure to defend the Supreme Court effectively. Senators McClellan and Ervin had the support of other southern Senators and conservative northern Republicans, but they needed the vote of Pennsylvania Republican Hugh Scott to defeat a motion to delete Title II in committee. Their liberal opponents could now cite recent studies of police interrogation which showed that Miranda had little effect on the ability of police to secure incriminating admissions, and a report from the National District Attorneys Association convention which indicated "that some of the heat had come out of the confession question."[103] As a symbolic issue in the forthcoming presidential election campaign, however, Miranda offered the Republicans a convenient target. Since the party's leading candidate, Richard Nixon, had already blamed the courts for going "too far in weakening the peace forces against the forces of crime," Senator Scott was fully aware that the party's interest would be served by capitalizing on public misunderstanding of Miranda. Nixon was soon to issue a policy statement approving measures to "correct the imbalance" resulting from Escobedo and Miranda. "From the point of view of the peace forces," the candidate declared, "the cumulative impact of these decisions has been to very nearly rule out the confession as an effective and major tool in prosecution and law enforcement."[104] Nixon was able to make this assertion because during the two years since Miranda the Justice Department had not communicated a full and accurate picture of its effects, except for Attorney General Clark's brief attempt in the spring of 1967.

With Senator Scott's support Title II went to the Senate floor along with the rest of the omnibus crime bill in May, 1968. In addition to admitting voluntary confessions and eye-witness identifications as evidence in federal trials, Title II severely restricted the powers of federal District Courts to review state criminal convictions and limited the appellate jurisdiction of the Supreme Court to prevent it from hearing state cases involving the admissibility of confessions. When Senate debate opened on the omnibus crime bill, legal scholars, leaders of the bar, and many judges recognized the threat Title II posed to the independence of the federal judiciary and to effective protection for due process of law in the states. Changes in the constitutional rules for federal trials were somewhat less dangerous than this wholesale restructuring of the relations between state and federal courts and the attempt to strip the Supreme Court of its jurisdiction. The A.B.A.'s board of governors, twenty-four law school deans, and the Judicial Conference of the United States, composed of all the chief judges of the federal appellate courts, registered their opposition to Title II. Attorney General Clark expressed "grave reservations" as to its constitutionality and gave every indication that the Administration was prepared to make a determined public fight to defeat it.[105]

Although President Johnson met privately with Senate leaders and A.B.A. officials during the Senate deliberations, he chose to remain publicly silent about Title II. The White House decided instead on a strategy similar to the way it handled the electronic surveillance issue. In order to secure passage of the crime bill, the President informed crucial Senators that he would accept a modified Title II if it only changed federal rules of procedure and did not contain the limits on Supreme Court jurisdiction and on federal court powers to review state convictions. Following the White House lead, the Senate passed the rules applying to federal trials and eliminated the measures directly threatening judicial power and independence. Attorney General Clark may have endorsed this strategy because he expected to see Title II deleted in the House-Senate Conference where House Judiciary Committee chairman Emanuel Celler would oppose it. When the House leadership permitted the Senate bill to come to the floor after Senator Robert Kennedy's assassination, and the choice was posed between no crime bill and the Senate version, the measure was overwhelmingly adopted.[106]

The Justice Department was now confronted with an omnibus crime control act which contained an electronic surveillance measure (Title III) and interrogation and line-up rules (Title II) it had opposed from the outset. Since a veto was impossible because of White House commitments, the need for federal grants to improve state and local criminal justice, and the danger of provoking more serious Republican campaign criticism, the President signed the bill and appended a message explaining the Administration's policy for implementing it. Calling upon Congress to reconsider and repeal the "unwise and potentially dangerous" electronic surveillance provisions of Title III, the President stated:

"Until that can be accomplished we shall pursue—within the Federal Government—carefully designed safeguards to limit wiretapping and eavesdropping. The policy of this Administration has been to confine wiretapping and eavesdropping to national security cases only—and then only with the approval of the Attorney General. This policy, now in its third year, will continue in force. I have today directed the Attorney General to assure that this policy of privacy is followed by all Federal law enforcement officers."

With regard to Title II's rules for the admissibility of confessions and eye-witness testimony, President Johnson did not urge their repeal but instead declared he had been advised by the Attorney General that "the provisions of Title II, vague and ambiguous as they are, can...be interpreted in harmony with the Constitution." Promising that federal practices would "conform to the Constitution," the President asked the Attorney General and the F.B.I. Director to assure that federal officers would continue the policy of consistently giving suspects "full and fair warning of Constitutional rights."[107]

The President's message did not spell out the Attorney General's logic in saying that Title II did not clearly conflict with the Supreme Court's interpretation of the Fifth and Sixth Amendments; but Columbia Law Professor Herbert Wechsler, director of the American Law Institute and a member of the crime commission, explained what may have been Clark's reasoning. Although the evident danger of Title II was that it might "force reconsideration of Miranda or Wade by the Supreme Court," Wechsler doubted it would operate in practice to do so:

"No responsible trial judge would jeopardize a criminal conviction by following the statute in his rulings on inadmissibility, nor would a sensible prosecution even seek a ruling in these terms since it would certainly invite reversal. It can, therefore, be predicted with confidence that the offending sections of the bill would be dead letters even in the district courts. The chance that the Supreme Court would be called upon to declare their repugnance to the Constitution is remote."

Accordingly, both Professor Wechsler and the Attorney General did not believe the presence of Title II in the bill justified a veto.[108] As long as the Johnson Administration remained in office, neither Title II nor Title III of the omnibus crime control act would affect federal law enforcement.

Nevertheless, the divisive debate over Miranda and electronic surveillance left the Department weak in the face of the Republicans' campaign emphasis on law and order. Richard Nixon's attack on Attorney General Clark threatened to turn the 1968 election into a referendum on the Department's policies, with Clark's refusal to engage in electronic surveillance and his adherence to Miranda as two of the main objects of criticism. Neither issue would have been so useful to the Republicans if Katzenbach and Vorenberg had defended the Miranda case adequately in 1966-67 or if Johnson and Clark had modified their adamant stand against wiretapping. The electorate's dissatisfaction went far beyond these two policies, however, for urban riots and youthful protest demonstrations had persuaded eighty-one percent of the public in the fall of 1968 that law and order had broken down in the country.[109]

The crime commission had produced some constructive results, providing guidance to state and local governments and the impetus for massive federal assistance to police and judicial administration. The commission's work would continue in the form of the Law Enforcement Assistance Administration, which gave the Justice Department the resources to influence the direction criminal justice would take in the years ahead. Most of the new agency's decisions on grants to states and cities would be in the hands of the kind of professional law enforcement experts whom the commission had consulted in drafting its reports. The L.E.A.A.'s overall priorities, however, would be established by the new Attorney General.

5. THE NIXON ADMINISTRATION
AND CRIMINAL JUSTICE, 1969

Richard Nixon's victory and the substantial vote captured by George Wallace provided an electoral mandate to reverse the direction of Justice Department policy. Since Nixon had explicitly endorsed Title II and Title III during the campaign, President Johnson's decision to bar wiretapping was likely to be reversed, and Professor Wechsler's expectations about the limited impact of Title II became unduly optimistic. During the new Administration's first year, the Justice Department remained a center of controversy. Only now the criticism came from civil liberties groups and those segments of the legal profession who had supported Ramsey Clark. Soon after taking office, Attorney General John Mitchell began to fulfill the President's campaign commitments by proposing an elaborate anti-crime program and revising the Department's own law enforcement policies.

When Mitchell testified at Senate hearings on his confirmation, he announced his intention to authorize electronic surveillance "against organized crime and other major crimes," following the standards of Title III. By mid-February the Department had begun electronic surveillance in several anti-racketeering investigations involving crime syndicate members; but it did not rush to use wiretaps or bugs in cases unrelated to organized crime, nor did Mitchell initially approve forty-eight-hour emergency surveillance without court order.[110] Most controversy during 1969 focused on the Department's policy for electronic surveillance of domestic political dissidents for national security purposes, rather than surveillance of organized crime. Since the Johnson Administration had also asserted its authority to wiretap and bug at its own discretion in national security matters, Attorney General Mitchell's policy (to be examined more fully in Chapter Four) did not entirely conflict with his predecessor's. In the summer of 1969 Mitchell announced that the amount of electronic surveillance for national security and organized crime investigations was less than when he took office. While several wiretaps had been installed under court warrants in criminal investigations under Title III, a greater number of national security taps had been discontinued because they were "not productive." The total of authorized electronic surveillance devices currently in use was less than the fifty-four acknowledged in the spring by F.B.I. Director Hoover.[111]

There were several reasons for Mitchell's cautious use of Title III in federal law enforcement. Before he took office, a House Republican Task Force on Crime, headed by Virginia Congressman Richard H. Poff, submitted a report to President-elect Nixon recommending that electronic surveillance "should be initially utilized on an extremely selective and carefully controlled basis" and that "the new Administration should be in less of a hurry to employ 'bugging,' or surveillance by microphone, than wiretapping, since legal and technical problems with 'bugging' are substantially greater than with wiretapping."[112] Furthermore, a Gallup poll taken in mid-1969 revealed that the public was evenly divided on the issue, forty-six percent approving wiretapping in general, forty-seven percent opposing, and seven percent undecided.[113] Most significant of all was the apparent decision of Justice Department executives to encourage local police instead of federal law enforcement agencies to engage in electronic surveillance under Title III.

In the first year after passage of the omnibus crime control act, seven states adopted electronic surveillance laws which met Title III's standards for court-approved wiretapping and eavesdropping, and at least six other states seriously considered such laws. While Title III limited federal surveillance to the investigation of certain specific offenses associated with organized crime, the act treated the states far more generously. Authorizing states to adopt electronic surveillance laws covering any crime "dangerous to life, limb, or property, and punishable by imprisonment for more than one year," Title III went greatly beyond the A.B.A. project's recommended standard for "important investigations" or "a limited class of designated violations."[114] This was one of the sections Ramsey Clark's Justice Department had opposed but had been unable to delete because of President Johnson's refusal to allow it to sponsor a narrower Administration bill. Even Robert Kennedy's 1962 bill and Professor Blakey's draft for the crime commission had more carefully circumscribed state surveillance powers.

Recognizing the wide scope Title III offered for local police wiretapping and bugging, Attorney General Mitchell chose to emphasize state rather than federal electronic surveillance. To set an example for states to follow, the Justice Department's anti-crime program for the District of Columbia included a proposal that Congress authorize Washington police to engage in court-approved electronic surveillance for virtually the entire range of offenses in the D.C. criminal code.[115] Moreover, the Law Enforcement Assistance Administration staged a series of regional conferences in 1969 to acquaint police with new law enforcement techniques. The lectures and workshops specifically covered the use of electronic surveillance. At least one of these meetings, held in Georgia, was devoted in part to demonstrating how to operate electronic listening devices. Although only two states in the region had electronic surveillance laws, the L.E.A.A.'s program conveyed an implicit message that effective anti-crime programs required such legislation.[116]

Attorney General Mitchell's encouragement of local wiretapping and bugging was accomplished quietly without arousing controversy. In an address to the A.B.A. convention, he emphasized his recognition that "because wiretapping is an invasion of privacy, a judgment must be made as to whether it is 'reasonable' to wiretap in a particular case in order to obtain information that is necessary to combat organized crime." Whenever a federal agency sought a judicial warrant for electronic surveillance, the Attorney General said he "insisted that each application and full supporting papers be personally presented to me for my evaluation." Mitchell had "refused to authorize a number of applications which, upon inspection, posed more dangers to personal privacy than would be warranted, in my opinion, by the information which the tap was designed to collect." The Attorney General did not mention, however, the growing local police surveillance over which he had no operational supervision. Yet by endorsing the view of "most recognized law enforcement experts" that wiretapping was "our most useful tool in obtaining information about the organized criminal syndicate," he gave local police further incentive to begin or expand their own wiretapping.[117] The Justice Department's failure to propose and secure passage of an electronic surveillance law strictly limiting local law enforcement had made this widespread invasion of privacy possible, and now the Department's program under John Mitchell made it more likely.

During President Nixon's first months in office, the Attorney General also considered what to do about Title II and Miranda. Soon after the 1968 election federal Circuit Judge Henry J. Friendly had offered a widely publicized proposal to amend the Fifth Amendment privilege against self-incrimination, and his amendment was introduced in the House by Republican Leader Gerald Ford.[118] A Gallup poll taken early in 1969 reported that seventy-five percent of the public thought the courts were not dealing harshly enough with criminals—up from sixty-three percent a year before.[119] At the same time F.B.I. Director Hoover issued his sharpest criticism in years of judicial decisions which "negate the enforcement of the law to ensure that the criminal is protected." The new Justice Department executives shared Hoover's view, as indicated when Assistant Attorney General Will Wilson, head of the Criminal Division, charged that Supreme Court rulings "made punishment for crime less swift and less certain."[120] In mid-April, therefore, the draft of a Presidential message calling for a broad study of criminal procedures was circulated in the Department.

The message asked Congress to examine the effects of Miranda, Wade, and other decisions governing police investigative practices with a view to considering either constitutional amendments or legislation to change the balance between defendants' rights and police authority.[121] Suggesting that Congress might apply the federal confession and eye-witness identification rules in Title II to the states, the draft message relied on Congressional power under Section Five of the Fourteenth Amendment to enact appropriate legislation to enforce due process of law in the states. That power had apparently been part of the constitutional authority under which Congress had adopted Title III, establishing rules for the admissibility of evidence obtained by electronic eavesdropping in state courts and administrative proceedings.[122] The Supreme Court had declared in 1966, however, that Section Five granted Congress "no power to restrict, abrogate, or dilute" the due process guarantees of the Fourteenth Amendment.[123] The alternative of amending the constitution had the support of the crime commission minority and Judge Lumbard of the A.B.A. criminal justice project, among many other legal experts. Justice Walter V. Schaefer of the Illinois Supreme Court, for example, made a powerful argument for restructuring pretrial interrogation procedures so that all questioning would be conducted by or before a judicial officer; but such a reform to eliminate police misconduct would not win support, Schaefer believed, unless the privilege against self-incrimination was modified to permit disclosure at his trial of a suspect's failure to answer questions.[124]

The comprehensive study of pretrial procedures contemplated in the Justice Department's draft message might have provided a valuable forum for developing similarly constructive responses to Miranda. If it concentrated on amending the constitution, rather than attempting to modify Supreme Court decisions by statute, it could render Title II irrelevant and avoid a direct challenge to the Supreme Court's authority. At the very least, it might have focused attention on the mounting empirical data showing that Miranda did not significantly affect police interrogation results.

After the appointment of Judge Warren E. Burger as Chief Justice and the resignation of Justice Abe Fortas, Attorney General Mitchell decided against recommending the draft message to the President. By offering President Nixon a chance to make a decisive shift in the composition of the Supreme Court, Justice Fortas' departure raised the prospect that his successor might join Chief Justice Burger and the three remaining Miranda dissenters to form a new majority which would reconsider past rulings and reorient the Court's future course. Before his appointment the New Chief Justice had expressed sympathy with proposals like Judge Schaefer's to reform pretrial questioning, although as head of the A.B.A. project's advisory committee on prosecution and defense, Burger had urged wider extension of free legal counsel to cover misdemeanor defendants and had supported the principle that suspects should be offered counsel routinely in the police booking process.[125] It was ironical if his nomination influenced the Attorney General to set aside the full-scale study of pretrial rules, because Chief Justice Burger had strongly advocated revision of criminal procedures through legislation based on research by special commissions rather than through court decisions.

Having discarded the idea of a constitutional amendment, the Justice Department turned back to Title II as a vehicle for persuading the newly constituted Supreme Court to modify Miranda and Wade. Assistant Attorney General Will Wilson, apparently without previously consulting the Attorney General, issued a memorandum directing federal prosecutors to take Title II into account in deciding whether to introduce confessions or eye-witness testimony as evidence in federal trials.[126] Attorney General Mitchell backed the new policy and later revealed his intention to seek a test of the Supreme Court's rules. Calling Miranda "a great psychological blow to the morale of our local police departments," he announced that the Department would no longer automatically concede error in cases where confessions had been obtained without the proper warnings. Since Title II said confessions could be admitted unless ruled "involuntary" and failure to warn a suspect of his rights did not necessarily make a confession involuntary, federal prosecutors were to present voluntary confessions as evidence even if a law enforcement officer "inadvertently fails to give a full warning."[127]

Mitchell's policy did not dispute the validity of Miranda's warning and right to counsel requirements since he still instructed federal officers to give the full warnings prior to interrogation. The precise issue for the courts would, therefore, be whether and under what conditions an inadvertent mistake might not prevent introduction of an otherwise voluntary statement as evidence. According to this interpretation Title II might be upheld as a constitutional way to lubricate the exclusionary rule where there were technical lapses by federal agents. The Supreme Court might find the statute to be a legitimate exercise of Congressional power to lay down federal procedural rules for enforcing Miranda's constitutional standards.[128] Since it did not affect state court procedures, Title II would have no bearing on the exclusion of confessions at that level. Several weeks after the Attorney General's announcement, however, Philadelphia district attorney Arlen Specter, backed by a resolution approved at the National District Attorneys Association convention, appealed a state court decision excluding a voluntary confession on Miranda grounds. The Philadelphia prosecutor contended that Title II required the courts to admit voluntary confessions in both state and federal trials.[129]

The Justice Department also implemented Title II's provision aimed at Wade. Mitchell declared, "Where we are convinced that the lineup was fair—for example, where the suspect was lined up with a number of suspects of similar physical characteristics—we will attempt to introduce the lineup identification on the ground that it was based on an independent recollection and not on any inherently coercive features of the lineup procedures." The Supreme Court might thus be compelled to reconsider its use of the exclusionary rule to protect suspects' right to the presence of counsel at this stage of the criminal process. Once again, the Department did not oppose in principle the Court's interpretation of the Sixth Amendment, but only the exclusion of testimony as a means to enforce a defendant's right.

In speeches delivered during the following months, Attorney General Mitchell did not defend his implementation of Title II as contributing to more effective police investigation. Unlike his arguments for electronic surveillance and preventive detention, which he said were required to solve specific law enforcement problems, his justification for using Title II was only that it would improve the morale of local police. The Administration's aim was "to reverse the psychological demoralization and frustration that. . .was particularly acute in the law enforcement community." The Attorney General made his decision to authorize the admission of voluntary confessions "which may not strictly adhere to all the requirements of the Miranda warning" in order to "demonstrate our support for law enforcement." Mitchell believed his action "had an enormous impact on the morale of the law enforcement community"; several groups of high-ranking police officials told him "that their previous pessimism is now replaced by optimism and enthusiasm."[130] Because Miranda had become a symbol of judicial restrictions on the police, implementation of Title II helped satisfy their emotional needs.

The importance of serving this function should not be ignored. Even Ramsey Clark had acknowledged in early 1968 that the police feeling that their hands were tied was "more psychological than practical in terms of police activity."[131] According to a report submitted to the National Commission on the Causes and Prevention of Violence in June, 1969, police across the nation were becoming politicized. Professor Jerome Skolnick, the report's author and a close observer of police behavior, described "the emergence of the police as a self-conscious, independent political power" which in many communities rivaled "even duly elected officials in influence." There was a growing tendency for the police "to see themselves as an independent, militant minority asserting itself in the political arena." Skolnick cited numerous instances where police brought pressure to bear on regular political institutions, ranging from organized support of political candidates to lobbying in state legislatures for broader authority to use deadly force. The election of Minneapolis Mayor Charles Stenvig, a police detective running as an independent and pledging "to take the handcuffs off our police," dramatized Skolnick's report.[132] Under these circumstances Justice Department policy could be defended as a deliberate attempt to prevent police frustration and anger from getting out of control and to reduce the feelings of alienation which were being expressed in growing police militancy and political activism.

Attorney General Mitchell's crime program included more than electronic surveillance and implementation of Title II. The Nixon Administration's proposal for pretrial detention of dangerous criminal suspects was its first and most controversial measure, while other changes in criminal procedures were advanced in legislative recommendations dealing with criminal justice in the District of Columbia, narcotics control, and organized crime. Much of the program inspired vigorous opposition from civil liberties groups, legal scholars, and the organized bar. Except for pretrial detention the Department's proposals received little public attention, and most had originated outside the Department. For instance, the District of Columbia crime commission appointed by President Johnson had endorsed pretrial detention in 1967 as a means of preventing criminal offenses by defendants out on bail. Several leading advocates of bail reform had long supported pretrial jailing of dangerous felony defendants under carefully circumscribed conditons with judges required to file written justification for denying bail. Just before the Nixon Administration took office, a Senate Judiciary Subcommittee headed by Senator Joseph Tydings held extensive hearings on the need for preventive detention.[133] While it raised serious practical and constitutional challenges, it was not entirely the new Administration's idea and could be defended as constitutional under at least one Supreme Court interpretation of the Eight Amendment proscription against excessive bail.[134]

Other elements of the Attorney General's program had different origins. The Department's D.C. crime and narcotics bills included a request that Washington police and federal narcotics agents be given "no-knock" authority to enter residences unannounced to seize evidence. Patterned generally after a New York statute, the measure would permit police to secure a special search warrant from a judge authorizing them to enter without knocking or identifying themselves. Warrants could be issued upon a showing by police that the evidence to be seized, i.e., drugs, might be easily or quickly disposed of. To secure entry officers could "break open an outer or inner door or window of a building." Defending the proposal Mitchell explained, "All too frequently violators are able to destroy contraband drugs while officers executing a search warrant are going through the process of knocking and announcing their authority and purpose."[135] In Ker v. California (1963) the Supreme Court had upheld an officer's failure to give notice before entry if he believed that a suspect "was in possession of narcotics, which could be quickly and easily destroyed."[136]

In a message on organized crime, President Nixon endorsed a recommendation from the National Commission on Reform of Federal Criminal Laws for changing witness immunity rules. As stated by the President, the new standard would provide that "a witness could not be prosecuted on the basis of anything he said while testifying, but he would not be immune from prosecution based on other evidence of his offense."[137] The purpose of immunity legislation, upheld previously by the Supreme Court, was to compel a person to testify in exchange for a guarantee that his words would not be used to incriminate him. Since current federal laws afforded absolute immunity against future prosecution for the offense to which the questions related, the reform commission believed they went beyond Supreme Court standards and could be modified for the sake of uniformity without infringing Fifth Amendment rights. Opposing this change, the A.C.L.U. charged that it would seriously undercut the privilege against self-incrimination because there would be "no effective way in which a defendant [could] really protect himself and overcome the government's contention that the evidence against him was obtained from completely independent sources." In reply Assistant Attorney General Wilson cited recent Court decisions "indicating that complete witness immunity from prosecution is not essential and that a witness' privilege against self-incrimination would not be violated if he were compelled to testify under an assurance that the evidence he gave could not be used against him, either directly or indirectly." Professor Robert G. Dixon, Jr., a consultant to the reform commission, also testified in support of the new immunity rules.[138]

The Justice Department also favored passage of an organized crime control bill produced in 1969 by Senator McClellan's

Judiciary Subcommittee. Among its controversial provisions were revival of the power of federal grand juries to make reports without returning indictments and imposition of thirty-year sentences on defendants found to be "special offenders." The Judicial Conference of the United States, the policy-making body for the federal judiciary headed by Chief Justice Burger, opposed broadening grand jury powers, apparently sharing the A.C.L.U.'s fear that "runaway grand juries" might make criminal-type accusations that would injure the reputations of individuals who could not defend themselves adequately. This provision was later amended to allow persons named in grand jury presentments to present witnesses in their behalf before the grand jury.[139] Criticizing the special offender category, which would include persons previously convicted two or more times of felony offenses, persons convicted once in certain conspiracies, and persons who committed a felony as "part of a pattern" of criminal conduct, the A.C.L.U. envisioned its possible use not just against organized crime, but to subject student militants or antiwar dissenters to thirty-year prison terms. Even Assistant Attorney General Wilson recognized that the special offender provision raised serious problems of due process in three areas—"specificity of definitions for categories of offenders, procedures for making determinations, and appeal provisions." Although Wilson suggested changes to avoid "successful constitutional attack," he opposed modifications which would limit the category to persons convicted of certain organized crimes and would require proof beyond a reasonable doubt, not merely a preponderance of the information, to place a defendant in the special offender class.[140]

While the grand jury report and special offender provisions of the organized crime bill raised serious policy questions, they were less significant than another section, Title VII, which posed the most direct challenge to the Supreme Court since the omnibus crime bill's anti-Miranda measure. In the spring of 1969 the Court ruled in Alderman v. United States that government files containing illegally obtained evidence against a defendant, i.e., the results of electronic surveillance violating the Berger and Katz standards, must be turned over to the defendant for his examination. Justice Byron White's opinion rejected the government's argument that the records should first be presented to the trial judge who would determine whether the contents were arguably relevant to the case and should be disclosed to the defendant. Instead, the Court held that the defendant must be "armed with the specific records of overheard conversations and with the right to cross-examine the appropriate officials in regard to the connection between these records and the case made against him." This requirement was found necessary to guard "against the possibility that the trial judge, through lack of time or unfamiliarity with the information contained in or suggested by the materials, will be unable to provide the scrutiny which the Forth Amendment exclusionary rule demands."[141]

Under the guise of organized crime control, the Senate Judiciary Committee with Justice Department approval sought to reverse the Alderman decision. Title VII required that before government records of illegally overheard conversations could be turned over to the defendant, the trial judge must determine that the information in the files might be relevant to the case and its disclosure was "in the interest of justice." Furthermore, the bill declared that illegal means of obtaining evidence could not be challenged if such conduct occurred more than five years before the defendant committed the offense with which he was charged. Thus the government would not have to produce all records of illegal electronic surveillance against the defendant. Having lost before the Supreme Court by a 5-3 vote, the Justice Department supported this attempt in Congress to overrule the decision. But Alderman was not subject to easy reconsideration after President Nixon's appointees reached the bench. The opinion was written by Justice White and joined by Justice Stewart, who both had dissented in Miranda; and even the dissents by Justices Harlan and Fortas did not challenge the majority's basic rule, but only urged an exception for "sensitive national security material." The sole member of the Court who might endorse Title VII's principle was Justice Black. Despite the Supreme Court's near unanimity in requiring disclosure of electronic surveillance records without judicial screening, the

Attorney General approved legislation in direct conflict with the Court's constitutional ruling.

When the House Judiciary Committee considered the Senate bill in 1970, it dropped the anti-Alderman provision from Title VII. The Senate accepted this change, so that the Organized Crime Control Act of 1970 only limited disclosure of illegally seized evidence and surveillance data obtained five years before an event relating to a criminal case. This legislative rule may be consistent with Court opinions holding that attenuation can dissipate the connection between illegal surveillance and the Government's proof at a trial years later.[142]

The Justice Department had thus modified its traditional relationship to the Supreme Court. Title VII indicated the Attorney General desired more than to offer psychological rewards to the police, as might have been justified in the political circumstances of 1969, or to strengthen law enforcement with measures like electronic surveillance, pretrial detention, and no-knock searches which were arguably within constitutional limits. Instead, he chose to challenge the Supreme Court's role as final authority on constitutional standards for criminal justice. If his implementation of Title II's anti-Miranda and Wade sections had been the only instance where the Department acted contrary to Court decisions, it might have been rationalized on the ground that Congress had already enacted the measure and wanted it tested in court. The attempt to reverse Alderman was different, however, for it placed the Executive Branch firmly on the side of an assertion of Congressional power to overrule constitutional decisions by simple legislation. The Justice Department no longer saw its function as that of reconciling conflicting demands for effective law enforcement and for protection of defendants' rights within the constitutional bounds established by the Supreme Court. It would disregard the Court's decisions as a guide for legislation when they stood in the way of what the Department believed was in its own interest.

6. THE JUSTICE DEPARTMENT
AND CRIMINAL JUSTICE

One of the greatest changes that took place in the legal system during the 1960's was the nationalization of law enforcement politics. The Supreme Court led the way, and the Justice Department followed by taking on responsibility for leadership in criminal justice policy-making. Before the decade began, the Department provided a few technical services to local police and secured their cooperation in solving federal crimes, but it did not attempt to develop a national criminal justice policy through either legislative standards or financial assistance programs. By 1970, however, the Attorney General was in a crucial position to influence state as well as federal policy and the course of constitutional interpretation. The character of criminal justice in America now depends to a greater degree on how the Attorney General weighs the various demands for stronger crime control, for protection of criminal defendants' rights, and for adherence to constitutional norms.

The experience of the 1960's demonstrated the Justice Department's limited capacity to reconcile these conflicting values into a coherent policy. Before crime became a national political issue, Robert Kennedy was able to sponsor measures to improve the fairness of criminal justice without arousing great controversy. His limited wiretap bill embodied the first federal legislative proposal to circumscribe the powers of local law enforcement to use illegally obtained evidence in state courts, in line with the Supreme Court's decision in Mapp v. Ohio. The Allen Committee's report led to passage of bills broadening the availability of legal counsel for federal defendants and reform-ing the bail system for federal courts. After the Escobedo decision in 1964, the Justice Department worked with legal scholars and bar association leaders to develop a constructive response to the Court's initiative. It was receptive to proposals for federal financial assistance for improving the quality of police departments, both as a means to combat crime and a way to curtail police misconduct. Since crime was not yet a highly visible subject, Attorney General Kennedy could develop policies that harmonized judicial and legislative actions with the concerns of the legal profession and the police.

The emergence of "law and order" as an issue in the 1964 Presidential campaign made it politically as well as technically advisable to create a national crime commission to survey problems of criminal justice. But the Department gradually lost its ability to maintain coherent policies as pressures increased for action to reduce crime and the Supreme Court moved ahead to give greater protection to defendants' rights. Although the crime commission offered an excellent opportunity to pursue a comprehensive strategy for coping with these tensions, it fragmented the Department's efforts instead. When Katzenbach permitted it to avoid studying the effects of Supreme Court decisions and President Johnson opposed its electronic surveillance recommendations, the commission was unable to serve as a useful ally in dealing with Congress. Hence, Ramsey Clark lost influence over Congressional enactment of Titles II and III of the omnibus crime bill; and massive federal aid to local law enforcement, as promised by Title I, did not satisfy the aroused emotions of the police and the public. The initiative passed to the Supreme Court's critics.

The President's stand on electronic surveillance prevented the Justice Department from working out a more acceptable compromise that would reconcile legislative and judicial interests. Despite the Supreme Court's willingness to accept a carefully drawn measure, Johnson refused to make the crime commission's electronic surveillance proposal a part of his legislative program. Thus the Attorney General was unable to narrow Title III's broad wiretapping and eavesdropping provisions. The President's decision not to implement Title III brought an almost complete breakdown in executive-legislative cooperation. By 1968 the main actors in the process of policy-making for criminal justice were in serious conflict with each other, largely because of the Justice Department's inability to bring them together.

After Attorney General Mitchell took office, the Department completely reassessed its program and tried to win back influence over Congress and local law enforcement. In doing so

Mitchell chose to maximize his immediate political support through legislative proposals and executive decisions designed to take advantage of public concern about crime. By refusing to adjust to the Supreme Court's decision in Alderman and by implementing Title II's anti-Miranda and Wade provisions, the Department failed to harmonize its policy with judicial standards and with those elements of the public and the legal profession who respected the Court's authority as constitutional policy-maker. While the political risks to the Attorney General were not great, the change in the relationships among legislative, executive, and judicial institutions implied by his action could undermine the stability of the legal system in the long run.

Passage of the crime control act had raised a basic question. Should Congress assert control over the establishment of standards for due process of law? Congress had reacted to Miranda, Wade, and Alderman with bills revising federal rules for the admissibility of confessions and testimony and disclosure of illegally seized evidence. These measures fell short of exercising legislative power under Section Five of the Fourteenth Amendment since they did not directly affect the states. But Title III's electronic surveillance standards were an assertion of that power, and the Nixon Administration came close to proposing similar legislation to deal with confessions in early 1969. The potential now exists for further Congressional efforts to redefine the rights of criminal defendants and to modify judicial procedures in criminal cases throughout the country.

The danger in legislative solutions is that they will be more influenced by partisanship and electoral politics than are judicial policies. Facing this prospect, the Supreme Court under Chief Justice Burger may adjust to the consequences of its earlier decisions. Attorney General Mitchell sought a reevaluation of the exclusionary rule, not just because of its effect on police, but because trial courts appeared overburdened with pretrial hearings on the exclusion of confessions, witness testimony, and evidence seized by the police. A judicial retreat from the Warren Court's rigid exclusionary rule might be justified, therefore, to avoid a shift in control over definition of due process of law to the political branches of the federal government. In one sense this would satisfy the Court's critics, but from a broader perspective it would maintain the orderly evolution of constitutional norms.

The Justice Department has a crucial role in determining whether Congress or the Supreme Court will establish due process standards in the future. Should it press test cases under Title II to challenge Miranda, it would place the Court in a dilemma. If the Court declared Title II unconstitutional, it might inspire renewed political attack; but deference to Congress would legitimize legislative revision of constitutional decisions by statute. This is the dilemma Ramsey Clark and Professor Herbert Wechsler hoped the good sense and discretion of federal prosecutors would avoid. Unless the Attorney General withdrew his support of Title II and bills like the anti-Alderman legislation, however, he would compel the Supreme Court to reconsider not only its past decisions, but its entire role in the legal system. As a result of the nationalization of criminal justice politics in the 1960's, the balance between legislative and judicial power over constitutional interpretation could be substantially altered.

3

BLACK

MILITANCY

"Law and order" pressures on the Justice Department during the 1960's represented far more than a concern for increasing rates of ordinary criminal behavior. Beginning with disorders in New York City's black ghettos during the summer of 1964, urban riots spread to virtually every major city, reaching their greatest intensity in 1967 and after the assassination of Dr. Martin Luther King, Jr., in the spring of 1968. Although prevention and control of civil disorders was mainly a task for state and local authorities, the Justice Department was involved from the outset in cooperative efforts to assist local officials and to explain the causes of urban riots to the public. These outbreaks raised serious issues of social reform, racial discrimination, police-community relations, and law enforcement strategy. Among the challenges posed specifically to the legal system was whether fears of mass black violence would lead to the repression of individuals and groups whose outspoken rhetoric of protest against poverty and prejudice might be held responsible for civil unrest.

At the same time that the Justice Department was developing a larger role in national policy-making for criminal justice, it was called upon to establish policies for dealing with black militant leaders and organizations in the context of civil disorders. Similar measures were required to cope with growing protest against the war in Vietnam, to be discussed in the next chapter. The Department's response to black militancy and antiwar dissent raised a different set of policy questions than did the criminal justice programs described in Chapter Two. The debate over procedural rules for criminal law enforcement compelled federal executives to strike a balance between demands for crime control and for equality and fairness in the system of justice. Black militants and white radicals, on the other hand, became the object of demands for political repression that forced the Justice Department to weigh the values of political liberty and impartial law enforcement against the desire to maintain stability and authority by suppressing unpopular groups.

A major difference between the Department's approaches to black militants and antiwar protesters was in the degree of direct federal law enforcement responsibility. Urban unrest placed more immediate pressures on local agencies, while Vietnam dissent focused to a greater extent on national government instrumentalities like the Selective Service System. The Department's role with regard to black militancy was, therefore, usually as a guide and supplement to local law enforcement. Nevertheless, as a carry-over from its concern about Communist subversion in the 1950's, the F.B.I. reported in 1964 that the Communist Party made a "constant effort" to exploit civil rights issues. On the basis of F.B.I. surveillance, J. Edgar Hoover declared that recent racial demonstrations had attracted Communists, "usually in a hidden role," and that legitimate leaders were "hard pressed to keep them out and minimize their influence."[1]

During the next several years the Justice Department under Nicholas Katzenbach and Ramsey Clark attempted to play down the F.B.I.'s role in coping with black militants. They sought other sources of advice and information and attempted to encourage constructive means of preventing racial disorders. Katzenbach and Clark hoped to persuade the public and law enforcement agencies that black militancy was a sympton of deeper social ills and a police-community relations problem, not a danger to the nation's internal security. Toward the end of the decade, however, black militant groups came to be perceived in much the same way as the Communist Party had once been. Congress adopted ill-conceived legislation to punish riot agitators, and one small but highly publicized group, the Black Panther Party, emerged as the focus for national fears of guerrilla warfare. While local and later federal prosecutions threatened to infringe freedom of speech, a more significant development was creation of a national intelligence surveillance network. What began as an effort to give technical advice to local police risked becoming an instrument for political repression.

1. THE STIRRINGS
OF UNREST, 1964-65

The first large-scale urban disorders of the 1960's occurred in New York City in August, 1964. During a week of sporadic rioting following police shooting of a black youth, at least 150 persons were injured and 520 arrested. Three days after the trouble began, President Johnson ordered a complete F.B.I. investigation to assist local authorities and determine whether there were any violations of federal law. No specific federal statutes were mentioned, but it was said to be normal procedure for the F.B.I. to conduct an investigation where there had been such an extensive and prolonged outbreak of violence. The most likely reason for President Johnson's public announcement was concern that Republican Presidential candidate Barry Goldwater might make political capital out of the disorders, which took place a week after his nomination. Charging the Administration with being lax in dealing with urban violence, Goldwater declared, "We would not be having the trouble we are having today in the cities if we had an Attorney General who was not always trying to be moderate and would go on and apply the law."[2]

On the same day as the President's statement, New York's Acting Mayor Screvane asserted that the disorders were incited in part by "fringe groups, including the Communist party and some other more radical groups." Two days later President Johnson confirmed at a news conference that on the basis of F.B.I. reports he had the impression "there are extremist elements involved, and at the appropriate time I think their identity will be made known." Meanwhile, city officials secured a court injunction barring demonstrations by William Epton, chairman of the Harlem Progressive Labor Club and the Harlem Defense Council, and rent-strike organizer Jesse Gray's Community Council on Housing. At a hearing on continuance of the injunction, police disclosed evidence to justify the court order. A tape recording was played of a street corner rally where Epton told a crowd, "We will take our freedom. We will take it by any means necessary. . .we will create a new government.

And in the process of smashing the state, we are going to have to kill a lot of these cops, a lot of these judges, and we'll have to go up against their army. We'll organize our own militia and our own army." At another meeting Jesse Gray allegedly called for a hundred skilled black revolutionaries ready to die to stop police brutality and to engage in guerrilla warfare. An F.B.I. statement later emphasized the role of Epton's Progressive Labor Movement in deliberately inciting disorders by printing and distributing thousands of handbills with a photograph of the policeman who shot the black youth under the headline, "Wanted for Murder."[3]

The F.B.I.'s description of Epton's activity was part of an analysis prepared for the President on the disturbances in New York and other cities during the summer of 1964. The White House released a summary of the F.B.I.'s findings in September. Although its overall conclusion was that "there was no systematic planning or organization of any of the city riots," the report did indentify the Progressive Labor Movement's role in New York. The F.B.I. labeled it "a Marxist-Leninist group following the more violent Chinese Communist line," and Epton was described as a former Communist Party member who resigned from the party because it was not sufficiently revolutionary. Other individuals "with histories of Communist affiliation" were said to have instigated riots elsewhere. The F.B.I. called attention to the growth of black militancy, asserting that "a number of violent agitators" had arisen. Its report specifically mentioned "one widely publicized ex-convict [who] announced a broadly based nationalist movement for Negroes only. In this announcement, which was frequently repeated and widely noticed, Negroes were urged to abandon the doctrine of non-violence and to organize rifle clubs 'to protect their lives and property.' "[4] This unnamed figure was undoubtedly Malcolm X, the former Black Muslim minister who had broken with the Nation of Islam and was traveling in Africa during the summer of 1964.

The Justice Department was deeply interested in the expanding black nationalism of Malcolm X. Alex Haley, who was assisting Malcolm X on his autobiography, agreed to meet privately with Civil Rights Division head Burke Marshall while Malcolm X was still abroad. According to Haley, Marshall was chiefly interested in Malcolm X's finances. Haley explained that payments from the publisher of the autobiography, fees for speeches, possible donations to his organization, and loans from his sister paid for Malcolm X's extensive travels.[5] Marshall had apparently considered the black nationalist leader's activities so sensitive that he chose not to rely on a routine F.B.I. interview. Perhaps he wanted to avoid giving an impression of Justice Department harassment by making contact openly rather than by instituting a covert investigation. In any event the assassination of Malcolm X in February, 1965, removed the leading black militant from the scene.

Another source of federal interest in black militant groups was an F.B.I. investigation of the Student Committee on Travel to Cuba, which led to a federal indictment in September, 1964, against eleven persons for conspiring to violate regulations prohibiting travel to Cuba without a valid passport. In the course of this investigation it was learned that several black participants in the trip to Cuba formed, upon their return, a Black Liberation Front in New York City. Since both the F.B.I. and New York police knew about the organization, New York police officials decided to place an undercover informant in the group. While the informant was a city policeman, local authorities shared his reports with the F.B.I. His information resulted in the F.B.I.'s arrest, in February, 1965, of three Black Liberation Front members and a Canadian woman for conspiracy to destroy government property. They had planned to dynamite the Statue of Liberty and other national monuments to symbolize a violent repudiation of American institutions. The undercover agent had traveled with the Front's leader, Robert Collier, to Canada to secure the dynamite and help bring it back to New York. Based on the informant's testimony, the four were convicted in federal court.[6]

While the Black Liberation Front case was a federal prosecution, New York authorities bore responsibility for bringing charges against William Epton under the state's criminal anarchy law, which had not been used since 1919 when Benjamin

Gitlow was convicted for distributing Communist pamphlets. District attorney Frank Hogan's office accused Epton of advocating and conspiring to advocate the violent overthrow of the New York state government. Another count charged conspiracy to riot. Epton was convicted in 1965 on all counts and appealed, but his case did not reach the Supreme Court for three more years. The evidence against him included not only the handbills he distributed and tapes of his speeches during the 1964 Harlem disorders, but testimony that he had formed "a group dedicated to armed revolt against the police under the direction of 'block captains' and with the assistance of 'terrorist bands,' equipped with Molotov cocktails that Epton himself had explained how to use."[7]

Upholding the conviction, the New York Court of Appeals found that the trial judge had properly interpreted the anarchy law to apply only where the defendant's speech created a clear and present danger of an attempt to overthrow the government. There was some doubt, however, about the judge's instructions to the jury on the riot conspiracy count, since he failed to make a distinction between constitutionally protected and unprotected overt acts in furtherance of the conspiracy. According to prevailing Supreme Court doctrine in Yates v. United States, for advocacy to be an ingredient of a crime it had to be advocacy "of action not merely abstract doctrine."[8] The judge had not specifically advised the jury to consider as overt acts only those speeches and writings which went beyond advocacy of abstract doctrine. As Justice Douglas later noted, the failure to make that distinction meant it was impossible "to determine whether a protected activity was employed to convict Epton of conspiracy to riot."[9]

When the case reached the Supreme Court in 1968, the Court decided not to hear the appeal. Separate opinions by Justices Stewart and Douglas gave some insight, however, into the Court's thinking. Stewart offered an explanation for the decision. Epton's one-year sentence for conspiracy to riot was to run concurrently with his one-year sentence for criminal anarchy. Since Stewart did not believe the riot conviction presented a substantial federal question, he concluded that the

Court was not required to consider whether the New York anarchy statutes, either on their face or as applied, violated the First and Fourteenth Amendments. The Court was following the rule that "there is no occasion to review a conviction on one count of an indictment if the judgment on another count is valid and the sentences are concurrent."[10]

Justice Stewart then suggested why the riot conspiracy conviction did not raise a substantial federal question. He thought it was "at least arguable that a State cannot convict a man of criminal conspiracy without first demonstrating some constitutionally unprotected overt act in furtherance of the alleged unlawful agreement." But the State had presented proof of activities that could "make no serious claim to constitutional protection." Justice Stewart implied, therefore, that because some of the overt acts were unprotected, the judge's failure to instruct the jury to disregard protected speech was not a fatal flaw. Justice Douglas disagreed. The charge to the jury had "made no qualifications whatsoever as to the permissible range of the use of speech and publications as overt acts." The conviction might thus "have rested in whole or in part on overt acts which had First Amendment protection." Before Epton's speeches and leaflets could be used against him, the judge should have instructed the jury "to determine that the particular speech or particular publication was not constitutionally protected." Justice Douglas apparently stood alone, however, in his view of the proper scope of conspiracy prosecutions.[11]

The basic free speech issues raised first in the Epton case were to come up again in the years ahead as black militancy grew in scope and intensity. State and federal conspiracy prosecutions provided a way to tie the political advocacy of a group to its illegal behavior. Without a clear constitutional rule that protected speech could not be used to support a criminal conviction, conspiracy trials could mix conduct with advocacy and discredit the expression of vigorous dissent. Moreover, law enforcement agencies could investigate all radical groups if legal political activity were admissible as evidence in a prosecution for conspiracy to commit illegal acts.

In its 1965 annual report the F.B.I. revealed for the first time that it "had under investigation a number of Negro nationalist groups which are antiwhite and actively promote racial hatred. These included organizations such as the Nation of Islam, frequently referred to as the 'Black Muslims,' the Muslim Mosque, Inc., the Revolutionary Action Movement and the Black Liberation Front." The F.B.I. had placed these groups under surveillance because they had "considerable potential for violence as evidenced by various recent incidents such as the plot by members of the Black Liberation Front to dynamite the Statue of Liberty and other national monuments."[12] Although it was not made public until 1969, the F.B.I. was using wiretapping to maintain surveillance of Black Muslim leader Elijah Muhammed under national security authorization from the Attorney General.[13] It is impossible to estimate the extent of F.B.I. surveillance through informants or electronic devices used against black militants, but the groups named in the Bureau's report were clearly receiving special scrutiny. Much data could easily be gathered by following news stories, collecting publications, or attending open meetings. The New York City Police Department's Bureau of Special Services, which was responsible for surveillance of the Black Liberation Front, shared information with the F.B.I. In most other cities, however, police had not developed their capacity for gathering intelligence about black militant groups.

2. THE EMERGENCE OF
"BLACK POWER," 1966-67

Far more than the New York disorders the year before, the Watts riot in Los Angeles during August, 1965, shocked the nation as ghetto dwellers turned to spontaneous arson and looting in response to wretched living conditions, frustrated hopes, and perceptions of police oppression. The Mayor of Los Angeles claimed the rioting was plotted "by a small vicious group of trained troublemakers"; but there were no substantial allegations of incitement by specific black militant groups.[14] In 1966 civil rights groups like the Student Nonviolent Coordinating Committee and the Council on Racial Equality articulated a new black aggressiveness, as such spokesmen as Stokely Carmichael of S.N.C.C. and Floyd McKissick of C.O.R.E. adopted the slogan "black power." Local political action under the black power label developed first in the South, where the Deacons for Defense and Justice were formed in Bogalusa, Louisiana, and the Lowndes County, Alabama, Freedom Organization took as its symbol a black panther.[15]

During the summer of 1966, while traditional civil rights groups debated the meaning and usefulness of the black power concept, disorders occurred in many northern cities including Chicago and Cleveland. In mid-July Attorney General Katzenbach announced that the F.B.I. had no evidence of the outbreaks being part of any conspiracy, and he rejected the idea that calls for black power had anything to do with the riots. When a Cleveland grand jury linked that city's disorders to extremist agitators, Katzenbach disagreed with its findings. Instead, he asserted, riots were fomented by "agitators named disease and despair, joblessness and hopelessness, rat-infested housing and long-impacted cynicism. These sources of agitation are not the product of Communists or Black Nationalists." The F.B.I. was closely following the activities of the Nation of Islam and a new group, the Revolutionary Action Movement, because of their "strong potential for violence." But in testimony before the House Un-American Activities Committee, the Attorney General specifically discounted a report that R.A.M., supposedly led by Negro expatriate Robert F. Williams who lived in Cuba, inspired disturbances.[16]

Nevertheless, other public officials like Chicago Mayor Richard Daley, Ohio Senator Frank Lausche, and Brooklyn district attorney Aaron Koota charged that organized outside agitators were at work in their communities. Taking up these allegations, Florida Congressman William Cramer introduced a bill to make it a federal crime to cross state lines with intent to incite or participate in a riot. Congress had to "protect citizens from the professionals who make a business of riots," Cramer declared, citing reports that the same persons had been seen taking part in disorders in different cities. In August the House passed Cramer's bill as an amendment to the civil rights bill by an overwhelming 389-25 margin, but it died when the Senate failed to override a filibuster against the civil rights measure.[17] Congressman Cramer's argument was apparently confirmed in early September, however, when S.N.C.C. chairman Stokely Carmichael was arrested in Atlanta for inciting to riot. Carmichael was present when an angry crowd, gathering after a policeman shot and wounded a fleeing Negro car theft suspect, turned into a riot in which sixteen persons were injured. S.N.C.C. filed suit in federal court to enjoin Atlanta authorities from prosecuting Carmichael on the ground that the state's riot incitement statute was unconstitutional. Within a month Congressman Cramer was defending his bill as a deterrent against "the Stokely Carmichaels who stir up the Negroes against everyone."[18]

When the Un-American Activities Committee announced plans to investigate the role of "subversive elements" in the riots, the more liberal House Judiciary Committee decided to hold hearings on the Cramer bill. Testifying for the Justice Department in October, Civil Rights Division head John Doar was skeptical about the need for a federal antiriot law since controlling disorders was essentially a local police function. Doar doubted the bill's effectiveness since it was difficult "to prove an intent to incite a riot at the very time the inciter crosses a state line." Noting the constitutional problems posed by any attempt to punish both conduct and speech, he warned that since the courts were vigilant in protecting First Amendment freedoms, Congress would place the bill in jeopardy "by appearing to reach too far, or by using vague or uncertain language in defining the crime sought to be punished." Congressman Cramer replied that juries would be able to determine an agitator's intent and that the First Amendment gave no one the right to incite a riot. Even Judiciary Chairman Emanuel Celler, who had opposed Cramer's bill in August, now agreed a federal response was needed to "the looting, vandalism, arson and bombing that has flared up in many communities."[19] As the 1966 session adjourned, it was not clear whether Congress would follow Celler's lead and move against only riotous acts, not speech.

By early 1967 the F.B.I. had stepped up its surveillance of black militant groups. In testimony before a House Appropriations Subcommittee in February, J. Edgar Hoover described the role of "violent, lawless, subversive and extremist elements" who were striving "ceaselessly to precipitate racial trouble and to take advantage of racial discord in this country." The Director paid special attention to the Progressive Labor Party, the Nation of Islam, and the Revolutionary Action Movement. According to Hoover, R.A.M. was "dedicated to the overthrow of the capitalist system in the United States, by violence if necessary, and its replacement by a Socialist system oriented toward the Chinese Communist interpretation of Marxism-Leninism." Although its membership was only about fifty, it had organized units in several large cities and its leaders had "participated in activities organized by the more militant civil rights leaders in order to expand its influence in racially tense areas." Hoover connected Stokely Carmichael to R.A.M., reporting that "in espousing his philosophy of black power, Carmichael has been in frequent contact with Max Stanford, field chairman of the Revolutionary Action Movement," and that Carmichael had "afforded Stanford assistance and guidance in forming a Black Panther party in New York city."[20]

The F.B.I. may have secured much of its data about R.A.M. from the New York police department, which had placed undercover agents in the group. Operating with the experience of its successful actions against William Epton and the Black Liberation Front, New York police chose to move against R.A.M. in June, 1967. Sixteen members were arrested in pre-dawn raids and indicted for conspiracy to advocate criminal anarchy. Two members, Arthur Harris and Herman Ferguson, were charged with conspiracy to assassinate N.A.A.C.P. executive director Roy Wilkins and Urban League director Whitney Young. After the simultaneous arrests and searches conducted by some 150 policemen, police spokesmen claimed to have seized thirty weapons, 1,000 rounds of ammunition, six boxes of literature, much of it allegedly following a Peking-oriented political line, and instructions on how to pull down power lines and make Molotov cocktails. The police department revealed it had begun surveillance of R.A.M. in July, 1965, and undercover agents had infiltrated the group to obtain information. Criticizing police for conducting a trial by publicity, the New York Civil Liberties Union declared, "Evidence that may or may not be admissible in court has been freely reported in an apparent effort to create an ineradicable impression of guilt in the minds of potential jurors."[21]

Several months later seven other members were charged in Philadelphia with plotting to kill President Johnson, J. Edgar Hoover, and the Mayor and police chief, again on the basis of reports by informants who infiltrated R.A.M.[22]

Lawyers for the sixteen indicted for criminal anarchy in New York blocked their trial by seeking a federal court injunction against the prosecution on the ground that the anarchy law violated the First Amendment. When the case reached the Supreme Court in 1969, counsel for the state argued that the charge was "not advocacy of ideas or opinions—it was advocacy of detailed revolution." Revealing some of the state's evidence, he explained that policemen who had infiltrated the group would testify about the details of its revolutionary training, including techniques for making Molotov cocktails, preventing police response by igniting gasoline in the streets, and disabling electric power facilities. They would also testify that two members staged a test run by firing shots from a car into store windows. "Their plans were made," counsel declared. "Their timetable was set. Weapons had been distributed—they were ready to go." When one Supreme Court Justice asked why the R.A.M. members were not prosecuted for substantive offenses like arson and weapons violations, counsel replied by citing the murder conspiracy case against Harris and Ferguson. Even though it held oral argument on the issue of whether a federal court could enjoin the criminal anarchy prosecution, the Supreme Court chose not to decide the case in 1969 and called for reargument the following term.[23]

The assassination conspiracy trial of Harris and Ferguson took place in 1968. Their defense counsel argued that the plot against Wilkins and Young was assisted, if not instigated, by a police undercover agent. The agent testified he had joined the other two in a three-man "terrorist cell," had helped them form a rifle club, and had driven Harris to Roy Wilkins' residence to seek an ambush site. The two were convicted, sentenced to three-and-a-half to seven years in prison, and appealed.[24] Like the Black Liberation Front case two years earlier, this prosecution raised the problem of complicity by undercover agents in the illegal activity they were supposed to be monitoring. Yet covert informant surveillance was thought necessary to provide intelligence for the F.B.I. and local police, at least in New York City.

The F.B.I.'s 1967 annual report made clear that it considered black militants primarily an internal security problem. J. Edgar Hoover also believed it was the role of law enforcement agencies to warn the nation about this new danger. The Student Nonviolent Coordinating Committee was now under F.B.I. surveillance, and both it and R.A.M. were said to constitute "a serious threat to our country's internal security." Hoover's report declared that militant organizations "preaching hatred for the white race. . .hope to disrupt the tranquility of our Nation with violence to further the concept of 'black power.' " Their leaders attempted to "spread domestic discord among Negroes by making inflammatory speeches and issuing hate-filled literature." Addressing police officials across the country, Hoover wrote in the F.B.I.'s Law Enforcement Bulletin that the general public was "becoming weary of persons who, for self-aggrandizement and monetary gain, exploit noble causes and agitate peaceful groups into rioting mobs." The F.B.I. Director urged public officials to "speak out and let everyone know that law and order will prevail."[25]

Despite the F.B.I.'s intelligence operations and its ties to local police, Justice Department executives decided in 1966-67 not to rely primarily on the Bureau for developing policies to guide local authorities in their response to civil disorders. Instead, Attorney General Katzenbach turned to the President's crime commission for technical advice. After holding a two-day conference with police and National Guard officials on the control of riots, the crime commission emphasized certain principles for handling disorders. It advised police not to react too quickly or with too much force to disorder "in the course of demonstrations." On the other hand, it urged strong law enforcement response, on the basis of advance planning and operational coordination, "in a true riot situation." How should police differentiate demonstrations from riots? One way would be for police and protest leaders to discuss in advance the appropriate times, places, and methods for demonstrations. In addition, the commission urged police to establish "procedures for the acquisition and channeling of intelligence. . .so that information is centralized and disseminated to those who need it." Thus the commission believed that both open contacts with militants and covert intelligence surveillance would help police reconcile their tasks of preserving order and protecting constitutional rights.[26]

The commission's Task Force on Police singled out New York, along with Washington and Philadelphia, for effectively handling potential riots. Instead of adopting the common police technique of using a massive amount of force to break up rioters into small groups as soon as possible, New York police had employed a different method successfully. When a mob formed, they did not try to break it up directly. The police blocked off streets but left an avenue of escape for the mob. No shots were fired in answer to sporadic sniping, and the emphasis was on restraint. Despite a week of disturbances in 1966, no major riot had resulted, police casualties had been light, and the department earned "considerable praise from the community."[27] New York's success may have influenced the commission's overall recommendation for expanded police intelligence programs, since the New York department's Bureau of Special Services was the most elaborate local intelligence operation in the country.

The commission may have thought it no accident that the police department with the greatest intelligence resources was most effective in coping with volatile ghettos. The Bureau of Special Services was undoubtedly the product of the intensity of radical political activity in New York and the need for tight security precautions to protect controversial national and international figures who appeared at the United Nations and elsewhere in the city. Focusing on riot control, the crime commission apparently ignored the New York bureau's other role in laying the foundation for criminal anarchy prosecutions against militant groups like R.A.M. Similar intelligence programs existed in few other cities. A year later after the riots in Detroit and Newark during the summer of 1967, another close observer who interviewed law enforcement officials still found full-fledged intelligence efforts to be "beyond the resources (both of money and experience) available to most city departments."[28]

In addition to the crime commission's report, the Justice Department distributed another publication offering guidance on how to reconcile the values of free speech and public order. A manual entitled *Prevention and Control of Mobs and Riots* was prepared with the assistance of the crime commission staff and an Army M.P. colonel. The F.B.I. then circulated it to 35,000 police agencies. In contrast to J. Edgar Hoover's views, it advised, "A peaceful or lawful demonstration should not be looked upon with disapproval by a police agency; rather, it should be considered as a safety valve possibly serving to prevent a riot. The police agency should not countenance violations of law. However, a police agency does not have the right to deny the demonstrator his constitutional rights." Although the manual did emphasize arresting the leaders of a riot, it also recommended against "the premature application of excessive force" and concluded that "the most effective method of preventing riot and mob situations is to eliminate the conditions which might lead to friction and misunderstanding" between police and minority groups. The manual's advice was consistent with the crime commission's observations that "demonstrations should not be confused with riots" and that riot prevention involved "maintaining proper police conduct."[29]

If the answer to civil disorders was good intelligence and careful planning as the crime commission suggested, then Congressional efforts to pass an antiriot bill were irrelevant to the problem. After a new wave of disturbances in cities like Tampa, Cincinnati, and Atlanta, and large-scale rioting in Newark early in the summer of 1967, the House considered the Cramer bill once again. Liberal Democrats questioned its constitutionality, and Judiciary Chairman Celler reported that Attorney General Clark opposed it. But Republican Congressman William McCulloch, long a civil rights advocate, endorsed the bill saying stiff penalties would have a powerful effect in deterring agitators from traveling from city to city. The bill passed, 347-70, giving Congressmen what one writer called "the satisfied feeling that comes only to a legislator when he had courageously and straightforwardly done something that cannot possible cost him any votes."[30]

While many House members shared J. Edgar Hoover's opinion that militant agitators were responsible for urban unrest, Nicholas Katzenbach and Ramsey Clark had not allowed the F.B.I. Director's views to influence their policy. The Justice Department recognized that protest could be a constructive safety valve. While it encouraged local authorities to develop their own intelligence programs to secure accurate information about potential riot situations, this to some extent downgraded the F.B.I.'s role by decentralizing intelligence operations. The crime commission emphasized better community relations rather than an internal security orientation for these programs, but it apparently failed to recognize the possible use of covert surveillance to bring criminal anarchy prosecutions against black militants. The desire for improved police intelligence as an aid in careful management of ghetto tensions carried with it the potential that surveillance might lead to local repression.

3. THE RESPONSE TO
CIVIL DISORDERS, 1967-68

Less than a week after the House passed the antiriot bill, serious violence erupted in Detroit, leading to the dispatch of federal troops at Michigan Governor George Romney's request. The Detroit riot marked a major turning point in federal policy since it demonstrated the inability of local and state forces to contain disorders. Federal civil and military authorities now faced the prospect of having to intervene in future civil disorders unless local agencies substantially improved their capacity to control or prevent mass violence. In addition, there was increasing danger that the public might believe charges made in the antiriot bill debate by Congressmen like Rules Committee Chairman William Colmer that the riots were an "organized conspiracy backed by the Communists." Deputy Attorney General Warren Christopher, who had recently taken office under Ramsey Clark, became the central official charged with the task of coordinating federal responses to civil disorders. He had served as executive director of a California commission to study the Watts riot in 1965. On July 27, 1967, President Johnson announced creation of a similar National Advisory Commission on Civil Disorders to investigate and make recommendations with respect to: "(1) The origins of the recent major civil disorders in our cities, including the basic causes and factors leading to such disorders and the influence, if any, of organizations or individuals dedicated to the incitement or encouragement of violence. (2) The development of methods and techniques for averting or controlling such disorders. . . ."

The F.B.I., in particular, was directed to "provide investigative information and assistance" to the commission. President Johnson emphasized that the F.B.I. would "continue to exercise its full authority to investigate these riots, in accordance with my standing instructions, and continue to search for evidence of conspiracy."[31] There was a brief flurry of concern at this time over the F.B.I.'s role, since former President Eisenhower stated that Senate Republican leader Everett Dirksen had told him the F.B.I. lacked authority to carry out an investigation to determine if there was a national pattern to the riots. Dirksen said he had been misunderstood and that the F.B.I. obviously had jurisdiction to investigate incidents in which there was even a "hint" of interstate action. But no federal official specified any statute involved. The President's statement implied, instead, that the F.B.I. was acting under his "standing instructions," possibly issued in 1964 when the Bureau investigated the Harlem riots and prepared its report on disorders for the White House.

At the commission's first closed hearings, Director Hoover reviewed some fifty-two disturbances since 1964. Illinois Governor Otto Kerner, the commission chairman, revealed afterwards that Hoover had presented "no intelligence on which to base a conclusion of conspiracy." The next day the commission's staff director, David Ginzburg, elaborated on Hoover's report. By the absence of a conspiracy, the F.B.I. Director meant he had found no relationship between the riots in one city and those in another; but the F.B.I. had found nonresidents taking part and agitating racial trouble in some cities where riots occurred. Asked if Hoover had characterized the outside agitators as Communists or subversives, Ginzburg replied that some "were characterized" but that Hoover had not attached much significance to their role. This account of Hoover's testimony explained that F.B.I. agents had photographed rioters, made notes of incidents, and investigated possible federal offenses, although they had made no arrests because looting and arson were local violations outside the F.B.I.'s jurisdiction.[32] Staff director Ginzburg made no mention of the legal basis for the F.B.I.'s authority to gather intelligence to protect the nation's internal security.

As the Kerner commission started work, the Senate Judiciary Committee began hearings on the antiriot bill. A Nashville police captain testified that Stokely Carmichael and his successor as head of S.N.C.C., H. Rap Brown, had joined other student leaders in organizing disorders in April and that their plans included teaching of violence and the manufacture of Molotov cocktails. The Cambridge, Maryland, police chief claimed that a speech by Brown was "the sole reason" for a riot in that city and played a tape recording of Brown's words: "Don't be trying to love that honk to death. Shoot him to death. Shoot him to death, brother, 'cause that's what he's out to do to you. Like I said in the beginning, if this town don't come 'round, this town should be burned down." When disorders followed his speech, Cambridge police had issued an arrest warrant against Brown for inciting to riot. Brown later said that the trouble started two hours after his speech and after he left the city. [33]

Because he symbolized all the fears of agitation and black militancy, Rap Brown became the focus of national attention and Justice Department action. On the day before the President announced creation of the Kerner commission, F.B.I. agents carrying out a federal fugitive warrant obtained by Maryland authorities arrested Brown at the Washington National Airport. The timing of the arrest to coincide with President Johnson's announcement may not have been coincidental, since Brown's lawyer claimed the Justice Department broke a promise to let him surrender in New York. While extradition proceedings were underway in Virginia, Brown was released on bail by a federal court; but he remained under federal surveillance. [34]

Within a month federal authorities arrested Rap Brown again and charged him with violating federal gun laws by transporting a rifle on an airplane from New York to New Orleans and back while under indictment in Maryland. There were hints the Justice Department charged Brown with this obscure firearms offense in order to preclude possible prosecution by New Orleans district attorney Jim Garrison. In any event, Brown was released again pending trial on the condition that he remain in New York except for travel in connection with court appearances in New Orleans and Virginia and for court-approved speaking engagements around the country. He was tried on the federal gun charge in May, 1968. Since he admitted carrying the rifle on the plane, the crucial issue was whether or not he was aware of the Maryland indictment at the time. Maryland officials had not notified him of it until after his flights to and from New Orleans; but the trial judge instructed the jury that Brown could be convicted if he had learned of the indictment from a nonofficial source, including newsmen or friends. On that basis the jury acquitted him on the first count covering his trip to New Orleans, but it found him guilty on a second count since it believed he was aware of the indictment before he returned to New York. Before sentencing, defense counsel William Kunstler told the judge, "I would hate to think my country used a little known law like this to persecute and silence this man." The maximum sentence of five years in prison was imposed.[35]

Rap Brown still did not go to jail, though, because his lawyers appealed the judge's refusal to let the defense see transcripts of electronic surveillance which the Justice Department admitted had "accidentally" recorded his conversations. A year later the Court of Appeals sent the case back for a new hearing in light of the Supreme Court's decision in Alderman. Meanwhile, Brown's trial in Maryland was postponed several times and removed from Cambridge to another county over the objections of the defense.[36] The result of all these legal maneuvers was to frustrate any intentions of state or federal officials to silence Brown, at least until 1970. The Justice Department's unwillingness to press vigorously for high bail for Brown after his arrest in 1967 tends to indicate that it was less interested in curtailing his immediate political advocacy than in showing that any law violation, even the most minor, would lead to the arrest of black militants under surveillance. F.B.I. Director Hoover continued to issue statements that much of the unrest among Negroes stemmed from speeches by Stokely Carmichael, Rap Brown, and other militants who "sowed the seeds of discord and hope to reap in 1968 a year filled with explosive racial unrest."[37]

The Impact of the Kerner Commission

Attorney General Clark explained the Department's policy at a news conference in January, 1968. Law enforcement agencies at every level would "watch all individuals who have extremist, violent capabilities." Although the government had evidence that there were some people "who like to cause trouble" and who "want that trouble to take the form of civil rights tension," it had no hard evidence of any "massive conspiracy or foreign effort" to promote riots. When asked what police should do to prevent agitation by militants like Stokely Carmichael, Clark replied that "police intelligence. . .identifying leadership that would endeavor to cause violence is of the highest priority" and that police should "move fast and firmly. . .against such leadership whenever a violation of law is found." Where there was no "unlawful conduct," the Attorney General emphasized, police should "rely upon their intelligence and their ability to act whenever any violation might occur."[38]

During the winter of 1967-68 the Justice Department and the Kerner commission reiterated the message that intelligence and planning were the keys to control of civil disorders. At a series of conferences with local law enforcement officials, Department and commission representatives urged every police department to establish an intelligence unit staffed with full-time personnel "to gather, evaluate, analyze, and disseminate information on potential as well as actual civil disorders. It should provide police administrators with reliable information essential for assessment and decision-making. It should use undercover police personnel and informants but it should also draw on community leaders, agencies, and organizations in the ghetto." To help law enforcement agencies improve their information and to determine what federal response, if any, would be required to meet trouble during the coming summer, the Justice Department established "a national center and clearinghouse. . .to develop, evaluate, and disseminate riot prevention and control data." The new Civil Disturbance Group and its Interdivisional Intelligence and Information Unit operated directly under the Deputy Attorney General and secured a computer to compile and correlate data from cities across the nation. The computer stored intelligence reports from the F.B.I., local police units, and the military services.[39]

Supplementing the Justice Department's clearinghouse, the Army had developed after the Detroit riots its own expanded facilities for domestic intelligence-gathering, including under-cover agents and a nationwide wire service network to provide daily and weekly reports to every major troop command in the United States.[40] Both Justice Department and Army intelligence focused not only on the danger of civil disorders in black ghettos, but on antiwar protest demonstrations like the October, 1967, march on the Pentagon (see Chapter Four).

The Kerner commission issued its report at the end of February, 1968. Its main aims were to allay public fears and promote social reforms by declaring that white racism, not any organized plan or conspiracy, was fundamentally to blame for urban riots. The commission "found no evidence that all or any of the disorders or the incidents that led to them were planned or directed by any organization or group, international, national, or local." In reaching this conclusion the commission, relying on F.B.I., C.I.A., State and Defense Department and other government intelligence reports, and its own investigative staff, had "studied the role of foreign and domestic organizations, and individuals, dedicated to the incitement or encouragement of violence. It considered the organizational affiliations of those who called for violence, their contacts, sources of financial support, travel schedules and, so far as possible, their effect on audiences." The commission did believe some groups had created "a climate that tends toward the approval and encouragement of violence as a form of protest. . . .

"Strident appeals to violence, first heard from white racists, were echoed and reinforced last summer in the inflammatory rhetoric of black racists and militants Throughout the year, extremists crisscrossed the country preaching a doctrine of black power and violence. Their rhetoric was widely reported in the mass media; it was echoed by local 'militants' and organizations; it became the ugly background of the violent summer.

"We cannot measure with precision of the influence of these organizations and individuals in the ghettos, but we think it clear that the intolerable and unconscionable encouragement of violence heightened tensions, created a mood of acceptance and an expectation of violence, and thus contributed to the eruption of disorders last summer."

Recognizing that further racial polarization "would provide fertile ground for organized exploitation in the future," the Kerner commission advised that "intensive investigations. . .by local police departments, grand juries, city and state committees, federal departments and agencies, and congressional committees. . .should continue."[41]

While none of these inquiries had identified any organized groups as having initiated any riots during the summer of 1967, the commission's predictions were not reassuring. Its overall message was that failure to begin massive social reform would create conditions under which "a rising proportion of Negroes in disadvantaged city areas might come to look upon the deprivation and segregation they suffer as proper justification for violent protests or for extending support to now isolated extremists who advocate civil disruption by guerrilla tactics."[42]

In its recommendations for control of disorders, the commission quoted with approval the federal riot manual's admonition against mistaking "lawful protest for illegal activities"; but it also declared that "a primary function of criminal justice in a riot situation is effectively to apprehend, prosecute and punish the purposeful inciters to riot." Many state laws against incitement needed revision, however, because they were "so broad that they might inhibit the consitutional right of free speech" and often provided "no definition of 'incitement' or comparable terms." Statutes defining a riot "in terms of groups containing as few as three persons" needed to be tightened since they could apply "in situations where nothing even approaching a truly riotous activity is taking place."

In addition, the commission gave qualified endorsement to federal antiriot legislation. Warning of the "risk that too broad a bill would encroach on the right of free speech and peaceful assembly," it emphasized that disorders should generally be controlled at a local level, that there were "few instances of interstate travel which would be subject to federal control," and that "no criminal legislation. . .comes to grips with the underlying causes of disorder." Nevertheless, the commission felt "that a tightly-drawn federal control statute might play a limited, but important, role in dealing with disorders. Even if there are only a few persons traveling with the intent of precipitating disorders, these few can do enormous harm."[43]

The Antiriot Act of 1968

President Johnson had already taken the opportunity of his February, 1968, message to Congress on crime to propose a federal antiriot act "to make it a felony, punishable by up to five years in prison, for any person to incite or organize a riot after having traveled in interstate commerce with the intention to do so." The President added that a narrow and carefully drawn bill would not impede free speech or peaceful assembly. Admitting it was not a solution to our urban problems, he urged the bill's adoption to "give the Federal Government the power to act against those who move around the country, inciting and joining in the terror of riots."[44] Attorney General Clark no doubt reluctantly endorsed the President's and the commission's proposals in the hope that they might narrow the scope of pending bills in Congress. When the civil rights-open housing bill reached the Senate floor a month later, however, a much broader antiriot amendment was added, 82-13. Sponsored by Senators Thurmond of South Carolina and Lausche of Ohio, the amendment was far different from the Administration's proposal. At its heart was Congressman Cramer's idea for punishing anyone who travels in interstate commerce "with intent (a) to incite a riot; (b) to organize, promote, encourage, participate in, or carry on a riot; or (c) to commit any act of violence in furtherance of a riot; or (d) to aid or abet any person in inciting or participating in or carrying on a riot or committing any act of violence in furtherance of a riot."

After the Senate Judiciary Committee had revised the Cramer bill the previous fall, it contained several other elements—some restricting, others expanding its scope. Four provisions tended to circumscribe the law. First, conviction required proof that a defendant had performed or attempted to perform an overt act, other than crossing state lines, for any of the purposes listed above. Second, a judgment of conviction or acquittal on the merits under similar state law barred any federal prosecution for the same acts. Associated with this rule was a declaration that the federal law did not deprive local authorities of responsibility for prosecuting acts which violate both state and federal law. Third, the law could not be construed to bar pursuit of "the legitimate objectives of organized labor, through orderly and lawful means." Finally, the terms "to incite a riot" and "to organize, promote, encourage. . .a riot" were deemed not to mean "the mere oral or written (1) advocacy of ideas or (2) expression of belief, not involving advocacy of any act or acts of violence or assertion of the rightness of, or the right to commit, any such act or acts." The last provision was designed to satisfy the Supreme Court's requirements in the Yates case for defining unprotected speech.

Two additional passages tended to toughen and broaden the bill. Despite the Kerner commission's advice, the term "riot" was defined as

"a public disturbance involving (1) an act or acts of violence by one or more persons part of an assemblage of three or more persons, which act or acts shall constitute a clear and present danger of, or shall result in, damage or injury to the property of any other person or to the person of any other individual or (2) a threat or threats of the commission of [the above act or acts]."

Anticipating that Attorney General Clark might not enforce the law, Judiciary Chairman Eastland inserted another provision requiring that whenever the Justice Department found a violation, it must "proceed as speedily as possible with a prosecution of such person. . .and with any appeal which may lie from any decision adverse to the Government." If the Department failed to do so, it was required to "report in writing, to the respective Houses of Congress, the Department's reason for not so proceeding."[45]

The version advanced by Senators Thurmond and Lausche also included language that was construed to create a presumption that a defendant had traveled across state lines with intent to incite a riot if a riot in fact broke out within fifteen days after he entered the state. Before approving the measure, however, the Senate removed this wording, thus making it necessary for the government to prove intent. Other parts of the bill made it a federal crime to manufacture or demonstrate the use of firearms, firebombs, or other explosive devices for use in a civil disorder, and to obstruct firemen or policemen engaging in suppressing a riot.

Fearful of jeopardizing the fragile coalition supporting the civil rights bill, Senate liberals put up only token opposition to the antiriot amendment. Attorney General Clark accepted it as part of the price for open housing legislation, and some observers believed the Department would consider the bill 'virtually unenforceable." Adoption of the antiriot amendment may, indeed, have helped dissipate some of the opposition to the open housing law, especially in the House where the Senate bill was passed in April following the assassination of Dr. Martin Luther King, Jr.[46]

In summary, President Johnson and Ramsey Clark had hoped the Kerner commission would reduce public fears by discrediting the view that civil disorders were the result of a black militant conspiracy. The commission had provided an alternative to the F.B.I. as a source of information and intelligence evaluation both for the public and for executive decision-making. Instead of relying on the F.B.I. for continuing review of intelligence, Clark set up his own Civil Disturbance Group under

Warren Christopher; and the Kerner commission further encouraged local police to establish intelligence programs. While the F.B.I. was still the normal channel of communication with the police, overall riot analysis was in the hands of other executives. The Attorney General also attempted to draw a clear line between unlawful conduct, like Rap Brown's federal gun law violation, and political advocacy. When Congress enacted a broader antiriot law than Clark or the commission requested, however, it gave the F.B.I. almost limitless jurisdiction to investigate political activity.

Portions of Clark's intelligence directives were made public in 1971. One memorandum stated, "We must make full use of and constantly endeavor to increase and refine the intelligence availability to us, both from internal and external sources, concerning organizations and individuals throughout the country who may play a role in either instigating or spreading disorders or in preventing or checking them." Another memo instructed the F.B.I. to "use the maximum available resources, investigative and intelligence," for this purpose. "As part of the broad investigation," the Attorney General continued, "sources or informants in Black Nationalist organizations, S.N.C.C., and other less publicized groups should be developed and expanded to determine the size and purpose of these groups and their relationship to other groups, and also to determine the whereabouts of persons who might be involved in instigating riot activity in violation of federal law." The Interdivisional Intelligence Unit was set up to provide "systematic means. . .of compiling, analyzing the voluminous information about various persons and organizations furnished to us by the F.B.I."[46a] The new Unit did not, however, supervise the F.B.I.'s implementation of Clark's broad orders.

4. MANAGEMENT OF
RACIAL TENSIONS, 1968

Dr. King's assassination triggered a wave of rioting in over a hundred cities, including serious disorders and widespread property destruction in Washington, D.C., as well as new charges of organized incitement. A special Mayor's panel in Pittsburgh reported some advance planning and preparation for the riots as indicated by the prompt printing of placards, the making of firebombs, and the selectivity in establishments chosen for destruction. Chicago's Riot Study Commission found that advocates of black racism had encouraged "political rebellion. . .violence. . .and conflict." Deputy Attorney General Christopher declared, however, that the disorders in Washington and elsewhere were "largely spontaneous outbreaks of violence, generally by groups of Negro youths, touched off by the assassination"; none had been "characterized by terrorist attacks against vital installations or by efforts to disrupt the governmental structure."[47]

Christopher's statement on terrorist attacks reflected his concern that law enforcement agencies and military officers, who had been called on to control the Washington disorders, might tend to believe the riots had reached the stage of guerrilla warfare. At the height of the Detroit riots in 1967, the Army's Assistant Chief of Staff for Intelligence had reportedly instructed his staff to get out their counterinsurgency manuals.[48] More recently Stokley Carmichael, who was in Washington during the violence there, had acknowledged a phone conversation with a Cuban radio commentator in which he stated, "It is going to become more and more a guerrilla—urban guerrilla—warfare, because it is clear that we cannot win with the police in open rebellion. So, more people are now beginning to plan seriously a major urban guerrilla warfare, where we can begin. . .serious revolution with this country to bring it to its knees."[49] The Deputy Attorney General sought to counter these impressions and reassure the public: "While no compelling evidence of conspiracy has yet appeared, we remain vigilant. To probe more deeply on this question, the F.B.I. has expanded its investigative effort and the Department of Justice has established an intelligence unit focusing solely on the disorder question. In time of disorder, teams of men are working around the clock trying to discern whether there is some pattern, testing whether there are pieces of a jigsaw which can be fitted together." He reasserted that the Department was "following the activities of certain individuals and organizations which may have the potential for inciting violence."[50]

Attorney General Clark faced demands that Stokely Carmichael be arrested and charged with inciting to riot. The morning after Dr. King's death Carmichael had told a news conference in Washington, "We have to retaliate for the deaths of our leaders. The execution for those deaths will not be in the courtroom. They're going to be in the streets. . . .There no longer needs to be intellectual discussion. Black people know that they have to get guns." On the streets in Washington and in a speech at Howard University, however, Carmichael urged blacks to stay off the streets because they were "not ready for the thing." Aware he was watched by federal agents, he was determined to give them no cause to arrest him. According to Washington Post reporters, F.B.I. undercover men "did not have much success keeping track of him. He was always suspicious of being followed and 'made' (spotted) any surveillance almost immediately." F.B.I. agents later interviewed dozens of witnesses to find out if any connection existed betweeen Carmichael and the riots. The Attorney General told complaining Congressmen, "If we find evidence that meets the standards of criminal justice that Stokely Carmichael has committed a crime against the federal government, he will be prosecuted with all of the diligence and all of the energies at our command." But Carmichael was never arrested or charged.[51]

The Poor People's Campaign

During the months immediately after Dr. King's death, the Department confronted the difficult problem of accommodating in riot-torn Washington the Poor People's Campaign, originally planned by Dr. King and now led by his successor, Rev. Ralph Abernathy. Dr. King had called for a nonviolent "massive dislocation of the capital" to demand Congressional action on jobs and income for the poor. While camped in Washington, the demonstrators were to engage in civil disobedience, with efforts made to disrupt the government by blocking entrances to federal buildings, including the Capitol. Prepared to face jail, Dr. King had predicted that "the Army may try to run us out," although he told a gathering at the National Cathedral on March 31 that he was not "coming to tear up Washington."[52] While he was leading protests in Memphis, the Southern Christian Leadership Conference's Washington representative, Rev. Walter E. Fauntroy, had begun negotiating with key federal officials to make plans for the Campaign and its Resurrection City encampment. President Johnson, while urging the group to follow constitutional methods and not to try to stop the functioning of the government, had promised in February that the Administration would "do all we can to work with all groups in this country to see that their views are heard, considered and acted upon with promptness and understanding."[53]

Dr. King had hoped his militant civil disobedience campaign would provide a constructive channel for the anger and frustration that erupted into riots. According to his plans, the demonstrations would be organized around a force of some 3,000 persons selected from ten cities and five rural areas and carefully trained in nonviolence. Everyone engaged in the campaign would be required to take a pledge of nonviolence for as long as he participated. Nevertheless, many officials were apprehensive about Dr. King's ability to maintain nonviolent discipline over a long period. Their fears were reinforced in late March when disorders occurred during a demonstration in Memphis, where Dr. King was supporting a sanitation workers strike. West Virginia Senator Robert C. Byrd, chairman of the District of Columbia appropriations subcommittee, proposed a court order to block the demonstrations; and Mississippi Senator Stennis urged that only a small delegation be allowed to come to Capitol Hill to present their case symbolically.[54]

This was the status of preparations when Dr. King was killed and the capital was disrupted by looting and burning. In mid-April negotiations between Rev. Fauntroy and government officials resumed since S.C.L.C. leaders decided to carry through with Dr. King's plans. In a Law Day address Deputy Attorney General Christopher outlined Department policy:

"Acts of civil disobedience are generally a far cry from the widespread violence that takes place during a civil disorder. But we must recognize that a demonstration which involves civil disobedience has a greater potential for disorder. Nevertheless, it would not be prudent to stop all demonstrations on the ground that they might lead to disobedience and thus disorder.

There are several reasons for this conclusion. First, the demonstration may well serve as an escape valve by permitting a public airing of grievances without violence. . . .Furthermore, most major demonstrations involve a good deal of planning by both those who are leaders of the demonstration, and by the concerned law enforcement agencies. With such planning, it is possible to build-in safeguards against violence and disorder.

The events in Memphis before and after Dr. King's death provide a useful example. You will recall that there was violence accompanying Dr. King's march in Memphis sup-porting the striking sanitation workers. There is general agreement that the lack of planning played a heavy role in the trouble. But as you also recall, there was no violence during the march in Memphis subsequent to Dr. King's assassination, despite the presence of a very large crowd. Good planning and careful control made the dif-ference."[55]

During the two months following Christopher's statement, Department executives tried their best to follow its principles as staff members of the Community Relations Service supervised the Poor People's demonstrations.

Only rarely was the guidance of the C.R.S. made public, for the agency had developed a pattern of quiet, behind-the-scenes influence in situations of potential disorder. Created by the 1964 Civil Rights Act as a means to conciliate racial tensions in the South, the C.R.S. had turned its attention to northern cities and was transferred from the Commerce Department to the Justice Department in 1966. Under its director Roger Wilkins, its tasks included helping improve police-community relations and developing a corps of specialists who could mediate in local disputes between ghetto residents and city officials. The C.R.S. had learned in December, 1967, of the plans for the Poor People's Campaign and was able to keep abreast of emerging strategies by making contact with S.C.L.C. leaders. Consequently, the Justice Department did not have to rely solely on undercover surveillance for such information. As various groups across the country began gathering people for the trip to Washington, C.R.S. field representatives moved from city to city, assessing the size and mood of the participants.[56]

Despite the objections of several Congressmen, including Senator McClellan who charged that armed militant advocates of violence were planning to incite rioting and looting, a permit was granted for use of a portion of West Potomac Park near the Lincoln Memorial as the cite of the Resurrection City encampment. The permit, due to expire June 16 but later extend to June 23, banned weapons and alcohol from the grounds and called for enough S.C.L.C. marshals to insure effective self-policing. Meeting with liberal Congressmen before the first demonstrators arrived, Rev. Abernathy pledged that civil disobedience would be used only as a last resort.[57] Sit-ins or other protests that might provoke arrest would be avoided, at least until after a mass Solidarity Day march to be held June 19, a month after the establishment of Resurrection City. During the intervening weeks, while protesters met with Congressmen and executive officials to discuss their grievances, the Justice Department would do all it could to minimize disruption by helping arrange meetings and attempting to prevent arrests through negotiations.

Some arrests could not be avoided, as when one protester began shouting in the House gallery and when three others interfered with police attempting to prevent tampering with the American flag outside the Supreme Court building. On at least two separate occasions, police were persuaded not to enforce strictly the rules against peaceful demonstrations on the Capital grounds, inside the Capitol, and on the steps of the Supreme Court building. During the first week S.C.L.C. leaders sent home two hundred unruly youths from Chicago and Detroit for what was termed failure to develop "any internal cohesion with poor people."[58] As long as Attorney General Clark had confidence in the leaders' intentions not to provoke confrontations, he was willing to stay his hand when small-scale peaceful demonstrations took place in violation of the strict letter of the law.

Two incidents illustrated the lengths to which Rev. Abernathy and Attorney General Clark would go to preserve cooperative relations. Resurrection City manager Jesse Jackson led more than a hundred marchers to the Agriculture Department, where they went into the employees cafeteria and ran up a $290 lunch bill. When the Attorney General learned that Jackson had declined to pay the bill, saying the amount was a token of what the nation owed the poor, Clark informed Rev. Abernathy via C.R.S. representatives that unless the bill was paid at once, Jackson might be taken before a grand jury on charges of theft by fraud. Embarrassed by the unnecessary confrontation and probably fearful it would undermine Clark's trust, Rev. Abernathy criticized Jackson; and their disagreement resulted in Jackson's replacement as supervisor of Resurrection City. The following week Attorney General Clark indicated his continued confidence by refusing to arrest a group of several hundred demonstrators who blocked an entrance to the Justice Department building, demanding to see the Attorney General. Instead, Clark agreed to meet the next day with a hundred representatives in the departmental auditorium, where he listened for two hours to vehement attacks on the government for failing to provide justice for the poor.[59]

On June 19 the Solidarity Day events took place without incident, as an estimated 50,000 persons marched from the Washington Monument to the Lincoln Memorial. Some 4,300 local policemen and National Guardsmen were deployed for march security, while about 1,000 marshals were recruited by S.C.L.C. from off-duty black policemen, firemen, and other city employees in New York. Speaking at the end of the Solidarity Day program, Rev. Abernathy announced that the Resurrection City demonstrators would intensify their protests even if their permit was not renewed past June 23. "Some people call this kind of defiance of government civil disobedience," he concluded, "but if that is so, it stands at the heart of the Judeo-Cristian tradition. . . .We may be placed in jail, but I know my God is able to deliver us."[60]

If the Attorney General had any intention of extending the permit, his plans were probably set aside the day after the mass march. Apparently without Rev. Abernathy's approval, a group of about 500 who had been conducting a vigil at the Agriculture Department began a spontaneous sit-in as employees began leaving work. Blocking exits and disrupting traffic, they courted arrest; and when police struck one marcher with night sticks, their mood turned hostile. Before S.C.L.C. leaders arrived and cooled tempers, police had arrested 82 demonstrators on charges of disorderly conduct. That night clashes occurred between youths and police, who used tear gas and claimed that S.C.L.C. leaders did not help keep the peace.[61] During the next two days conditions in Resurrection City deteriorated, fights and thefts were reported, passing cars were stoned.

Not only had Campaign leaders lost control of their followers, but the Justice Department also seemed unable to restrain federal park police who overreacted to the increased provocations in the early morning hours of the Sunday, June 23. According to Washington Post reporters, after a few youths threw missiles at passing cars and police, the park police bombarded the encampment with tear gas. Aroused from their sleep by clouds of tear gas, hundreds of residents ran out "choking, vomiting, and screaming." One Justice Department official drove quickly to the area and put on a gas mask. He located several persons overcome by gas and took them to ambulances. S.C.L.C. leader Rev. Andrew Young called the gassing "worse than anyting I ever saw in Mississippi or Alabama. You don't shoot tear gas into an entire city because two or three hoodlums are throwing rocks."[62] Against this background S.C.L.C. officials arranged with the Department for a final act of nonviolent civil disobedience that would allow peaceful clearance of the Resurrection City site after its permit expired.

On the morning of June 24, Rev. Abernathy led most of the group on a march to the Capitol, while about a hundred remained at the campsite to be arrested peacefully when a force of 2,000 police cleared the area. At the edge of the Capitol grounds Rev. Abernathy and over two hundred other marchers submitted to arrest on the charge of engaging in an illegal assemblage. Another 150 of the most youthful and militant demonstrators avoided arrest and marched to the local S.C.L.C. headquarters in the Washington ghetto, where a crowd of local youths gathered with them on a streetcorner. Although most of the Poor People's Campaigners were soon bused to a distant church to be fed and housed temporarily, the neighborhood youths remained and began breaking store windows. Washington police, uneasy through the tense day, reacted with an overwhelming show of numbers and tear gas, ignoring efforts by S.C.L.C. officials in the area to quiet the crowd. The mayor proclaimed a state of emergency and ordered a curfew into effect. The disorders soon ended, but they marred the impression of what otherwise had been a nonviolent conclusion to the Poor People's Campaign in Washington.[63]

Despite occasional flare-ups during the six-week protest and its unruly end, Justice Department policy toward the Campaign served as an object lesson that it was possible to entertain strong dissent in the nation's capital, even to the point of civil disobedience, without producing serious disorder. Attorney General Clark recalled later that he became "red-eyed" reading intelligence reports of impending violence, including forecasts that Potomac bridges would be blown up, but he persisted in believing that the consequences of curtailing the demonstrations would be worse.[64] On the other side, S.C.L.C. leaders retained their confidence in the Department because it negotiated openly and candidly. Yet Rev. Abernathy was not Stokely Carmichael, and Resurrection City attracted few of the most militant blacks for whom nonviolence was a doctrine of weakness and guns were a symbol of strength.

The Spectre of "Guerrilla Warfare"

Perhaps because the upheavals after Dr. King's death exhausted the riot impulse or as a result of improved police capacity to handle street violence, there were fewer serious disorders during the summer of 1968. Instead, a number of reported armed clashes between police and black militants suggested that the decline in the scale of riots coincided with an increase in more strategic acts of violence. In the fall a leading black journalist wrote that "guerrilla warfare, long a part of the rhetoric of Negro militants, now appears to have the potential for coming into practice. Indeed, that phase may have already begun."[65]

During August and September shoot-outs between police and blacks in the ghetto were reported in New York, Cleveland, Memphis, St. Louis, Pittsburgh, Los Angeles, and elsewhere. While the exact nature of most of these incidents was not clear from published reports, one clash in Cleveland received national publicity. A brief gun battle there resulting in the deaths of three policemen, three black nationalists, and a bystander, appeared to mark the first documented case of organized black violence against the police. Although his group was not involved, new S.N.C.C. chairman Phil Hutchings (Rap Brown's successor) claimed the shooting was the first stage of revolutionary armed struggle. Cleveland's Negro Mayor Carl Stokes tried to counter this interpretation by declaring that there was no evidence of a plot to ambush police and blaming the incident on "spontaneous actions taken by a group who were armed and emotionally prepared to do violence." A local grand jury later substantially agreed with the mayor's analysis; and Attorney General Clark said a federal investigation had produced no indications of a conspiracy. Clark called the outbreak the random act of a handful of very extreme and violence-prone militants, and he wondered "why it hasn't happened before in other cities." There seemed to be "even less evidence now of militant agitation or conspiratorial efforts to cause them than in the past several years."[66]

The Cleveland shootings provided the most frequently cited example of guerrilla warfare, despite official repudiation of that theory. Because of its widespread notoriety, the Cleveland shoot-out was examined in detail by a team from the Civil Violence Research Center at Case Western Reserve University, whose findings were submitted to the National Commission on Violence (appointed by President Johnson after Senator Robert Kennedy's assassination). According to this account, on the day before the clash the Cleveland police department's special intelligence unit obtained a report from an F.B.I. informant warning that a local black militant group planned to assassinate Mayor Stokes, three other prominent Negroes, and a white policeman two days hence. There was a possibility of simultaneous outbreaks in other cities. The truth of these reports was questionable. Not only were there inconsistencies in the informant's story, but other intelligence sources did not corroborate it, and those who talked to the informer on the telephone suspected he was under the influence of drugs. Since the informant claimed the militant group had collected semi-automatic weapons and possession of such arms was illegal, police might have had probable cause for obtaining a search warrant. But police executives chose not to do so because it would blow the informant's cover. Instead, they decided to subject the home of the black militant leader to intensive surveillance by roving police cars. Enough cars were available for an effective moving surveillance, and the Police Department would assign to the task as many Negro officers as it could.

Meanwhile, a black city councilman agreed to talk personally with the militant leader. At their meeting the leader "poured out his apprehension about the police surveillance. There were, he said, even police on the roof. The police had harassed him before; he was afraid the surveillance was leading up to another incident. He urged [the councilman] to try to get the surveillance removed." After the meeting the councilman, knowing he could do nothing on the scene since the surveillance was in the hands of a special unit, telephoned Cleveland's Safety Director who advised him to call Mayor Stokes. Before their conversation was over, the mayor was informed that shooting had begun at the militant leader's home.

Who shot first? And at whom? Various accounts of where, how, and why the shooting started appeared. Even after extensive investigation, questions remained unanswered. The study team concluded that, rightly or wrongly, the militant leader "regarded the obvious presence of the surveillance cars over several hours' time as threatening." These fears apparently led to the shooting. The councilman recalled that he "saw an unmarked car 'full of white people.' It was glaringly evident that the police had established a stationary surveillance rather than a moving one." Two cars containing only white officers were in plain view of the militant's home.[67]

The analysis implicit in the study team's report was that at some point after police executives' decision to begin intensive moving surveillance by Negro policemen, the top-level order either was modified to permit stationary surveillance by white officers or was disregarded by the special surveillance unit. At the militant leader's trial for murder in 1969, the defense brought out that a coroner's examination of two of the policemen who were killed showed they were legally drunk at the time of death. A pathologist testified that one of the black militants was killed by a gun held no more than six inches from his head and hence by a policeman. The prosecution relied on one eye-witness (a police tow-truck driver) and extensive circumstantial evidence, including reports of arms purchases and the militant leader's belief in "revolution by force." He was convicted of first degree murder and sentenced to death.[68] Far from confirming a guerrilla warfare theory, however, the report on the Cleveland shoot-out supported a conclusion that police surveillance policy, involving unreliable informants and failure of the special unit to follow orders, was largely to blame for the violence.

Cleveland's experience demonstrated two rival styles of managing racial tensions, one championed by Ramsey Clark and the other embodied in the F.B.I.'s undercover surveillance. By example during the Poor People's Campaign and through advice from the Community Relations Service, Clark attempted to persuade police that their new intelligence programs should stress open contacts and accurate information, not covert operations and unverified rumor. If police considered black militants solely as a threat and communications broke down, the potential for violence by both sides increased. The Attorney

General had few ways to influence the police, however, except in a passive sense: his reluctance to declare black militants a danger to internal security might avoid exacerbating tension. Hence Clark may have been responsible for J. Edgar Hoover's comparative silence throughout 1968.

The Black Panther Party

Other widely publicized clashes between police and militants occurred in California and involved the group that was becoming the object of most fears—the Black Panther Party. Formed in Oakland in 1966 as a small ad hoc group to institute armed patrols for black self-defense, the Black Panther Party had grown by mid-1968 into a national organization with a program for black political action in alliance with white radicals. Its original leaders, Huey P. Newton and Bobby Seale, were joined in early 1967 by writer Eldridge Cleaver, who was released from prison in 1966 after serving nine years of a one-to-fourteen-year sentence for rape. Cleaver had won public attention when his prison writings were published in the magazine Ramparts. Although they were in contact with S.N.C.C. members and briefly merged the two groups in 1968, Newton, Seale, and Cleaver saw their role as that of carrying on what Malcolm X had advocated just before his death: not primarily antiwhite black racism, but a radical political program asserting black grievances in the urban ghettos.

The Panthers first won national attention in the spring of 1967 when Cleaver addressed a mass antiwar rally in San Francisco and a delegation of armed members entered the California state capitol. In October, 1967, Newton was arrested following an isolated confrontation with Oakland police in which one policeman was killed; and both black militants and white radicals across the country took up the slogan "Free Huey." Later in 1967 the Panthers formed an alliance with the small white radical Peace and Freedom Party, which ran Cleaver as its presidential candidate in 1968.[69]

In January Cleaver's San Francisco apartment was invaded by police without a warrant, and a month later Bobby Seale was arrested after a similar search turned up two illegal guns in his Berkeley apartment. (The search of Seale's apartment was later ruled illegal.) Following these raids and other incidents of alleged harassment by Bay Area police, the Panther officers issued a general order declaring that "those who approach our doors in the manner of outlaws, who seek to enter our homes illegally. . .will henceforth be treated as outlaws, as gangsters, as evildoers. We have no way of determining that a man in uniform, involved in a forced outlaw entry into our home, is in fact a Guardian of the Law. He is acting like a lawbreaker and we must make an appropriate response." The order mandated that all party members "must acquire the technical equipment to defend their homes and their dependents and shall do so."[70] Like the black nationalist group in Cleveland, the Panthers were preparing armed resistance against what they perceived were illegal police assaults.

Meanwhile, publication of Cleaver's book, *Soul on Ice,* turned him into a national figure, appearing on television and replacing Stokely Carmichael and Rap Brown as the most highly publicized black militant spokesman. Following Dr. King's assassination the Panthers were given credit for keeping Oakland quiet, adopting the position that riots would only provide an opportunity for police attacks. "We don't want anything to break out that will give them a chance to shoot us down," explained one member. "They are hoping that we do something like that but we are passing the word to our people to be cool."[71] Nevertheless, two days after Dr. King's death, Eldridge Cleaver was involved in a shoot-out with Oakland police which resulted in the death of party treasurer Bobby Hutton. Steps were immediately taken to revoke his parole, and he spent the next two months in jail. In June, however, a California court ordered his release, observing in its decision, "The peril to his parole status stemmed from no failure of personal rehabilitation, but from his undue eloquence in pursuing political goals, goals which were offensive to many of his contemporaries. Not only was there absence of cause for cancellation of parole, it was a product of a type of pressure unbecoming, to say the least, to the law enforcement paraphernalia of this State."[72] Cleaver was released on bail pending the state's appeal and began an extensive speaking tour. Bobby Seale was free awaiting trial for gun violations, while Huey Newton's murder trial was scheduled for July and did not end until September.

In mid-1968 the Black Panthers set out to become a national organization. In New York alone the party reportedly signed eight hundred members in June under Seale's direction. Since many imitation Black Panthers had formed elsewhere, the Oakland leaders began to contact and amalgamate these groups under a single strategic program stressing tight organization and rejecting spontaneous violence that might dissipate their strength. The Panthers apparently took advantage of previous organizational work by S.N.C.C. in the ghettos of Cleveland, Chicago, and other cities. While they began a school breakfast program in Oakland, their most frequent demand was for decentralization of police forces with policemen required to reside in the area where they work. The Panthers' ten-point platform presented an essentially Marxist analysis of society, condemning capitalism and urging that housing, land, and the means of production be placed in the hands of the community. Such a large-scale, short-term recruitment drive undoubtedly brought police informants into many local chapters. It also enlisted many members who did not understand the Oakland leaders' carefully thought-out policy.[73] By the end of the summer instances of sniper fire at policemen were being blamed on Black Panthers and, given the party's rapid growth and lack of discipline, some were probably responsible.

The intensity of police hostility to the Panthers was evidenced in September when a crowd of over one hundred whites including many off-duty policemen assaulted several party members in the Brooklyn criminal court building. A week later Huey Newton was convicted in Oakland for killing the white policeman; but he was found guilty only of manslaughter, not first or second degree murder, and was given only a two-to-fourteen-year sentence. Soon after the verdict the party headquarters in Oakland was fired upon by drunken policemen who were later apprehended and dismissed from the force.[74] In late September a California appeals court overturned the decision that had released Eldridge Cleaver, on the ground that the probation agency had not exceeded its discretionary authority in revoking his parole. Ordered to return to jail in November, Cleaver disappeared.

The Justice Department's response to Cleaver's flight indicated how careful it still was to respect legal procedures. With the exception of the case against Rap Brown, Attorney General Clark had taken no federal legal action against leading black militants. When the California Attorney General's office asked for a federal fugitive warrant after Cleaver's disappearance, United States Attorney Cecil Poole in San Francisco declined to authorize one since he did not believe the state had sufficient evidence of flight across state lines. Not until two weeks later, after the F.B.I. submitted proof that Mrs. Cleaver had withdrawn $33,000 from a local bank and had flown to New York with the money, did Poole approve a federal complaint charging unlawful flight to avoid custody. The remaining original Panther leader, Bobby Seale, successfully blocked his state gun law prosecution in January, 1969, when a California judge ruled that the search which uncovered the guns was illegal.[75]

Under Ramsey Clark the Justice Department had treated the Black Panther Party as just one militant group among many. No attempt was made to single out the Panthers as a special danger, despite their growing membership and program for violent self-defense. The Department refused to usurp local responsibility until absolutely necessary. For over two years it had followed a complex policy that combined encouragement of local police intelligence in conjunction with better police-community liaison. While the F.B.I. had stepped up its surveillance of black militants, the analysis of intelligence was in the hands of officials who worked directly under the Deputy Attorney General. Clark continued to distinguish illegal conduct from protected political advocacy, despite Congressional passage of the antiriot law. The Black Panthers posed a serious test for Clark's style of managing racial tensions, but he did not remain in office long enough to demonstrate whether his policy could prevent renewed violence.

5. THE NIXON ADMINISTRATION
AND BLACK MILITANCY, 1969

Although Cecil Poole remained United States Attorney in San Francisco throughout 1969 as the only Negro in such a position, the Justice Department under the Nixon Administration substantially changed federal policy toward the Black Panther Party. Soon after taking office, Attorney General Mitchell permitted the F.B.I. to engage in electronic surveillance of the Panthers under his national security authorization. By July J. Edgar Hoover pictured the party as "the greatest threat to the internal security of the country. Schooled in the Marxist-Leninist ideology and the teachings of Chinese Communist leader Mao Tse-tung, its members have perpetrated numerous assaults on police officers and have engaged in violent confrontations with police throughout the country. Leaders and representatives of the Black Panther party travel extensively all over the United States preaching their gospel of hate and violence not only to ghetto residents, but to students in colleges, universities and high schools as well."[76] If the Justice Department had limited itself to increased intelligence surveillance of the Panthers and regular condemnations of the group by the F.B.I. Director, it would have remained roughly consistent with prior policies as applied to groups like R.A.M. and S.N.C.C.

Instead, the Department went much farther and singled out the Panthers for intensive prosecution under statutes like the antiriot act and the Smith Act, which had not been enforced since the 1950's when anti-Communist fervor declined and the Supreme Court narrowly interpreted its scope. Why did the Department adopt these measures in 1969? Three factors were (1) the political commitments of President Nixon during the 1968 campaign, (2) perceptions of the nature of the Black Panthers in the current ghetto environment, and (3) the interaction of federal and local police surveillance agencies. Each element along might have influenced the Department to focus on the Panthers; in combination they produced a new policy toward black militants.

In his most detailed address on civil disorders delivered in March, 1968, during his primary campaign, President Nixon had made a commitment to order. Citing Watts, Harlem, Detroit, and Newark as "a foretaste of what the organizers of insurrection are planning," he declared that the nation must "prepare to meet force with force if necessary, making it abundantly clear that. . .retaliation against the perpetrators and the planners of violence will be swift and sure." Nixon believed the "best time to display both power and the will to use it is before trouble starts—to make transparently clear to a potential aggressor that the price of aggression is too high and the chances of success to slight." Viewing threatened domestic violence as "more in the nature of a war than a riot." Nixon saw it not as a spontaneous outburst but as "subject to advance planning." Thus he asserted, "if those threatening war can plan, those being threatened can also plan."[77] During the fall campaign Nixon merely referred to his "detailed program for freedom from fear issued during the primary campaigns," while his running mate Spiro Agnew served as spokesman for his commitment to deal swiftly with the forces of violence.[78] As the candidate's campaign manager, John Mitchell undoubtedly shared and perhaps influenced these conceptions of urban unrest and the necessary federal response.

When the new Administration took over, how did it assess prevailing conditions in the cities and the role of the Black Panthers? Early in 1969 two national organizations devoted to social reform, the Urban Coalition and Urban America, Inc., reported, "There was no evidence that any more than a small minority of the nation's Negro population was prepared to follow militant leaders toward. . .the tactical use of violence. The minority, however, continued to have an impact beyond its numbers, particularly on the young." Since the mood of blacks was not moving in the direction of patience, their report repeated the Kerner commission's warning that failure to begin massive urban reform might lead to greater support for "extremists who advocate civil disruption by guerrilla tactics."[79] With the new Administration unwilling to press for such social measures immediatley, therefore, the dangers of organized urban violence must have appeared high.

If this was the prevailing image of the ghettos, how did Justice Department executives perceive the nature of the Black Panther Party? One indication is a study prepared for the National Commission on Violence by sociologist Morris Janowitz, who saw riots "giving way to more specific, more premeditated, and more regularized uses of force."

"It is almost appropriate to describe these outbursts as political violence or political terror, or even conspiratorial violence. It is not inaccurate to describe this shift as one from expressive outburst to a more instrumental use of violence. . . .There was an element of organization, at least to the extent that activists are concerned with personal survival and avoidance of the police. There was an element of organization to the extent that the target seems to be selected, and the patterns repeated for a specific purpose. . .of developing solidarity in local gangs and paramilitary groups."

While Janowitz admitted it was difficult to draw the line between random outbursts and these forms of political violence, he found obvious the "focused selection of police personnel as specific and delimited targets." It was "much rarer but perhaps indicative of emerging trends that a formal organization such as the Black Panthers finds itself in repeated gun battles with Oakland police."[80]

This picture of conspiratorial activity was probably not far removed from the Justice Department's perception of the Panthers. It was reinforced by a widely noted editorial in the N.A.A.C.P. publication *The Crisis* which condemned "the exhorters who summon Negro youths to death in futile shoot-outs with the police" and declared "that responsible leaders who speak out against the extremists have been subjected to threats of violence."[81]

Whether or not the Panthers fit this description, in whole or in part, Department executives chose to operate on the premise that they did. Yet there are indications that during the winter of 1968-69 the Panther leadership, especially Bobby Seale who was the party's best organizer, was aware of a lack of coherence in the organization. At an unpublicized meeting of top-ranking officers from every chapter in December, Seale concentrated on training in political and revolutionary theory. Concerned about the number of arrests for robberies and other crimes committed by members, as well as infiltration by informants, the Panthers expelled several hundred from the nationwide membership for violating party discipline. These steps were consistent with the party leaders' strategic opposition to acts which might only provoke repression. The group was sufficiently diverse, however, to permit some chapters to remain more independant of the Oakland-based leadership, especially where members had experience in earlier black militant groups.[82] It deserves repeating that Panther leaders saw violence as legitimate for self-defense and as a possible stage on the revolutionary agenda when the time was ripe, but not as a useful offensive tactic in the short run. Nevertheless, many members may have found the more sophisticated revolutionary concepts, with their stress on organization and the refusal to dissipate strength "spontaneously," difficult to comprehend.[83]

The Justice Department's first legal action in 1969 against the Panthers showed its failure to perceive this crucial distinction between leaders and followers. In early March Bobby Seale was indicted with seven antiwar movement leaders under the antiriot law for conspiracy to incite disorders at the 1968 Democratic convention in Chicago. Seale's inclusion was puzzling since he had no role in organizing the demonstrations, and Chicago Mayor Daley's post-convention report did not blame him (as it did five of the others) for inciting violence. Appearing as a substitute for Eldridge Cleaver, he had been in Chicago for only two days. The charge against him was based primarily on a Lincoln Park speech in which he urged the audience to "barbecue some pork."[84] More light was shed on the decision to prosecute Seale several months later when an Illinois A.C.L.U. official told of a comment made by the new head of the Civil Rights Division, Jerris Leonard, whom Attorney General Mitchell had assigned to supervise the drafting of the Chicago indictments. "The Black Panthers," Leonard asserted, "are nothing but hoodlums and we've got to get them."[85]

Treating the Panthers like organized criminals could mean strategic prosecutions designed to maximize disruption within the organization by focusing on its leaders. With Huey Newton in jail and Eldridge Cleaver out of the country, Seale was the last remaining original Panther leader. Yet other officials emphasized alternative means to counter the Panthers without placing the burden of control on the legal system. For example, San Francisco Mayor Joseph Alioto, who also called the Panthers "a gang of hoodlums," told a House committee that their ability to mobilize followers in his city's slums had been blunted by indirect measures that could be used elsewhere. These tactics were to work closely with what he called "true" black militants on projects to improve housing, education and recreation facilities.[86]

Within the Justice Department this position was voiced by the Community Relations Service, whose officials believed that "creative disorder" should be encouraged in the cities. Peaceful demonstrations and organized protests to win black employment opportunities and other reforms tended to create enough infectious excitement to drain community energy to the point where it would not normally be expended in more violent ways. The C.R.S. policy was to influence local officials to cooperate with community activists who sought to channel black efforts in constructive directions. C.R.S. Director Ben Holman saw changing attitudes among urban blacks—many of the most militant leaders were counseling against violence, in part because blacks were beginning to feel they were coming into ownership of their neighborhoods.[87] Later in the year at its first formal press conference, the C.R.S. issued a report on student unrest in high schools, where the Panthers had a widespread appeal. Predicting more disorders, the C.R.S. warned against the use of police by school officials, since it tended to heighten school tensions and increase the polarization between administrators and student protestors.[88]

Despite Jerris Leonard's view of the Panthers, his Civil Rights Division also had a continuing responsibility to be concerned about police harassment of blacks. A century-old civil rights statute made it a federal crime for state officers willfully to deprive any person of his constitutional rights. The statute had been invoked in 1967 to support a federal prosecution of policemen who shot several blacks during the Detroit riots in the so-called "Algiers Motel incident." It was also the basis for prosecuting seven Chicago policemen in companion cases to the antiriot indictment arising out of the convention disorders.[89] Later in 1969 the Civil Rights Division secured indictments against five Paterson, New Jersey, policemen for violating the rights of two college students during disorders in the spring. The policemen were accused of assaulting and injuring the students, who were supporting black demonstrators at the school. The F.B.I. investigated these and other police brutality complaints, such as an incident in Alexandria, Virginia, where black residents charged that a white policeman beat a black youth without provocation.[90]

Assistant Attorney General Leonard apparently adopted a more cautious policy, however, for starting these investigations. Previously the F.B.I. had standing instructions to institute preliminary investigations on its own initiative "immediately upon receiving a complaint in civil rights cases involving brutality on the part of law enforcement officers."[91] But in the Alexandria case the inquiry was specifically requested by the head of the Civil Rights Division, and a Department spokesman said the Assistant Attorney General would not order such an investigation unless he first received a complaint "from somebody with knowledge of the case."[92] Leonard's change in policy for police brutality investigations was possibly a recognition of the close working relationship between the F.B.I. and local police in dealing with black militants.

The third factor involved in shaping Justice Department policy toward the Panthers was, therefore, the interaction of federal and local police surveillance agencies. Cooperation might be hindered by automatic F.B.I. inquiries into complaints of police misconduct. More important, local prosecutions and police action against the Panthers became intertwined with national policy during 1969. The decision by New York district attorney Frank Hogan's office to move against the Panthers in April, 1969, set off a chain of events that led to F.B.I. raids on

Panther offices across the country and probably brought about the establishment of a special unit within the Justice Department to coordinate federal action against the Panthers. The momentum of these operations produced a special grand jury investigation in San Francisco, other inquiries into the activities of white supporters of the Panthers, a concentration of federal gun law enforcement against the Panthers, and a flurry of intelligence reports to local police preceding massive raids in December against Panther offices in Chicago and Los Angeles.

Given the Administration's conception of how to combat urban unrest and its image of the Panthers, it is somewhat surprising that neither the Justice Department (after Seale's antiriot prosecution) nor local authorities took immediate measures against the party specifically for its political activities. The explanation may lie with the Supreme Court, which in the spring of 1969 decided cases raising crucial issues in the definition of protected speech. Although failing to rule on the R.A.M. appeal, it chose to decide whether the First Amendment barred the conviction under Ohio law of a Ku Klux Klan leader for advocating "violence, or unlawful methods of terrorism as a means of accomplishing. . .political reform." In a per curiam opinion, the Court reversed the conviction because neither the statute itself or the construction of it by state courts nor the indictment or the trial judge's instructions to the jury drew the necessary distinction between "mere advocacy" and "incitement to imminent lawless action." The Court laid down the principle

> "that the constitutional guarantees of free speech and free press do not permit a State to forbid or proscribe advocacy of the use of force or of law violation except where such advocacy is directed to inciting or producing imminent lawless action and is likely to incite or produce such action."[93]

The decision in Brandenburg v. Ohio in effect revived and restated in more specific language the clear and present danger test.

In another decision, Watts v. United States, the Court reversed a conviction under a 1917 federal statute prohibiting any person from knowingly and willfully making any threat to take the life or to inflict bodily harm upon the President of the United States. The defendant had declared at a 1966 rally on the Washington Monument grounds, "If they ever make me carry a rifle the first man I want to get in my sights is L.B.J. . . .They are not going to make me kill my black brothers." Defense counsel stressed that the statement was made during a political debate, that it was expressly made conditional upon the speaker's induction into the Army, and that the crowd's response was to laugh. Given this specific context, the Supreme Court did not believe that the kind of political hyperbole indulged in by the speaker met the statutory requirement of a true "threat." The defendant's remarks were just "a kind of very crude offensive method of stating a political opposition to the President." Although the Court did not find it necessary to rule on what constituted "willfulness," it expressed grave doubts about the lower court's interpretation that the willfulness requirement was met "if the speaker voluntarily uttered the charged words with 'an apparent determination to carry them into execution.'" Since the statute was to be "interpreted with the commands of the First Amendment in mind," the Court held that such threats should be distinguished from constitutionally protected speech. In light of the Brandenburg decision, an unprotected threat had to mean incitement.[94]

The Supreme Court's stringent limitations on laws punishing speech made explicitly repressive prosecutions less likely. Since the Court did not decide the R.A.M. case, authorities in cities like New York could not use criminal anarchy laws or other statutes threatening free speech without risking a federal court injunction barring the prosecution. But there were other alternatives available for using legal processes to discredit black militant groups. The Court's handling of the earlier Epton case had left open the possibility of using political advocacy in a prosecution for conspiracy to commit illegal acts.

The New York "Panther 21" Case

New York district attorney Frank Hogan chose the conspiracy route to move against the Black Panther Party in the spring of 1969. Instead of charging advocacy of revolutionary violence as he had in the past, Hogan secured an indictment against twenty-one Panthers for conspiracy to engage in overt illegal conduct—to bomb department stores, railroad tracks, and police stations, and to possess weapons and explosives illegally. In simultaneous early morning raids on members' homes, police claimed to have seized arms and ammunition, three homemade bombs, blasting powder, and other bomb components. Attorney Gerald Lefcourt, representing the defendants at their arraignment, said the Panthers believed the conspiracy indictment was an attack directed from Washington.[95]

To what extent might the Justice Department have influenced the decision to prosecute the "Panther 21?" The same week of the arrests, the State Department acted to deny visas to seven Cuban diplomats attached to the Cuban mission to the United Nations. A federal source disclosed that the Cubans had given financial and directional aid to militant groups such as the Black Panther Party, that at least fifteen Panthers had been observed entering the Cuban mission, and that other Panthers had visited Cuba during the previous year. (Eldridge Cleaver later turned up in Cuba before traveling to Algeria.) No evidence linked the Cubans to the alleged bombing conspiracy. "They are interested in promoting revolution among Negroes and white radicals," said the official, "and right now that does not mean bombing to them." According to this source, punitive action against the Cubans had been sought by the F.B.I.[96] Did the F.B.I. also desire local prosecution of the Panthers? The answer is not clear.

As noted earlier, the F.B.I. and the New York police department's Bureau of Special Services both engaged in surveillance of groups like the Panthers. They undoubtedly shared their findings. J. Edgar Hoover explained to a House appropriations subcommittee that "where pertinent, state and local authorities have been advised of information developed and the prompt dissemination of such information often enables them to take preventive measures to forestall acts of violence as it develops."[97] Since New York's bureau was highly experienced and efficient, however, it may not have relied on F.B.I. informants.

At hearings to set the defendants' bail, the prosecution produced a bomb seized by police which was characterized as "exactly like" one that had exploded the previous week in a Chicago department store, killing a woman clerk. The F.B.I. may have communicated apprehensions that the Chicago bombing was the work of black militants and might spread to other cities. Even the slightest intelligence indicating that New York Panthers were thinking about bombings would, therefore, have compelled immediate preventive action. The arrest of a lone white man for the Chicago bombing came too late to change the initial perception of an imminent threat.[98] The indictments were rushed through the grand jury (another grand jury returned superseding indictments several months later), and the arrests were made as soon as possible. In addition to the bombing plot, the Panthers were charged with illegal possession of guns and explosives, and individual defendants were alleged to have previously planted bombs at police stations and attempted to ambush policemen. Arrests for these offenses were not made earlier because the police probably did not want to blow the cover on their informants until more serious violence seemed possible.

This explanation of the decision to prosecute does not take account of the way the district attorney's office prepared the indictment and presented it to the public. By casting the charge as a sweeping conspiracy covering past and future acts, the prosecution focused attention on the Black Panthers as a group rather than on the individuals who allegedly had committed or planned to commit specific crimes. "During the course of the conspiracy," the indictment read, "the defendants were members of the Black Panther Party which utilized a para-military structure and discipline in pursuit of its objectives in the City of New York. The members of the party were required to wear uniforms and carry guns."[99] Although the indictment nowhere specified that the defendants planned any action on a particular day, district attorney Hogan told a rare televised press conference called to announce the indictment that they intended to bomb department stores "today." When it was noted that the explosives seized by police were far from sufficient to carry out the conspiracy's aims, a spokesman for the prosecutor said, "We believe they have other material cached away."[100] Finally, the district attorney's office persuaded the courts to set such high bail that most of the defendants were held in jail pending trial, unable to aid effectively in the preparation of their defense or to engage in further political activity.

The prosecution's strategy not only risked prejudicial pretrial publicity, but put the Black Panthers as a group on trial. It contributed greatly to the informed public's impression of the Panthers as a terrorist organization, despite the efforts of national Panther leaders several months earlier to bar spontaneous violence inconsistent with their revolutionary theories. Perhaps due to their own preconceived ideas some members of the New York chapter may have engaged in or planned violent acts. For example, one of the defendants, Robert Collier, had been convicted for the Black Liberation Front conspiracy to bomb national monuments in 1965. There is the added possibility, suggested by the role of police informants who participated in the Black Liberation Front and R.A.M. actions, that such agents might have encouraged or facilitated this departure from national Panther policy. As Morris Janowitz warned in his study for the Violence Commission, undercover operators often begin to believe they should spread distrust within these organizations.[101]

Incentives to prepare an all-encompassing conspiracy case focusing on the Black Panther Party came from a least two likely sources. First, the decision to blow the cover on its informants meant that the police—F.B.I. intelligence community in New York would want those agents to be able to reveal in court all they knew about the Panthers—not just the specific testimony related to particular criminal acts. A series of prosecutions concentrating on the individuals involved in each separate offense would lose the impact of a single comprehensive case. Furthermore, Attorney General Mitchell's prior decisions to prosecute Bobby Seale and to permit electronic surveillance of the Panthers as a threat to national security indicated to New York officials that their move would be consistent with national law enforcement policy. Whatever the immediate incentives for bringing the prosecution, the criminal anarchy cases against Epton and R.A.M. had already established a pattern for the district attorney's office to follow in dealing with black militants.

The New York case took on wider ramifications with the murder of Alex Rackley, a member of the New York Panther chapter, whose mutilated body was found in a river north of New Haven, Connecticut. In May eight New Haven Panthers were arrested and charged with kidnaping Rackley, bringing him to New Haven, and torturing him to death because he was thought to be a police informant. According to the local police chief, there was a "direct link" between the killing and the New York conspiracy case; and interstate implications had brought in the F.B.I., which was looking for other suspects outside the state.[102] During the following weeks F.B.I. agents entered Panther offices in Chicago, Detroit, Washington, Salt Lake City, and Denver in search of these suspects, apprehending at least three to be extradited to New Haven. Justice Department officials explained that the raids were to execute fugitive warrants and were conducted at early morning hours to avoid attracting crowds that might turn into riots.[103]

The A.C.L.U. later described law enforcement actions in Chicago "where police and F.B.I. agents undertook a June 4th dawn raid on Panther headquarters with an arrest warrant for George Sams, but no search warrant. Upon smashing down the door of the office and failing to find George Sams, enforcement officials broke up furniture, confiscated literature, lists of donors and petitions and arrested eight Panthers on charges so flimsy they were later dismissed. The following day a similar raid was made in Detroit, the door broken down, documents photographed, three Panthers arrested on specious charges and later released."[104] When small-scale disorders unrelated to the F.B.I. searches erupted in San Francisco, Indianapolis, and Sacramento, local police also raided nearby Panther offices. These and other incidents led Bobby Seale to charge a national plot to destroy the organization and to call a conference with white radical groups to develop "a united front against Facism in America."[105]

In late August Seale was arrested by the F.B.I. as a result of a warrant issued in New Haven charging him with complicity in the Rackley killing. Two members of the local chapter were ready to testify that they had participated in the murder and that Seale had personally ordered them to do so while at Yale to deliver a speech. Both later pleaded guilty to reduced charges of second degree murder and conspiracy to kidnap resulting in death. While Seale's attorneys attempted to block his extradition to Connecticut, he was taken secretly by federal marshals to Chicago, where the trial of the convention riot conspiracy case was about to begin.[106]

The Justice Department Task Force

By mid-1969 the Justice Department had decided not only that the Black Panthers were a special danger to the nation's security, as J. Edgar Hoover asserted, but also that it should take more direct action against them. Apart from Bobby Seale's Chicago indictment, the other previous cases against the Panthers had primarily local origins. Will Wilson, head of the Criminal Division, now chose to abandon Ramsey Clark's policy of deferring to city and state law enforcement. When Seale was taken to Chicago in August, his defense lawyer Francis McTernan claimed the Justice Department had prepared a special file in connection with a program of harassment against Panther leaders all over the country. The Department confirmed that it had formed a special interagency intelligence task force for dealing with black militants. The task force would coordinate the activities of the Criminal, Internal Security, and Civil Rights Divisions with other federal agencies such as the Treasury Department.[107]

The search for New Haven fugitives was not the only reason for creating the Panther task force. When police raided party offices in Sacramento, that city's Mayor had made a personal inspection and was "shocked and horrified" at the evidence of bullet holes, broken typewriters and damaged food resulting from the police action.[108] A federal grand jury then began to look into the police-Panther clashes in Northern California. After the grand jury started to work, Assistant Attorney General Wilson dispatched a team of five attorneys from the Criminal Division to handle the inquiry. "They sent them in without prior warning to me or consultation," United States Attorney Cecil Poole revealed later. "Whatever they say they're doing, they're out to get the Black Panthers. . . .I don't know whether they trust me or not. If it were anybody but the Black Panthers, though, I think I'd be prosecuting." According to the United States Attorney, the original authorization for the special attorneys' role in the grand jury probe, signed by Assistant Attorney General Wilson, was ruled insufficient by the presiding federal judge. Attorney General Mitchell was forced to give his personal approval in sealed orders.[109] Establishment of the Panther task force accompanied Wilson and Mitchell's decision to take control of the San Francisco grand jury.

The new task force had ready access to the facilities and resources developed in 1968 under Ramsey Clark and Warren Christopher for gathering intelligence about potential civil disorders. James T. Devine, Director of both the Department's Civil Disturbance Group and its Interdivisional Intelligence and Information Unit, disclosed several months later that the unit's computer was used to produce a special print-out report on the Black Panther Party. While F.B.I. reports were the chief source of data feeding the computer, it also contained information supplied by the Army, the United States Attorneys offices, and other federal agencies such as the Treasury Department's alcohol and tobacco tax division, which enforces federal gun laws, and the Secret Service (which began assembling a data bank of its own). The computer's normal function was to produce each week a four-volume intelligence report containing a city-by-city assessment of the potential for civil disorder, including what marches, rallies, or meetings are occurring, the organizations and individuals sponsoring them, and the city's disturbance history. From this information the Interdivisional Intelligence Unit sent pertinent data to the Attorney General and the appropriate divisions.[110]

During the fall of 1969 the Department's coordinated efforts against the Panthers began to produce federal legal action. In October two white members of the Friends of the Panthers, including the daughter of the leader of the Canadian New Democratic Party, were arrested in Los Angeles and charged with illegal possession of hand grenades.[111] Two officers of the International Committee to Defend Eldridge Cleaver received a subpoena in November, directing them to produce all committee records for a Philadelphia grand jury investigation into possible mail fraud violations. The subpoena stemmed from an advertisement in the New York Times a year earlier denouncing harassment of the Panthers and soliciting funds for Cleaver's legal defense. When committee officials appealed the District Court's refusal to quash the subpoena, contending that disclosures of contributors' names would violate the freedom of association and that the government had not shown probable cause for suspecting mail fraud, the Justice Department dropped its request for the names of contributors. The Department still wanted other records to discover any mishandling of funds or misleading of contributors, perhaps because money may have been used to aid Cleaver's escape rather than his legal defense. The Court of Appeals permitted the committee to withhold the data while it considered the issues.[112]

Federal agencies moved not only against white supporters, but against individual Panther leaders. On November 7 Panther field marshal David Cox was arrested in New York and charged with federal gun violations.[113] David Hilliard, the party's highest ranking official still functioning outside prison, was arrested by Secret Service agents on December 3 for threatening the life of President Nixon. The charge stemmed from a speech he made on November 15 at a San Francisco antiwar rally. According to evidence presented to the grand jury investigating the Panthers, Hilliard referred to the President as "the man that's responsible for all the attacks on the Black Panther Party nationally," adding, "We will kill Richard Nixon." After his release on $30,000 bail, his defense attorney accused the government of taking Hilliard's "rhetoric of the ghetto" out of context and predicted that a conviction would be impossible under the First Amendment.[114] The Supreme Court's decision in Watts v. United States made Hilliard's prosecution questionable, especially if the government had to prove actual incitement.

At the same time the San Francisco grand jury, under the guidance of the team of lawyers sent out from Washington, was investigating party finances and activities and was considering evidence of possible violations of the antiriot law and of Smith Act provisions against advocating violent overthrow of the government and calling for revolution through assassination of public officials.[115]

Few of these federal actions received any publicity. Instead, public attention in the fall of 1969 focused on the role of Bobby Seale in the Chicago convention riot conspiracy trial, which began in September over Seale's objection. Since his attorney, Charles Gerry, was undergoing an operation, he requested postponement of his trial until Garry could be present as his defense counsel. Judge Julius Hoffman denied this request and refused to let Seale act as his own counsel or to sever the case from the others. When witnesses began to testify about Seale's activities, he attempted to cross-examine them and was physically restrained—even bound and gagged—by order of the judge. Judge Hoffman eventually severed Seale's case and imposed a stiff contempt of court sentence. Seale's dramatic attempts to defend himself and the judge's response were vividly conveyed by the news media and created a widespread impression that the Panthers had no respect for the courts or the legal process.[116]

All across the country law enforcement agencies were now sensitive to every move the Panthers made. While Seale's case and the New York conspiracy prosecution were the most publicized, Panthers were being arrested in other cities for a wide variety of local offenses. If local authorities were so closely following their activities, why did the Justice Department believe it necessary to base the San Francisco grand jury inquiry on such a constitutionally dubious statute as the Smith Act? United States Attorney Poole offered one obvious explanation. Department executives were interested in the Panthers not only because they appeared to represent a serious internal threat to the country, but for political motives as well. Criminal Division head Will Wilson was "really after showing the people of the United States, and particularly the voters, that the Department of Justice is going to put an end to this foolishness of rioting in the streets by the blacks." Because of its "commitment to do those things which furbish its image as a tough law enforcement agency," Poole believed the Department was "apt to tread dangerously close to those actions we thought we'd progressed beyond" and to become "heavily involved in the area of one's beliefs and ignore the sensibilities of the Bill of Rights."[117]

The December Panther Raids

By moving beyond a policy of prosecuting for overt illegal acts, by intensifying surveillance, and by no longer deferring to local law enforcement, the Department was on the verge of overt repression. At this point events occurred which significantly altered the political context. Two massive pre-dawn raids on Panther offices were conducted by police in Chicago and Los Angeles on December 4th and 8th to execute search and arrest warrants issued by local courts authorizing seizure of illegal weapons. Both raids precipitated shoot-outs: in Chicago two Panthers, state leader Fred Hampton and Mark Clark of Peoria, were killed and four others wounded; in Los Angeles three policemen and three Panthers were wounded after a four-hour gun battle. Even Los Angeles Mayor Yorty expressed doubts about the wisdom of police tactics, while the Chicago deaths inspired a nationwide reaction. Three Chicago aldermen, the Afro-American Patrolman's League, the Illinois A.C.L.U. and N.A.A.C.P. immediately called for an independent investigation; nine Democratic Congressmen asked the Violence Commission to conduct a credible inquiry; and in Los Angeles three state legislators joined a rally supported by the N.A.A.C.P. and the Urban League demanding investigation of the clash there.[118]

Within ten days the Justice Department announced that the Civil Rights Division and the F.B.I. would begin an investigation of allegations that undue force may have been used by local police in carrying out their obligations. Among those requesting the inquiry had been Roy Wilkins, Whitney Young, and members of the Chicago Lawyers Committee for Civil Rights Under Law, who wired the Attorney General asking him to convene a special grand jury composed entirely of lawyers to look into the shooting. Lacking confidence in the Department, twenty-six prominent civil rights leaders, lawyers, and church officials formed a citizens' Commission of Inquiry into the Black Panthers and Law Enforcement Officials. Organized by Legal Defense Fund director Jack Greenberg, the commission included former Justice Arthur Goldberg and Ramsey Clark. The United States Civil Rights Commission, asked by Illinois Senator Charles Percy to make an investigation, was unable to secure from the White House the authority for additional funds it thought necessary to do a thorough job with sufficient staff. Another inquiry conducted by five black Congressmen heard testimony in Chicago questioning the Justice Department's impartiality. It was there that Jay Miller, Illinois Director of the A.C.L.U., recounted Civil Rights Division head Jerris Leonard's comment the previous spring that "the Black Panthers are nothing but hoodlums and we've got to get rid of them."[119]

The Department's official position was that it "had never had any policy of concerted activity with local police in order to harass any members of the Black Panther Party. . . .The recent incidents of violence took place when local police departments were attempting to serve warrants. The violations alleged in the warrants were infractions of state law and were not under Federal jurisdiction. No Federal officials participated in the police actions."[120] There were, however, some indications that federal agencies had influenced the local police decisions to seize illegal weapons, which were probably known to be in Panther possession for some time, in two major cities within four days. A journalist with extensive contacts among law enforcement officials reported that federal intelligence had produced a recent "flurry" of F.B.I. reports on the Panthers to police departments in various parts of the country.[121] Several weeks later the Treasury Department's chief investigator in New York revealed that his agency had infiltrated the Panthers and exchanged information about gun violations with police. The Mayor of Seattle disclosed he turned down a request by Treasury agents in January, 1970, for city police to conduct a search of Panther headquarters.[122] Even if federal agencies did not specifically request the Chicago and Los Angeles raids, it is reasonable to believe that intensive federal-local intelligence cooperation facilitated police action.

In late December the A.C.L.U. released a survey of nine major cities describing the pattern of punitive harassment against the Panthers during the year:

"In San Francisco, Los Angeles, Chicago, Philadelphia and New York, police have made repeated arrests of Panthers for distributing papers without a permit, harassment, interfering with an officer, loitering and disorderly conduct—stemming from incidents where police have challenged Panthers as they attempted to distribute their newspaper or other political materials. Seldom have these charges held up in court. . . .

"A.C.L.U. affiliates in New York and Indiana report infiltration by government informants into black groups thought to be Panthers for the purpose of entrapment. The evidence indicates that government agents have attempted to induce black militants to burglarize, in one case offering automatic weapons, in another providing a map of the likely target, a getaway car and the offer of weapons. . . .

"A common police procedure reported to us by A.C.L.U. affiliates in New York, Connecticut, Illinois, California,

and Wisconsin is that of excessive traffic stops by police of
Black Panther Party members. These challenges by police
are so frequent in number and so forceful in manner as to
be unconstitutional. They have rarely resulted in traffic
violations, arrest of a known fugitive or charges of illegal
possession of weapons. They more often produce the
traditional catch-all charges of the police roust—disorderly
conduct, interference with an officer, resisting arrest."

While the A.C.L.U. did not allege a concerted national campaign
to get the Panthers, it charged that "high officials, by their
statement and actions, have helped create the climate of
oppression and have encouraged local police to initiate the
crackdown." Citing J. Edgar Hoover and Vice President
Agnew's description of the Panthers as a "completely irresponsible, anarchistic group of criminals," the A.C.L.U. concluded,
"This official federal posture makes it easy for the president of
the Cleveland Fraternal Order of Police to suggest, 'the country
doesn't need the Black Panther Party, to my way of thinking,
they need to be wiped out.' "[123]

The furor over repression of the Panthers triggered by the
Chicago deaths finally brought to light the San Francisco grand
jury investigation. Department attorneys explained its purposes
and revealed that officials of the party newspaper had been
subpoenaed to produce its records and the original manuscripts
of articles which allegedly included threats against President
Nixon, statements in support of North Vietnam, calls to "do
away with pigs," and remarks about armed struggle and
revolution. One attorney, whose career extended back to the
prosecution of Communists in the 1950's, observed, "When you
read those issues, they should give you a clue as to why the
government is interested in their activities." A White House
statement asserted, however, that the investigation focused only
on individual members of the party, not on the organization
itself.[124]

Among the evidence supporting a possible Smith Act
indictment was a story published by the New York Times in
mid-December. Reporter Earl Caldwell quoted David Hilliard as

saying, "We advocate the very direct overthrow of the Government by way of force and violence. By picking up guns and moving against it because we recognize it as being oppressive and in recognizing that we know that the only solution to it is armed struggle." Hilliard claimed that the Panthers were "prepared to lose more members, to go to jail and to be shot in the streets to bring this repressive system to a grinding halt."[125] Similar statements made by Eldridge Cleaver in a CBS television interview from Algeria led the federal prosecutors to issue subpoenas for production of the out-takes (unused portions) of the CBS film and all records and correspondence relating to the interview. A week later Earl Caldwell was served with a subpoena directing him to appear before the grand jury with the notes and tape recordings of his interviews with Hilliard and Raymond "Masai" Hewitt, managing editor of the party newspaper.[126]

The Department's decision to issue these subpoenas probably reflected a desire to avoid surfacing its undercover informants before the grand jury. There was no need to blow their cover if enough information could be obtained from the news media and reporters' testimony. Although the Department had other sources of information, it wanted Caldwell to relate what Panther officers had told him about the aims and purposes of the organization, its officers, staff, personnel and members. While CBS reluctantly complied with its subpoena, noting a departure from previous practices of negotiating before the issuance of subpoenas to news media, Caldwell refused to comply. His lawyer moved in court to quash the subpoena, arguing that his mere appearance before the grand jury under the terms of the subpoena would infringe his rights and jeopardize his ability to function effectively in his profession. Seventy black journalists joined in a statement charging that Caldwell was subpoenaed because it was felt that as a black man he had special access to information in the black community. Thus the role of every black newsman had been put into question.[127]

Under pressure from the news media and after three former Department executives asserted that newsmen's files and notes had never before been subpoenaed, Attorney General Mitchell admitted that past policies had mistakenly not been followed. He agreed to resume the practice of entering into negotiations to reach an acceptable compromise before issuing subpoenas to reporters. Although federal prosecutors no longer insisted on obtaining all the material first demanded from Caldwell, they still sought his appearance before the grand jury.[128] As the reporter's attorney submitted briefs for judicial consideration of the issue, the San Francisco grand jury postponed indefinitely any indictments, and the attempt to prosecute Panther leaders was at least temporarily curtailed.

While outrage over the Chicago shootings and the subpoenas to journalists was limited to portions of the legal profession, civil rights groups, and the news media, it was enough to bring a pause in Justice Department action against the Panthers. Since the F.B.I. and Civil Rights Division were compelled to investigate police misconduct in Chicago, the Department no longer stood in the position of tacitly approving all local anti-Panther moves. The flow of events might strengthen the influence of agencies like the Community Relations Service committed to alternative policies for dealing with black militancy. What had been during 1969 a relatively unpublicized federal effort against the Panthers was now out in the open. Civil rights groups, the news media, and concerned lawyers were now subjecting the Department's actions to closer scrutiny.

6. THE JUSTICE DEPARTMENT
AND BLACK MILITANCY

Federal policy toward black militant groups during the 1960's was marked by two contrasting styles of managing racial tension. Nicholas Katzenbach and Ramsey Clark, with support from both the President's crime commission and the Kerner commission, saw urban riots as a symptom of economic deprivation and racial inequality. Although basic social reforms were needed to reach the causes of unrest, their immediate program for preventing disorders combined efforts to improve police-community relations with development of better intelligence to predict possible outbreaks. They refused to blame black militants for riots or to use them as a scapegoat to avoid confronting problems of poverty and racial discrimination. Justice Department policy made sharp distinctions between illegal behavior and protected political advocacy, between federal and local law enforcement responsibility. Before 1969 an opposite point of view was urged by many Congressmen and F.B.I. Director Hoover, and adopted in some cities. They chose to emphasize the dangers of black militant activity and more aggressive legal action that would cross the line between conduct and speech. Hoover denounced specific organizations as threats to internal security, while New York district attorney Hogan instituted criminal anarchy and sweeping conspiracy prosecutions. When John Mitchell became Attorney General, the F.B.I. Director's approach was adopted by the Department.

Ramsey Clark and John Mitchell had significantly different conceptions of the functions of intelligence surveillance over black militant groups. Clark envisioned decentralized operations in each major city, with national guidance mainly to anticipate civil disorders and to gather information necessary for making the decision to use military resources if local law enforcement broke down. By mid-1969, however, Mitchell had allowed the Criminal Division to set up a task force that planned to use intelligence data as a basis for concerted federal prosecutions against the Black Panthers. Chapter Five examines in more detail the implications of domestic intelligence surveillance over both black militants and antiwar dissenters.

As in the controversies over criminal due process, the Supreme Court and Congress took opposing positions on constitutional standards for protection of militant political rhetoric. The Court's decisions in Brandenburg and Watts supported Ramsey Clark's firm distinction between advocacy and conduct by defining unprotected incitement as speech both intended and likely to cause immediate illegal acts. The Court's influence was somewhat mixed, however, since its refusal to decide the Epton case left open the possible use of protected speech in conspiracy prosecutions. Congress was more concerned about taking action that would let the public know that riot agitators would be punished. Although Ramsey Clark and the Kerner commission tried to advance carefully limited alternatives, they failed to win passage of legislation defining riots as large-scale disorders and specifying the same requirements for proof of incitement that the Supreme Court laid down. Adoption of the antiriot act created the conditions for conflict between Congress and the Court, unless the Justice Department enforced the law according to narrower judicial standards.

Within the Department itself various agencies contended for influence over the direction of federal policy. The F.B.I. and Will Wilson's Criminal Division had different reasons for moving against groups like the Black Panthers. J. Edgar Hoover's personal style reinforced his Bureau's traditional preoccupation with what it saw as dangers to internal security. Even though the Communist Party had little relevance to black militants, the revolutionary rhetoric and Marxist ideology espoused by the Panthers could fit in with Hoover's long-standing concern about Communism. Wilson, on the other hand, was probably motivated more by his desire to serve the political interests of the Nixon Administration. Consequently, he did not hesitate to override United States Attorney Poole and to send Criminal Division attorneys to take control of the San Francisco grand jury investigation. The F.B.I.'s voice had been muted under Ramsey Clark, who sought other sources of intelligence analysis; but Wilson's task force allowed the F.B.I. to use its intelligence operations to facilitate federal prosecutions and possibly to encourage local police action.

In contrast to the F.B.I. and the Criminal Division, two other branches of the Department represented different policy objectives. The Community Relations Service urged police and city officials to develop open regular communications with black organizations and even to be receptive to protests as a safety valve. Its conception of creative disorder meant that police should tolerate demonstrations and militant rhetoric for their own self-interest in the long-run maintenance of order. When law enforcement agencies used unnecessary force, the Civil Rights Division investigated and prosecuted under the criminal statutes punishing willful deprivation of constitutional rights. Although Jerris Leonard's hostility to the Panthers led him to approve Bobby Seale's antiriot indictment early in 1969, his Division's ongoing duty under the civil rights statutes compelled him to investigate the Chicago police shooting of Fred Hampton in December. Both the Community Relations Service and Civil Rights Division might counter the F.B.I.'s influence over the Attorney General.

The Department was, therefore, far from a monolithic organization even under John Mitchell. The various functions of these separate agencies tended to prevent any single policy from dominating for any length of time. Clark's preference for community relations answers did not keep him from prosecuting Rap Brown, while Mitchell backed away from the Criminal Division's attempt to bring Smith Act charges against the Panthers. Because of these divergent impulses, the Attorney General could not easily provide consistent national leadership. Law enforcement officials who looked to the Justice Department for advice might see J. Edgar Hoover's criticism of demonstrators rather than the Community Relations Service's stand on the positive functions of protest. Local police could follow the Criminal Division's example and single out the Panthers for arrest and prosecution, but their tactics of harassment might provoke the Civil Rights Division to expose police misconduct. In short, there was no coherent Department policy for dealing with black militants.

Former U.S. Attorney Poole has called charges of a conspiracy between federal and local officials to eliminate militants like the Panthers "utter, sheer nonsense." When he said the Department was "out to get" them, he did not mean it was interested in their deaths. It was concentrating instead on getting evidence against the Panthers for federal prosecutions. Nevertheless, Poole believed that to move exclusively against them took "a peculiar kind of hard shell, weighing the bad they stand for against their value as a cohesive force in the black community."[129] Regular cooperation among law enforcement agencies had been transformed from a means for anticipating and controlling civil disorders into an instrument that threatened repression. The structure of intelligence surveillance developed in response to urban riots would not be easy to dismantle.

4

ANTIWAR

DISSENT

The Justice Department's policies toward black militant groups in the 1960's were paralleled by measures adopted to deal with dissent against the war in Vietnam. A similar program of intelligence surveillance was developed, and there were demands for prosecutions that would go beyond illegal action to reach political advocacy. Sometimes the two strains of black unrest and antiwar protest became intertwined, as when Congressmen called for the prosecution of Stokely Carmichael for counseling draft evasion and when Bobby Seale was included in the Chicago conspiracy indictment. For the most part, however, organized activity against the Vietnam war was a white-dominated endeavor. Black and white radicals shared a common antipathy for the structure of economic and political power in America; but while blacks went into the streets of the ghettos in outrage against wretched living conditions, antiwar protests focused on the instrumentalities of national authority—the Selective Service System, military recruitment agencies, the Democratic national convention, and time and again the nation's capital.

Before the Vietnam war expanded, the Department had the remnants of the legal and administrative structure that had been created during the cold war years to combat domestic Communism. The F.B.I.'s main interest in 1964 was still the moribund Communist Party and the possibility that the party might "inflitrate legitimate nonsubversive groups for the purpose of gaining a dominant role in their policy-making machinery." Since 1936 the F.B.I. had gathered such domestic intelligence under the authority of a directive from President Roosevelt.[1] From its various sources, public and private, the F.B.I. reported in 1964 that Communists were criticizing the involvement of American troops in South Vietnam: "The Party has charged that these 'imperialistic policies' have disgraced the United States before the world and endanger world peace. It has conducted an intensive campaign for the withdrawal of American forces from South Vietnam. . . ."[2]

During previous wartime periods before Vietnam, political liberty was endangered by repressive federal prosecutions. The worst abuses occurred in World War I when literally thousands of people were convicted of sedition and conscientious objectors to military service received little sympathy. World War II's experience was somewhat better, except for the evacuation and detention of Japanese-Americans on the West Coast. Nevertheless, even civil libertarian Attorney General Francis Biddle approved conspiracy prosecutions under laws like the Smith Act against Trotskyite radicals and right-wing groups who favored Nazi Germany. The cold war years of international tension with the Soviet Union saw more extensive Smith Act prosecutions after the Supreme Court sustained the conspiracy conviction of national Communist Party leaders in 1951. When the search for subversives in and out of government reached a peak in the early 1950's, a new word entered the language. McCarthyism symbolized an attitude of intolerance and a policy of suppression that almost silenced radical criticism of American society.

The war in Vietnam offered another test of the legal system's capacity to maintain freedom of speech during times of national crisis. As opposition to the war became more widespread, the Justice Department had to decide whether legal sanctions should be imposed on the most vigorous critics. With the draft emerging as a focus for dissent, Selective Service enforcement policy created deep divisions among federal executives with the Attorney General and the Selective Service Director on opposing sides. Added burdens were placed on the Department by Congressional demands that it disregard consititutional standards and by antiwar protests that compelled it to develop policies for handling mass demonstrations. Because of these pressures the Department revived its internal security intelligence surveillance operations and ultimately returned to the conspiracy trial as a device to satisfy, at least symbolically, demands for suppression of dissent.

1. THE ESCALATION OF
ANTIWAR PROTEST, 1965-66

The escalation of the war in Vietnam during the spring of 1965, with increased American troop commitments and regular bombing of North Vietnam, aroused the first substantial organized protests against the war. Concentrated on university campuses and among left-wing organizations and pacifists, antiwar activity initially meant teach-ins and peaceful marches. Student energies previously devoted to civil rights work and occasional demands for university reform, as represented by the Mississippi Summer Project and the Berkeley Free Speech Movement in 1964, were turned to protest against President Johnson's Vietnam policy. On campuses the non-doctrinaire Students for a Democratic Society was far more popular than other radical organizations like the Young Socialist Alliance, the Progressive Labor Party's May Second Movement, and the Communist-affiliated W.E.B. DuBois Clubs. In April, 1965, S.D.S. won national attention when some 20,000 persons took part in an antiwar march in Washington. Protest demonstrations began to be planned by organizations that served as umbrellas under which various groups could join for specific action—the Berkeley Vietnam Day Committee, the Fifth Avenue Vietnam Peace Parade Committee in New York, and a loose National Coordinating Committee to End the War in Vietnam with offices in Madison, Wisconsin.[3]

F.B.I. intelligence-gathering focused early on the campus antiwar movement. A professor at the State University of New York at Brockport revealed later that he was approached by an F.B.I. agent after he had defended Administration policy during a Vietnman teach-in in April, 1965. He was asked to watch and report on the activities of professors who attacked Administration policy during the teach-in, but he had refused.[4] A Duke University student recounted how he was invited to report on college protests:

"During my freshman year (1964-65), I had noticed a good deal of antiwar literature on campus that described such things as American advisors torturing Vietnamese women, etc. According to the manner in which I was brought up, these flyers and handouts seemed less than patriotic and so I gathered several and mailed them to F.B.I. headquarters in Washington.

"Shortly thereafter—in early spring of 1965—a special agent who lived in Durham. . .contracted me and questioned me concerning why I sent the material, where it had been posted, etc. I gave him what information I had. Sometime later the same agent contacted me and we met for a short time. I furnished him more complete information and answered certain questions concerning what I knew of the University Liberal Action Committee and gave him some general information concerning several individuals. The agent was careful to note what my source of information was."[5]

The F.B.I. clearly believed that gathering comprehensive information about antiwar activities was a legitimate part of national security surveillance or its law enforcement duty. Director Hoover reported at the end of the year that the Communist Party and other subversive groups had supported and participated in demonstrations against the war, including the April student march in Washington and a Washington Summer Action Project in August.[6]

During the summer of 1965 the House and Senate Armed Services Committees were informed by Selective Service officials that some antiwar protesters had publicly burned their draft cards to symbolize their defiance of the draft and the war. Acknowledging "the deep concern expressed throughout the Nation over the increasing incidences in which individuals and large groups of individuals openly defy and encourage others to defy the authority of the Government by destroying or mutilating their draft cards," the House committee proposed a bill specifically making such action a federal crime. Current laws already punished forging, altering, or in any manner changing a draft card and failure of registrants to keep their cards in their personal possession. But the House committee felt that "in the present critical situation of the country" destroying draft cards posed "a grave threat to the security of the Nation." The Senate committee agreed that such defiant and contumacious conduct "by dissident persons who disapprove of national policy" represented a potential threat to the exercise of the power to raise and support armies. As passed by the House, 393-1, and by a voice vote in the Senate, the measure provided that a person who knowingly mutilated or destroyed a draft card was subject to a fine of not more than $10,000 and imprisonment for up to five years.[7]

Congressional action did little to discourage increasing antidraft activity. In September an S.D.S. national conference adopted a plan for a visible national antidraft program whose purpose would be to build an antiwar movement around the draft issue and possibly make the draft system function less smoothly. One step was to set up workshops and distribute literature encouraging men to register as conscientious objectors.[8] Selective Service law authorized conscientious objector classification for men who by reason of religious training and belief were opposed to participation in war in any form. The statute specifically excluded essentially political, sociological, or philosophical views or merely a personal moral code; and it defined religious belief as "belief in a relation to a Supreme Being involving duties superior to those arising from any human relation." Early in 1965, however, the Supreme Court interpreted the statute to apply whenever "a given belief that is sincere and meaningful occupies a place in the life of its possessor parallel to that filled by the orthodox belief in God of one who clearly qualifies for the exemption."[9] Nevertheless, the Selective Service System did not modify its form requiring applicants to affirm or deny their belief in a Supreme Being, and draft officials still emphasized proof of religious background and belief.[10]

S.D.S. attacked the Selective Service System as undemocratic because it did not allow young men to make the basic individual moral decision of whether to kill—or die—in a war not of their own making. Its antidraft activities provoked Senators Stennis and Jackson of the Armed Services Committee to charge that peace groups were illegally counseling draft evasion. Referring to S.D.S. plans to jam the draft boards and to cause the government to spend thousands of dollars in investigations and paper work by advising men how to file as conscientious objectors, Senator Stennis demanded that the Justice Department "immediately move to jerk this movement up by the roots and grind it to bits."[11] Meanwhile, in California several hundred students associated with the Vietnam Day Committee tried to block trains carrying troops bound for Vietnam. War protest activity culminated on October 15 and 16, 1965, in a series of demonstrations across the country coinciding with worldwide International Days of Protest.

When these demonstrations took place, Attorney General Nicholas Katzenbach informed President Johnson that his Department would begin a national investigation of the antiwar movement. Announcing his intentions at the end of the weekend of protests, Katzenbach cited the draft card burning law, provisions of the Selective Service law against urging or abetting draft evasion, and federal sedition laws as the basis for the investigation. "We may very well have some prosecutions," he added, leaving the impression that S.D.S. was associated with a mimeographed sheet found in Berkeley called "Ways and Means of Beating and Defeating the Draft" which advised such tactics as faking homosexuality, bribing doctors for disability certificates, and arriving drunk or high at physical examinations. The Attorney General made clear that S.D.S. was one of the groups to be investigated and that Chicago (the location of S.D.S. national headquarters) and California (where the Vietnam Day Committee was most active) were the prime targets of the inquiry. F.B.I. agents, draft officials, and local police would cooperate with the United States Attorneys offices in the investigation; but Department officials in Washington would decide whether to prosecute.

Katzenbach emphasized that antiwar demonstrators had the right to express their views, and he cautioned against calling their activities treason. When asked whether Communists were involved in S.D.S., he replied that the identities of Communists in S.D.S. were known but that, by and large, Communists were not leaders in S.D.S. President Johnson fully endorsed the investigation, although his press secretary noted it was initiated by the Justice Department, not by the White House. The President was reported to be concerned that even well-meaning demonstrators could become the victims of Communist exploitation and hopeful that the investigation would be concluded as soon as possible.[12]

Among the statutes cited as a basis for the inquiry was a section of the 1940 Smith Act punishing any person who distributes or attempts to distribute any written or printed matter which advises, counsels or urges insubordination, disloyalty, mutiny, or refusal of duty by any member of the military or naval forces of the United States. Thus part of the investigation focused on a leaflet printed for the Berkeley Vietnam Day Committee urging servicemen not to fight "any more than you have to," which was distributed during the October protests and later mailed to soldiers in Vietnam. Another possible sedition investigation resulted from a report that Hanoi radio broadcast tape recordings produced in the United States and forwarded to North Vietnam through Canada. The recordings suggested ways for soldiers to avoid service in Vietnam and included the message, "We're not asking you to shoot your commanding officer or sergeant in the back yet—not at this time."[13] Other groups that were probably scrutinized closely included the U.S. Committee to Aid the National Liberation Front in South Vietnam and the May Second Movement which attempted to send supplies and medicine to the enemy.

The first draft card buring arrest was made on October 18, 1965. David J. Miller, a member of the Catholic Worker organization, burned his card at a New York rally shown on national television news programs. Admitting he had violated the law, Miller challenged its constitutionality by asserting that his act was a public expression of protest protected by the First Amendment and that Congress in adopting the measure had not intended it as a legitimate improvement of Selective Service operations but as intimidation of dissent. The decision to arrest draft card burners was made by Justice Department attorneys, who instructed F.B.I. agents not to make arrests on public platforms in order to avoid lending themselves to public spectacle. Since F.B.I. agents had to verify whether draft cards were in fact being burned, their presence was required at most large antiwar rallies. Not all apparent violations were prosecuted. Of five men who burned cards at a November demonstration in New York, only the four eligible for induction were indicted while the fifth who was not charged was over thirty-five. This age distinction may have been made on the ground that the Selective Service System's need for eligible men to carry their draft cards was greater than for overage men, thus reinforcing the government's argument that the law was justified to aid Selective Service administration, not to intimidate dissenters.[14] By mid-1966 the Department reported fourteen indictments under the statute, eight in New York, five in Massachusetts, and one in Iowa.

During the October Days of Protest, several University of Michigan students were arrested by Ann Arbor police for a sit-in at the local draft board office. They were convicted under city ordinance for trespassing, but they appealed (ultimately without success to the Supreme Court). The Ann Arbor sit-in was not the first demonstration to focus on draft offices; but coming as it did at the peak of the nationwide protests, it provoked Selective Service Director Lewis Hershey to advise the draft boards of the arrested students to withdraw their student deferments. Hershey's position was that Selective Service regulations permitted reclassification of registrants found to be delinquent and that the students were delinquent because their protest interfered with draft board operations. Hershey also recommended that draft card burners be reclassified for the same reason. While the Director's views did not bind local boards, twelve Michigan students were reclassified 1-A because of their sit-in.

At the request of a group of law professors, Michigan Senator Philip Hart took objections against Director Hershey's policy to Assistant Attorney General Fred M. Vinson, Jr., head of the Criminal Division. He charged that Hershey's directive gave draft officials the right to bypass the courts and assess punishment without trial. Draft boards could determine that registrants had obstructed selective service operations by their protests or by destroying draft cards and then withdraw their deferments, without their having been convicted of violating federal or state law. Even though the Ann Arbor trespass convictions were being appealed, the Michigan students had still been reclassified. Assistant Attorney General Vinson agreed with Senator Hart. After failing to persuade Hershey to change his ruling, Vinson wrote the Senator, "As a matter of both law and policy, the sanctions of the Universal Military Training and Service Act cannot be used in any way to stifle constitutionally protected expression of views." While in the past registrants had been reclassified if they failed to report a current address or otherwise violated draft regulations, Vinson distinguished those situations from the case where the conduct involved was the expression of an opinion, even if the method of expression transgressed the law. If the protesters violated the law, then the criminal sanctions which attached to the offense were all that should be applied. Vinson declared that if any Selective Service decisions were contested in the courts, the Justice Department "would conduct the litigation and would act in accordance with the views I have here expressed."[15]

Accompanying General Hershey's move against draft protests was a vigorous attack on student demonstrators by Associate F.B.I. Director C. A. DeLoach, who delivered a widely publicized address to the American Farm Bureau Federation convention in December, 1965. Referring to extreme opponents of the Vietnam war and draft card burners as "morally and emotionally immature misfits who have cast a shadow of disgrace across the streets of many American communities and the campuses of some of our educational institutions," De-Loach assailed defiance of the law as a malignant disease. He condemned "the arrogant nonconformists, including some so-called educators, who have mounted the platform at public gatherings to urge 'civil disobedience' and. . .those members of the self-proclaimed 'smart set' who consider it a sign of 'sophistication' to ridicule decency, patriotism, respectability and duty."[16] Several weeks later J. Edgar Hoover reported the Communist Party was playing an ever-increasing role in generating opposition to the United States position in Vietnam and was planning to "take advantage of the upsurge in 'radicalism' among American youth." Communists had taken part in the International Days of Protest in October, as well as a March for Peace in Vietnam and a National Antiwar Convention in Washington during November.[17]

Justice Department opposition to General Hershey's directive was matched by its refusal to echo F.B.I. officials' rhetoric. Apart from the fourteen draft card burning cases and an increase in draft evasion cases from 369 to fiscal 1965 to 642 in fiscal 1966, the Department's investigations of antiwar dissent produced no prosecutive action.[18] Whatever their feelings about the war, Department executives believed repressive prosecutions could not be legally justified, and they recalled the McCarthyism of the Korean war period with distaste. Two top men remembered those years vividly. Deputy Attorney General Ramsey Clark's father, Justice Tom C. Clark, had served as Attorney General in 1945-49 during the early years of postwar fear of subversive activities; and Assistant Attorney General Vinson's father was Chief Justice of the United States from 1946 to 1953. They could also look to an Associated Press survey of eighty-five colleges and universities reporting that members in antiwar organizations were only a minute fraction of the students on each campus. In addition, strong defense of civil liberties came from Defense Secretary Robert McNamara. Speaking at commencement exercises for Chatham College where his daughter was graduating, McNamara said, "There is a serious dimension to the protest among some students today. But whatever comfort some of the extremist protest may be giving to our enemies—it is clear from Hanoi's own statement that it is—let us be perfectly clear about our principles and our priorities. This is a nation in which the freedom of dissent is absolutely fundamental."[19]

While the Department brought no prosecutions, the F.B.I. continued its investigations of S.D.S. and similar groups. After a series of demonstrations in March, 1966, the Dean of Wesleyan University disclosed he had refused an F.B.I. agent's request for

names of all Wesleyan student members of S.D.S. The dean
feared the F.B.I.'s inquiries would create a climate of suspicion
"that might lead some students to be more circumspect than
the situation requires. Things like this can be a danger to a free
and open community if men change their behavior because of
it." When Wesleyan student government officers criticized the
inquiry as hostile to academic freedom, F.B.I. Director Hoover
replied that the charge was "so irresponsible as to cast serious
doubt on the quality of academic reasoning or the motivation
behind it." According to Hoover, the Attorney General had
publicly instructed the F.B.I. in October, 1965, "to determine the
extent of Communist infiltration into the Students for a Democratic Society." This was the purpose of the Bureau's contact with
the Wesleyan dean, and there had been no attempt to intimidate
any students or university officials. Hoover added,

> These investigations are initiated in a straight-forward
> manner without apology to anyone and are conducted
> objectively, truthfully and impartially to determine the
> facts. An F.B.I. investigation of certain members of an
> organization is not a judgment but a gathering of facts, to
> be studied by duly constituted legal authorities. In
> performing its duties, the F.B.I. has not and will not
> exceed its authority; neither will it shirk its responsibil-
> ities."

The F.B.I. Director cited the agency's duties under the Internal
Security Act, Executive Order 10450 (the federal employee
security program), and orders from the Attorney General.[20]
  The Internal Security Act of 1950 and the federal employee
security program both required the Attorney General to take
specific legal action against subversive or Communist-front
organizations. Under Executive Order 10450 issued in 1953, the
Justice Department was to prepare a list of the names of groups,
membership in which would be used to evaluate the loyalty of
federal employees. Since 1959 the Attorney General had made
no changes in the list of 274 organizations, most of which no
longer existed; but the F.B.I. continued its investigations on the

presumption that new groups could be added at any time. The Internal Security Act authorized the Attorney General to petition the Subversive Activities Control Board to designate groups as Communist fronts. In 1963 a petition was filed against Advance and Burning Issues Youth Organizations, with headquarters in New York City. Information obtained by the F.B.I. concerning infiltrated groups was referred to the Internal Security Division for consideration in instituting such proceedings.

In the spring of 1966 the Department made clear that the Internal Security Act was still alive when it petitioned the Subversive Activities Control Board to require the W.E.B. DuBois Clubs, a Marxist youth organization with headquarters in San Francisco, to register as a Communist front. The petition charged the DuBois Clubs were substantially directed, dominated, and controlled by the Communist Party and operated primarily to give aid and support to the party. One other indirect measure taken against an antiwar dissenter was the Secretary of State's withdrawal of Yale professor Staughton Lynd's passport following his unauthorized trip to North Vietnam in December, 1965, with S.D.S. founder Tom Hayden and Communist Party theoretician Herbert Aptheker.[21]

Since the Justice Department was not directly prosecuting war protesters, Congressmen began to explore ways of expanding the scope of federal criminal statutes. As the National Coordinating Committee to End the War in Vietnam announced plans for summer activities in conjunction with S.D.S. and several antiwar Congressional campaigns, the House Committee on Un-American Activities prepared to hold hearings. Texas Congressman Joe Pool sought to build public support for a bill making it a crime to interfere with troop movements, distribute propaganda affecting the morale of the armed forces, or provide aid to hostile forces. The committee's hopes must have risen when President Johnson began issuing patriotic appeals, called dissenters "Nervous Nellies," asked "every American to put our country first if we want to keep it first," and won enthusiastic cheers for his impromptu emotional attacks on war critics during a Midwestern political tour.[22]

The Un-American Activities Committee's hearings in August, 1966, turned out to be a farce. Even Republican Senate leader Everett Dirksen commented, "This spectacle can do Congress no good." Witnesses like Jerry Rubin of the Berkeley Vietnam Day Committee refused to take the investigation seriously, arriving dressed in the uniform of the American Revolution; and members of the Progressive Labor Party loudly proclaimed their revolutionary aims and support for the National Liberation Front in South Vietnam. The hearings ended abruptly after Congressman Pool ordered the arrest of civil liberties lawyer Arthur Kinoy, who was seized by marshals and dragged from the room, and other lawyers withdrew on the grounds that they could not properly counsel their clients in an atmosphere of intimidation.[23]

A week after these embarrassing incidents, Deputy Attorney General Clark testified against the committee's bill. Clark reported that the miniscule handful of extremists who tried to aid the enemy and obstruct the movement of troops had been totally ineffectual. There was no evidence that money or supplies had ever reached North Vietnam, and the one attempt to halt troop trains in 1965 had easily been dealt with by local police. Clark believed such activities were essentially a propaganda effort. Existing laws already protected the national interest, and the bill might risk infringement of constitutional rights of free speech by making it a felony to advise, urge, or solicit aid for anyone acting in hostile opposition to the armed forces of the United States. After Clark's testimony the committee dropped this provision, but retained sections prohibiting collecting money for the enemy and obstructing troop movements. Sensing the mood of the House as the 1966 elections approached, Congressman Richard Ichord of the Un-American Activities Committee asserted that if Congress did not pass such a law, "the American people are just not going to understand it." The bill soon passed in the House, 265-63, but the Senate took no action since both majority leader Mansfield and minority leader Dirksen reportedly opposed it.[24]

As if to make clear no new legislation was necessary, the Administration saw to it that existing laws governing trading with the enemy were strictly enforced. Since all financial and commercial transactions with North Vietnam and the National Liberation Front had been barred in 1964, the Treasury Department directed American banks not to honor checks payable to the Canadian Friends Service Committee which was sending medical supplies to Hanoi. Post offices were instructed to turn away parcels the Quakers wanted to send to Canada, and the Treasury Department even froze the bank accounts of several organizations. The State Department, which officially authorized these measures, rejected the argument that the medical supplies were meant only for noncombatants.[25]

Throughout 1966 the Justice Department rejected demands that it prosecute under sedition statutes or for counseling draft evasion. Sedition charges of urging insubordination or disloyalty in the armed services had last been considered by the Supreme Court during World War II. In Hartzel v. United States the Court reversed a conviction for circulating pamphlets injurious to military morale because neither the circumstances surrounding their preparation nor the writings themselves showed a specific intent to cause insubordination or disloyalty. Citing Justice Holmes' classic formula, Justice Murphy added that a second element necessary for conviction was "a clear and present danger that the activities in question will bring about substantive evils which the Congress has a right to prevent."[26] These principles would also apply to cases of counseling draft evasion. When Stokely Carmichael announced he would go to jail if drafted and urged Negroes not to serve in the armed forces, several Congressmen including Senate Judiciary Committee Chairman James Eastland, called on the Attorney General to prosecute him for inciting draft resistance. A Department spokesman replied that it was "keenly conscious and aware of the allegations and the factual background" and would take prompt action when and if the facts warranted it under the law as determined by the courts. Department attorneys believed that mere expression of personal views about the draft, short of counseling specific persons to evade their military duty, would be protected by the courts under the First Amendment.[27]

Federal executives seemed firmly committed to a policy of minimizing the effects of antiwar protests by playing down their significance. Even the F.B.I.'s annual report for 1966 omitted statements that appeared a year earlier about Communist involvement in the peace movement.[28] Despite his caustic words during the summer, President Johnson appointed an Advisory Commission on Selective Service chaired by former Civil Rights Division head Burke Marshall, indicating a desire to redress grievances based on the unfairness and certainty of the draft. In addition, the Justice Department was waging a quiet battle against General Hershey's directive advising draft boards to reclassify student demonstrators. The Department had the support of House Judiciary Committee chairman Emanuel Celler, who accused Hershey of demeaning the Selective Service act and jeopardizing the honor of the armed forces by using the draft to punish and discourage political dissent. Celler endorsed Assistant Attorney General Vinson's view that Selective Service violations should be punished by the courts, not by draft boards.[29]

The controversy entered the federal courts in 1966. Two New York residents who were reclassified because of the Michigan protest had filed suit, with New York Civil Liberties Union assistance, asking a federal District Court to issue an injunction directing their draft board to restore their original student deferments. The District Court refused, and the students appealed. Carefully drafting its argument, the Justice Department declined to defend the Selective Service System's action, but opposed the suit on the grounds that the courts could not remedy draft board errors by granting injunctive relief. Under prevailing Supreme Court precedents and Federal statutes the students did not have the right to bring the issue before the courts until after they had exhausted their appeals within the Selective Service System and were either inducted or prosecuted for refusing induction. However, by making no effort to show the students had disrupted Selective Service operations, the Department left uncontested the charge that they were reclassified solely because they had protested against the war.[30] This was almost an open invitation to the Court of

Appeals to reverse the lower court and declare an exception to normal review procedures for draft cases posing clear challenges to First Amendment rights.

Taking the opportunity offered by the Department's argument, the Court of Appeals ruled in January, 1967, that draft boards could not punish these registrants by reclassifying them 1-A because they protested as they did over the government's involvement in Vietnam. Federal courts could grant injunctive relief because the threat to First Amendment rights was of such immediate and irreparable consequence to not simply these students but to others as to require prompt action by the courts to avoid an erosion of First Amendment rights. It was unnecessary to exhaust Selective Service appeals since, in view of Director Hershey's statements condemning demonstrators and approving local board actions, attempts to secure relief within the Selective Service System would be futile. Judge Harold R. Medina's opinion concluded, "Thus the allegations of the complaint in this case that the draft boards have unlawfully suppressed criticism must take precedence over the policy of nonintervention in the affairs of the Selective Service System."[31]

While the Court of Appeals' decision appeared to authoritatively repudiate Director Hershey's position and did quiet him temporarily, it left a wide loophole. By presuming that the Michigan demonstrators did not interfere with draft functions and that the primary reason for reclassification was to deter expression of opinion, the Court had not provided guidelines applicable to registrants who did, in fact, obstruct Selective Service operations by demonstrations or by destroying draft cards. If the Justice Department had said the sit-in interfered with draft administration, the Court would have confronted the problem of who should determine guilt. Could a draft board substitute reclassification for criminal prosecution as a means of punishing such action? Was this just an extension of the traditional power of draft boards to reclassify a registrant who became delinquent by failing to report changes in his address or eligibility status? In reply to Congressman Celler's criticism, Hershey had stated that registrants would not lose deferments merely for demonstrating or stating views, but would be reclassified and inducted if they burned their cards or conducted obstructive sit-ins at local board offices. The Court of Appeals did not persuade him to reconsider or withdraw these recommendations.

The federal courts' civil libertarian policies reached a peak in April, 1967, when the Court of Appeals in Boston held the draft card burning statute unconstitutional. Six months earlier the Court of Appeals in New York had upheld the law, ruling that it was reasonably related to the power of Congress to raise and support armies and refusing to examine the motives for its adoption. The Supreme Court had declined to review the New York court's decision. The Court in Boston held, however, that the measure served no proper purpose and on its face was precisely directed at public as distinguished from private destruction of draft cards. Publicly burning a draft card was a symbolic form of protest protected by the First Amendment. "In singling out persons engaged in protest for special treatment," Judge Bailey Aldrich declared, "the amendment strikes at the very core of what the First Amendment protects. It has long been beyond doubt that symbolic action may be protected speech." Draft card burners could still be punished under older Selective Service act provisions against failure to retain possession of their certificates.[32] The conflict with the earlier holding in New York practically insured that the Supreme Court would finally decide the issue. The Justice Department's defense of the draft card burning statute was consistent with its view that violation of draft regulations should be punished through criminal procedures, not by reclassification and induction.

Concern within the executive branch for the rights of young men affected by the draft also reached a high point early in 1967 when the Marshall commission issued its report. Since the Selective Service act was up for renewal in Congress, the commission's recommendations were aimed at influencing the President to propose reforms. Although it seemed to ignore the problem of reclassifying draft protesters, the commission nevertheless put forward structural changes implying serious criticism of the Selective Service System. Greatest publicity was given to its proposal for a nationwide random lottery selection procedure; but the commission's recommendations for more centralized administration challenged the basic conception the system had operated under since 1940. Instead of following a policy of discretion, applied by local boards within general guidelines, the commission wanted to introduce a new controlling concept into the Selective Service System: the rule of law. Its report deplored the lack of uniformity resulting from decentralization and saw an overriding need to achieve the greatest possible degree of equity through impartial standards uniformly applied throughout the nation.

A majority of the commission was moved by the uncomfortable realization that the efforts by individual local boards to assess the justification of student deferments on a case-by-case basis without binding guidelines had led to some of the worst and most widespread unevenness in the administration of the whole Selective Service System. Perhaps fearing that its administrative reforms might not be adopted, the majority proposed that no new student deferments be granted in the future. In effect, this would gradually end most of the problems raised by Director Hershey's reclassification policy since students would no longer have deferments which local boards could revoke to punish demonstrators. The commission's minority, however, preferred to maintain undergraduate deferments and only to end most deferments for postgraduate study in order to make sure students could not get a total exemption from military service. Along with its structural reorganization proposals, the commission majority believed its recommendation to phase out student deferments would eliminate possible repressive uses of draft board discretion.[33]

The Marshall commission's report was the high water mark of official civil libertarianism toward antiwar dissent. It sympathetically considered the argument that a conscientious objector should be able to object to fighting in a particular war, although a majority rejected the idea on the grounds that selective pacifism was essentially a political question and that "political opposition to a particular war should be expressed through recognized democratic processes and should claim no right of exemption from democratic decisions." The commission's attempt to apply the rule of law to Selective Service procedures reflected the influence of members like Yale President Kingman Brewster, Rev. John Courtney Murray, S.J., Southern Regional Council director Vernon E. Jordan, and probably retired Marine Corps commander David Shoup and the chairman, former Assistant Attorney General Burke Marshall.

In conjunction with the federal court decisions barring draft reclassification of protesters and holding the draft card burning law unconstitutional, the commission's report seemed to indicate that after two years of a troublesome war in Vietnam, the government could tolerate and even adjust to antiwar dissent. The Justice Department had resisted demands to prosecute abrasive speech, and Congress had seen its champions of repression made to look foolish by a handful of noisy witnesses. Dissent could be tolerated during the early years of the war because neither the President nor his associates seriously attempted to mobilize public support for a military victory. A majority of the public continued to tell poll-takers that it agreed with the decision to send troops to fight in Vietnam and to bomb North Vietnam. Yet the Johnson Administration was reluctant to arouse public emotions, perhaps as a result of its own internal divisions. Top Defense Department policy-makers had become progressively disenchanted with the President's Vietnam policy. "Appalled by the catastrophic lack of proportion that had overcome the U.S. military effort," they were now "earnestly trying to guide the war toward de-escalation and settlement."[34] Somewhere the tension between hawks and doves in Washington was bound to emerge and influence the direction of law enforcement policy.

2. "RESISTANCE TO
ILLEGITIMATE AUTHORITY," 1967

In the early months of 1967, antiwar activities grew in scope and intensity. Senator Robert Kennedy proposed halting the bombing of North Vietnam to bring about negotiations, while Dr. Martin Luther King urged Negroes and whites to become conscientious objectors to military service. Leaders of older liberal organizations like S.A.N.E. (a nuclear disarmament group) and Americans for Democratic Action joined officials of such religious bodies as the National Council of Churches and the American Jewish Congress to form an association called "Negotiation Now" to press for an unconditional end to the bombing of North Vietnam. More radical groups came together under the coordination of the Spring Mobilization Committee to End the War in Vietnam, set up in November, 1966, which organized mass demonstrations for New York and San Francisco on April 15. Militant pacifist David Dellinger, editor of *Liberation* magazine and vice-chairman of the Spring Mobilization Committee, emerged as a leading figure in the antiwar movement after returning from a visit to Hanoi.

Two weeks before the April protests, the House Un-American Activities Committee charged that the Spring Mobilization was dominated by Communists, who did in fact participate along with a wide variety of other groups. In New York an estimated 125,000 persons took part, and another 30,000 marched in San Francisco. Following these demonstrations a group of more moderate students began planning a Vietnam Summer project, which was ultimately to involve some 26,000 volunteers in 700 communities.[35]

On the day of the April protest marches, the White House disclosed President Johnson was reading a report on antiwar activity from F.B.I. Director Hoover. Secretary of State Rusk declared in a television interview that "the Communist apparatus is very busy indeed in these operations," although he did not mean to say by that that all those who had objections to the war in Vietnam were Communists. Rusk added that because North Vietnam might misunderstand the protests, their net effect would be to prolong the war and not shorten it. Then on a tour of South Vietnam, Richard Nixon told reporters, "The enemy realizes they will never win the war here, but think they may win it in the United States." A week later General William Westmoreland, the American field commander, reiterated that criticism of Administration policy gave comfort to the enemy and might cost American lives by prolonging the war. High-ranking federal executives explained Dr. King's decision to join the antiwar movement as merely a search for money and headlines after setbacks in his northern civil rights program and as a result of radical influences on his staff.[36] These concerted efforts began to arouse public sentiment against Vietnam war protesters.

Even before the spring demonstrations President Johnson had rejected the Marshall commission's proposals to reorganize the draft. While he endorsed the lottery selection system, the President refused to submit to Congress the commission's unanimous recommendation for centralizing and unifying the Selective Service System. Observing that the system had done a good job for America and had been flexible and responsive, Johnson praised the current draft board structure. "We cannot lightly discard an institution with so valuable a record for effectiveness and integrity," Similarly, the White House set aside the proposal for eliminating student deferments, instead announcing only an end to deferments for non-medical graduate study. Opposition to the Marshall commission came not only from Director Hershey, but from the House Armed Services Committee which had appointed its own eight-member panel headed by retired General Mark Clark to examine the draft. Some Administration officials also apparently feared that abolition of undergraduate deferments might lead to massive defiance with a high proportion of college students refusing to serve if drafted.[37]

The Armed Services Committees soon began hearings on renewal of the Selective Service act. General Clark's panel charged that there was far more draft evasion and draft delinquency than prosecutions by the Justice Department. Detecting a "soft attitude" on the part of officials who seemed to view prosecutions as administratively bothersome, time-consuming, and expensive, the panel demanded "that 'teeth' be put into procedures for identifying all such offenders and that a vigorous program of punitive action against them be under-taken." Finding "an element of treason" in draft card burnings, General Clark urged that all violations be severely and expeditiously punished. He criticized the Supreme Court's 1965 decision in Seeger v. United States, which widened the grounds of conscientious objector claims based on belief in a Supreme Being, for making it possible for "anti-Vietnam people. . .to escape through the conscientious objector route."[38] Assistant Attorney General Vinson defended the Criminal Division's record of convicting draft law violators; but in answer to House committee chairman Rivers, he admitted that no one had been prosecuted for aiding and abetting others to evade the draft. Asked why no action was taken against Stokely Charmichael, Vinson replied that those who advised others in a general way to evade the draft were protected by the First Amendment. Congressman Edward Herbert then urged him to "forget about the First Amendment" even if the prosecution would be rescinded by the Supreme Court. The Assistant Attorney General repeated that the Department felt no one has violated the law, but he added that it might decide future utterances did constitute a clear and present danger to the country.[39]

A Department statement later explained that counseling draft evasion meant attempting to persuade specific persons to evade such a duty and there were no court decisions indicating that counseling evasion contemplated expressions of views and opinions made to a general audience. Under First Amendment standards, "before any speech can be suppressed there must be convincing evidence that grave harm and danger to the Nation would otherwise follow." Another Department official recognized antiwar groups were "becoming more and more vociferous and threatening" and said the government was following closely the activities of some of these groups.[40]

While the Department withstood pressures for prosecutions, it had less success in blocking restrictive legislation. Attempting to reverse the effects of the Seeger decision, the House Armed

Services Committee deleted the Supreme Being clause from the Selective Service law in the hope that greater emphasis would be placed on the exclusion of conscientious objector claims based on beliefs that were essentially political, sociological, or philosophical, or a personal moral code. When it reenacted the Selective Service act, Congress adopted this change as well as another directed against the Justice Department. Department hearings were eliminated from the conscientious objector appeal procedure, with the result that objectors were henceforth processed through ordinary Selective Service channels. In reaction to the Court of Appeals decision on reclassification of protesters, Congress reinforced the rule against injunctive relief for Selective Service abuses. A registrant wishing to challange his draft classification had either to submit to induction and then bring a habeas corpus action to win his release or to refuse induction and make his contention as a defense to a draft evasion prosecution. Finally, in order to prevent the President from acting on the Marshall commission's proposal to end college student deferments, Congress made undergraduate defer-ments mandatory rather than discretionary, as they had been under the expiring law. All these changes represented an attempt by the Armed Services Committees to insulate the Selective Service System from judicial and executive inter-ference.[41]

The televised burning of a flag at New York's Spring Mobilization rally in April inspired a Congressional move for legislation to punish flag desecration. Most of the bills would make it a federal crime to "publicly mutilate, deface, defile, or defy, trample upon or cast contempt" upon the American flag "either by word or act." After hearing testimony that state laws were too lenient or unenforced, the House Judiciary Committee reported out a revised bill, deleting the provision covering words as well as deeds. Attorney General Clark did not oppose the measure and promised to enforce it vigorously, but he told the committee the number of flag burnings was "infinitesimal" and he would prefer to leave prosecution to the states. The nation had survived 179 years without a federal law punishing persons who desecrate the flag. "Should their number ever become substantial," Clark observed, "then their conduct would be a matter of deepest concern, which all history shows a mere statute cannot resolve." Congressional action provided symbolic satisfaction for the impulse to counter an equally symbolic form of dissent. "Who can vote against something like this?" Congressman Celler asked. "It's like motherhood." The measure provided further reason for F.B.I. agents to monitor any antiwar demonstration where such acts might occur.[42]

All these developments led the A.C.L.U. to warn in mid-1967 that "clear and discernible pressures are rising for restraint and punishment of those who oppose the war. . . .Unless the right and importance of dissent are reaffirmed and defended, the nation could slip back into a new era of McCarthyism, with its dangers to a free society—fear, conformity and sterility." The A.C.L.U. was still relatively optimistic, however, since the state of civil liberties law had vastly improved as the result of judicial decisions and because a new generation of people unstained by experience with McCarthyism was proudly exercising their rights of free speech.[43] College students who provided the bulk of support for the antiwar movement did not seem intimidated by the prospect of repression, nor did the writers, clergy, and professionel men who signed "A Call to Resist Illegitimate Authority" in August. The sponsors and signers of the Call expressed their belief "that every free man has a legal right and a moral duty to exert every effort to end this war, to avoid collusion with it, and to encourage others to do the same. . . .

Each must choose the course of resistance dictated by his conscience and circumstances. Among those already in the armed forces some are refusing to obey specific illegal and immoral orders, some are attempting to educate their fellow servicemen on the murderous and barbarous nature of the war, some are absenting themselves without official leave. Among those not in the armed forces some are applying for status as conscientious objectors to American aggression in Vietnam, some are refusing to be inducted. Among both groups some are resisting openly and paying a heavy penalty, some are organizing more resistance within the United States and some have sought sanctuary in other countries.

We believe that each of these forms of resistance against illegitimate authority is courageous and justified. Many of us believe that open resistance to the war and the draft is the course of action most likely to strengthen the moral resolve with which all of us can oppose the war and most likely bring an end to the war.

We will continue to lend our support to those who undertake resistance to this war. We will raise funds to organize draft resistance unions, to supply legal defense and bail, to support families and otherwise aid resistance to the war in whatever ways may seem appropriate. . . .Now is the time to resist."[44]

The men who drafted the Call believed it was "the sort of speech that under the First Amendment must be free," but they recognized "that the courts may find otherwise, and that if so we might all be liable to prosecution and severe punishment." During subsequent months the original 150 sponsors, including Dr. Benjamin Spock, former chairman of S.A.N.E., Yale Chaplain William Sloane Coffin, and writer Mitchell Goodman, were joined by thousands more signers.

Meanwhile, David Dellinger's Spring Mobilization Committee, reorganized and expanded in May as the National Mobilization Committee to End the War in Vietnam, began planning for a mass demonstration at the Pentagon in October. As Vietnam Summer volunteers concluded their grass roots political activity, most antiwar groups met for a National Conference on New Politics in September. Draft resistance groups announced that 1,500 people would send their draft cards back to their draft boards during the week before the Pentagon protest. The rallying cry was, "Disrupt the Pentagon war machine."[45]

In Washington the Justice Department began counter-preparations, while legal counsel for the General Services Administration, which was responsible for Pentagon security, entered into negotiations with Mobilization chairman Dellinger over march permit conditions. Department intelligence sources, including F.B.I. reports and Army intelligence surveillance recently activated after the Detroit riots, warned of two dangers posed by the march on the Pentagon. Some antiwar groups publicly proclaimed their intention to assault the Pentagon, while others expressed openly their plans to engage in nonviolent civil disobedience. The prospect of confrontations between demonstrators and law enforcement officials was less frightening, however, than the possibility that attempts would be made to exploit racial tensions in Washington. There were reports that black power groups would split off from the bulk of the marchers and would go into the city to stir up black neighborhoods, perhaps leading to riots such as occurred two months earlier in Newark and Detroit. In consultation with the Attorney General, therefore, the Defense Department developed detailed contingency plans to rush 25,000 or more troops to Washington if rioting erupted. Seventeen hundred uniformed National Guardsmen were deputized to make arrests and patrol city streets, while a 2,900-man brigade of paratroppers was airlifted to Andrews Air Force base and helicopters were assembled at the base from posts along the Atlantic seaboard. At the Pentagon itself more than 2,500 troops were placed inside the building in advance of the demonstrations. City police in Washington and federal marshals at the Pentagon were responsible for crowd control.[46]

Attorney General Clark has said that he could have called off the march on the Pentagon because of the seriousness of intelligence reports, but he believed the consequences of trying to prevent the demonstration might have been worse. The government's first position in the permit negotiations was that there could be no march unless the Mobilization Committee repudiated civil disobedience, but David Dellinger held to his belief in nonviolent civil disobedience as a way to "move impressively into a new period of determined resistance." The government then agreed to allow the demonstrators to hold a rally at the Lincoln Memorial and a march to the Pentagon for another rally in its north parking lot. In addition, a large stretch of grass adjacent to an entrance to the Pentagon was set aside for what a government negotiator called "protest activities." One executive later said that a principal reason for permitting the demonstrations around the Pentagon was to insure that most of the protesters would be across the Potomac rather than in Washington itself, in order to reduce the likelihood that disorders would spill over into the city. Since the demonstrations were planned for a weekend, most federal employees could stay home, and there would be relatively little real disruption of their normal routine.[47]

The October 21 march on the Pentagon was a disorganized and even chaotic event involving over 50,000 participants, but no truly serious violence occurred and Washington remained calm. Plainclothes agents of the F.B.I., the Secret Service, Army intelligence, and the Washington police mingled with the crowd to keep watch on potential troublemakers. Young Army intelligence men even rode with protesters in buses to the city, although they had no way to communicate their observations to their superiors after they arrived. At the Pentagon scores of violent clashes took place between demonstrators and federal marshals, and hundreds of arrests were made for various breach of the peace or trespass violations. Altogether 580 persons were convicted, of whom fifty-one served jail terms of up to thirty-five days, while the rest were given suspended sentences on the condition of good behavior and payment of fines.[48] The national impact was somewhat reduced by network decisions not to televise the march and by low official estimates of the number taking part.

From the point of view of future federal policy, the Pentagon demonstration was matched in importance by other protest activities earlier in the week. Draft resistance groups held pre-march rallies around the country, collecting draft cards to be returned to draft boards or turned over to the Justice Department. On the day before the march, ten antiwar leaders including Dr. Spock, Yale Chaplain Coffin, and writer Mitchell Goodman, who all had sponsored the "Call to Resist," attempted to present a briefcase filled with draft cards to Department officials. Addressing a crowd outside the building, Rev. Coffin announced,

"The law of the land is clear. Section 12 of the National Selective Service Act declares that anyone who 'knowingly counsels, aids, or abets another to refuse or evade registration or service in the Armed Forces. . .shall be liable to imprisonment for not more than five years or a fine of ten thousand dollars or both.'

"We hereby publicly counsel these young men to continue in their refusal to serve in the Armed Forces as long as the war in Vietnam continues, and we pledge ourselves to aid and abet them in all the ways that we can. This means that if they are now arrested for failing to comply with a law that violates their consciences, we too must be arrested, for in the sight of that law we are now as guilty as they."

Goodman and Dr. Spock followed with short speeches, then collected draft cards from individuals and group representatives and delivered them to the Attorney General's office where an assistant refused to take them. Leaving the briefcase on a table, they returned outside where Rev. Coffin declared, "Here was an officer of the law facing clear evidence of an alleged crime, and refusing to accept the evidence. He was derelict in his duty." The F.B.I. took the cards into custody later.[49]

Within a little over two months the Justice Department charged Dr. Spock, Rev. Coffin, Mitchell Goodman, and two others with conspiracy to counsel, aid, and abet violation of the Selective Service law. The others charged were Marcus Raskin, a writer and former White House aide who had taken part in the return of draft cards at the Justice Department, and Michael Ferber, a Harvard graduate student who organized a pre-march meeting in Boston's Arlington Street Church where draft cards were collected. The decision to prosecute these five men seemed a major departure from the Department's earlier position that under First Amendment standards convictions for counseling draft resistance could be based only on attempts to persuade specific persons to evade their duty, not on statements addressed to a general audience. What led Attorney General Clark to approve the prosecution? Was it simply his objective belief that the defendants had committed acts in violation of the law and that their concerted efforts threatened grave harm and danger to the nation? Or did the case have political implications which affected Clark's decision?[50] Whatever the answer, the Spock prosecution did serve to relieve heavy political pressures on the Attorney General that developed after the Pentagon demonstration. These pressures came from two sources—Selective Service Director Hershey and the Congressional Republican leadership.

On October 26 Hershey sent a letter to all local draft boards reviving his policy of reclassifying protesters and even extending its scope by advising that interference with military recruitment should result in reclassification. Changing his legal rationale, Hershey adopted an argument advanced earlier by two lawyers on the staff of the Army's Judge Advocate General in the *American Bar Association Journal*. Deferments were granted only when they served the national interest, Hershey asserted. "It follows that illegal activity which interferes with recruiting or causes refusal of duty in the military or naval forces could not by any stretch of the imagination be construed as being in support of the national interest." Thus he encouraged each local board to reclassify protesters whenever it believed their deferments were no longer in the best interests of the nation.[51]

Previously Hershey's policy had been limited to reclassification of registrants who disrupted draft offices, destroyed their cards, or were delinquent in complying with Selective Service regulations. Even that policy had not been reiterated since the Court of Appeals ruling in the spring. But now the Director was asserting the power of draft boards to order the immediate induction of anyone they found to have committed what they thought was illegal action interfering with military manpower recruitment or impairing the morale of the armed services. The Selective Service System would, in effect, substitute itself for criminal law enforcement procedures as the vehicle for imposing sanctions on the war resistance movement. Some Selective Service officials may have realized the weakness of the Director's legal position, for they submitted to the Justice Department a proposed Executive Order which would have given Presidential backing to Hershey's policy. When Attorney

General Clark refused to approve it, Hershey declared he did not need it and would revoke his recommendations only if told to do so by the President.[52]

In the uproar following Hershey's letter, Congressmen, university presidents, and even Labor Secretary Willard Wirtz and Supreme Court Justice Abe Fortas criticized the Director. By late November reports appeared of reclassifications for turning in draft cards at the October antiwar rallies. The American Council on Education representing the nation's colleges asked the White House to officially disavow Hershey's statement. As opposition grew, Presidential aide Douglas Cater, who was contacted personally by several university presidents, asked lawyers from the Justice Department and the Selective Service System to come up with a compromise that would effectively tie Hershey's hands without forcing the President to repudiate him directly. Hershey met at the White House with Deputy Attorney General Christopher, but they were unable to arrive at a settlement after a three-hour conference. Agreement was finally reached the next day on a joint statement to be released without comment by either side.

The compromise document contained three elements. First, the Department instructed all United States Attorneys to expedite investigation and prosecution of draft law violations, and the Attorney General announced creation of a special unit in the Criminal Division to coordinate these prosecutions. The Attorney General noted, however, that draft prosecutions were already at an all-time high, although the number and percentage of men who failed to report for induction was substantially lower now than during the Korean war. (Selective Service cases filed had risen from 642 in fiscal 1966 to 1,388 in fiscal 1967.) Second, local draft boards were warned that "lawful protest activities, whether directed to the draft or other national issues" could not subject registrants to reclassification or any other special administrative action by the Selective Service System. Third, the statement described the types of violations which would result in reclassification as offenses affecting the registrant's own status, such as giving false information, failure to appear for examination, or failure to have a draft card. The

Department hoped the emphasis on registrant-status offenses would persuade draft boards to ignore Hershey's advice about other kinds of action, like disruption of draft offices or interference with military recruitment, while the Director was not explicitly overruled. An essential part of the compromise was to make no mention of the crucial issue—whether a draft board could determine that acts not affecting a registrant's own status were illegal and could order immediate induction. Department attorneys wanted to include a statement that such actions were punishable only by criminal prosecution, but Hershey would not accept it.[53]

Although part of the agreement was to let this document speak for itself, Hershey dismayed the Department by telling reporters it did not affect his policy. He argued that all it did was to make clear criminal prosecution was an alternative that foreclosed reclassification, but violations not prosecuted could still be the basis for removing deferments. Hershey suggested a rough division of labor between the Selective Service and the Department: prosecutions would be directed against those too old or otherwise ineligible for the draft, while eligible registrants would be taken care of by induction into the Army. Clark and Hershey met for two hours to try to renew their agreement; but when this failed, a Department official said, "We're right back where we started."[54]

Three weeks later the Spock indictment was returned. After praising the Department for doing "a fine job in getting them indicted. . .a job that ought to be done," Director Hershey became relatively silent about reclassification policies. Author Jessica Mitford reports that the special unit created by the Attorney General went to work on the Spock case at once; and she quotes the lawyer in charge as explaining, "The prosecution came about as a result of our flap with Hershey about his October 26 letter to the draft boards."[55]

If the Spock case did in fact result from a desire to satisfy Hershey, then responsibility for the prosecution rests largely with the White House for refusing to take sides and compelling the Department to reach a compromise. Yet the Department's original stand in the negotiations was already a compromise. By admitting that registrant-status violations of draft regulations could result in reclassification, the Department agreed at the outset that registrants who had turned in their draft cards in October could be immediately inducted. The Attorney General did not raise the argument that certain deferments, like those for ministers and divinity students, were not within the discretion of draft boards to remove. Nor did he press the point that Congress, by making undergraduate deferments mandatory rather than discretionary in the 1967 Selective Service act, had similarly blocked reclassification of college students. These points would later be crucial in the federal courts, and Solicitor General Erwin Griswold would consider them sympathetically; but the Attorney General chose not to advance them forcefully in his negotiations with Selective Service officials. Instead, the issue between Clark and Hershey was solely over reclassification of protesters who did not destroy or return their draft cards. The White House still failed to back Clark firmly.

President Johnson was involved personally in another sequence of events that built pressure on the Attorney General. In late November House majority leader Carl Albert declared that the march on the Pentagon had been basically organized by international Communism, and Secretary of State Rusk was reported to have said privately that Communists were instrumental in staging the protest but the government would not emphasize the fact to avoid a new wave of McCarthyism. Provoked by these statements, House Republican leader Gerald Ford called on the White House to make public a report which he said the President had used in briefing Congressional leaders about the protest in October. After Attorney General Clark visited Ford to argue against release of the information, the Republican leader urged that "the President order a full report made to the American people on the extent of Communist participation in organizing, planning and directing the disgraceful display which took place at the Pentagon last October 21." Ford believe the public was "now mature enough to receive such information and to react without hysteria." The Justice Department replied by citing an official statement made the day before the demonstration which said that while the

National Mobilization Committee did contain some Communists, there was no evidence that the Communist Party was in control of or in charge of the rally and march.[56]

Dissatisfied with this response, Congressman Ford decided to reveal the contents of the President's briefing which had persuaded him that the demonstration was conceived and directed from Hanoi. The report had detailed the travels of protest leader David Dellinger to Hanoi in November, 1966, and during the summer of 1967 and his meeting with Vietnamese Communist officials in Czechosolvakia in September. It also had traced the international movements of three or four other unnamed leaders. Most of this information was readily acknowledged by Dellinger and had appeared in the newspapers. Dellinger scoffed at the idea that a message from Hanoi could get 200,000 people to demonstrate in the United States. He placed a different interpretation on his travels, contending he was not influenced by the North Vietnamese but instead urged them and leaders in other countries to stage rallies to coincide with those in the United States.[57] In the context of these charges, the Spock case served to shift public attention away from the claim that antiwar protests were controlled by Communists, since the defendants did not have Communist connections.

Just as Rev. Coffin had virtually invited prosecution in October, so Dr. Spock took the occasion of a demonstration at the Whitehall Street induction center in New York on December 5 to announce his intention to provoke prosecution for urging refusal of service in the armed forces. "But the Government is not likely to prosecute us," Dr. Spock predicted. "Its bankruptcy in the moral sense is proved by its refusal to move against those of us who have placed ourselves between the young people and the draft."[58] Attorney General Clark was able, therefore, to escape serious criticism for bringing the prosecution since Rev. Coffin and Dr. Spock seemed only to have gotten what they asked for. Many failed to realize at first that the five defendants were not charged with substantive crimes of counseling evasion of service, but with a broad conspiracy to counsel, aid, and abet violation of the Selective Service law.

The Spock case could have focused on one crucial event, the turning in of draft cards to the Justice Department on October 20. Four of the defendants were present at the confrontation in the Attorney General's office, while Michael Ferber had assisted in gathering the draft cards in Boston. At the very least they were aiding registrants in violating the Selective Service requirement that draft cards be kept at all times. The most intriguing question about the case is why the Department chose not to charge conspiracy to commit these specific acts, but instead developed a sweeping conspiracy indictment based on the "Call to Resist Illegitimate Authority." The core of the case became the Call, which allegedly demonstrated the defendants' shared purpose to incite open resistance to the war and to the draft. On this theory many other persons who knowingly signed the Call appeared liable to prosecution. In this respect the case was similar to the mass sedition trial of Nazi sympathizers in 1944 and the Dennis case against Communist Party leaders in 1948, since the defendants were accused of being part of a larger political movement with illegal aims. Emphasis on the Call and the resistance movement it represented may have been thought necessary not just to tie the defendants to one another but to show that their actions were part of an enterprise which constituted a clear and present danger to the country, thus satisfying First Amendment requirements.

Perhaps Attorney General Clark believed a conviction would be reversed on appeal? There have been instances in the past, for instance Francis Biddle's decision to bring the first Smith Act prosecution in 1941 against Trotskyite leaders, where an Attorney General has begun a test case with the hope of ultimate reversal.[59] Since the indictment was returned in Boston and defendant Ferber may have been included primarily to take the trial to that city, any conviction would be appealed to the Court of Appeals which had declared the draft card burning statute unconstitutional on First Amendment grounds. By selecting Boston, therefore, the Department may have hoped to insure the closest possible appellate scrutiny of any free speech issues. A conviction would lead the Court of Appeals to examine fully the permissible scope of sweeping conspiracy prosecutions affecting First Amendment rights. Another explanation of the prosecution is equally plausible. Harvard Law Professor Alan Dershowitz has observed, "It seems entirely possible that the government made a deliberate decision to increase the risks of ultimate reversal in order to charge the kind of crime—a loosely knit, widespread and uncircumscribed conspiracy—that would have the greatest impact on discouraging organized opposition to the Vietnam War."[60]

The Spock trial may have had less effect on other antiwar activists because the defendants chose to respect the trial court's authority, thus avoiding a dramatic spectacle such as occurred during the mass sedition trial in 1944 and the Communist trial in 1949. The amount of publicity surrounding the trial was thereby reduced. After the judge ruled out defense arguments on the legality of the war, the defendants contended they had never advised anyone to violate the draft laws, but had intended only to support men who decided on their own to resist in this fashion. The jury rejected the argument and convicted four defendants, acquitting Marcus Raskin. The four others were given two-year prison sentences and appealed.

The Spock case culminated a year of increasing pressure on the Justice Department during 1967. The Armed Service Committees of Congress had not only acted to insulate the Selective Service System from executive revision and judicial review, but also demanded the prosecution of draft resistance advocates. After the Pentagon demonstration Congressional leaders of both parties took up the charge that the antiwar movement was Communist-inspired. By using intelligence reports to reinforce this image of protest leaders, by failing to endorse the Marshall commission's proposals for draft reform, and by asserting that dissent prolonged the war, President Johnson had made conflict between the Attorney General and the Selective Service Director more likely. His reluctance to overrule Hershey's November directive made compromise necessary. While the White House may not have ordered Ramsey Clark to prosecute, the President created the conditions which virtually required at least symbolic legal action against men like Dr. Spock and Rev. Coffin who publicly challenged federal law enforcement authority.

3. THE SPREAD OF
STUDENT UNREST, 1968

At the beginning of 1968 the Johnson Administration believed the war in Vietnam was going fairly well. General Westmoreland and Ambassador Bunker returned to Washington with glowing reports of success, while the President's domestic political position seemed strong despite Senator Eugene McCarthy's antiwar candidacy. Within three months all this changed. The massive Tet offensive at the end of January undermined the Administration's credibility; its public support as measured by opinion polls fell precipitously by the end of March; and Senator McCarthy's strong showing in the New Hampshire primary brought Robert Kennedy into the race. President Johnson's announcement of bombing limitations and his decision not to seek reelection climaxed a major reversal of government fortunes. A Defense Department executive later observed that these "decisions by the incumbent of perhaps the most powerful office on earth created a new situation that virtually precluded a return to the old."[61]

In the spring of 1968, therefore, antiwar dissent was channeled into the McCarthy and Kennedy campaigns. Campus unrest rather than war protests became an official concern, especially when a student strike closed Columbia University following New York police clearance of buildings occupied by S.D.S., many less radical sympathizers, and a black student group. Speaking for the Justice Department, Solicitor General Erwin Griswold, former dean of Harvard Law School, condemned those who occupied buildings and disrupted universities. In dealing with student unrest the Solicitor General believed the answers could not be "found in the law alone. We must find answers to problems of group psychology. We must be patient, and as persuasive as we can, never vindictive, but firm in the last resort to make it plain that those who are to stay in our educational institutions are those who are worthy to join the company of educated men." Griswold recognized, however, that the military draft had all but made effective academic discipline impossible by converting academic penalties into something far more serious. Since expelled or suspended students were likely to be drafted, "many Faculty members, who usually participate in disciplinary actions, have not been willing to take such a responsibility." Faced with this dilemma, the Solicitor General feared that "these young people may be in the process of destroying our centers of higher learning, and that would be a. . .national calamity. . . ."[62]

Citing an incident where students took papers from the Columbia president's office, Congressman Louis Wyman of New Hampshire proposed a measure to bar federal grants, fellowships, and loans to students who took part in campus disorders. The House adopted his amendment to a bill authorizing aid to higher education in May. During subsequent months the Administration tried to soften its impact, persuading the House Education and Labor Committee to propose an alternative that would give colleges and universities complete discretion as to when to suspend federal aid to students. Congress passed a compromise version in September, which the Administration reluctantly accepted as part of the overall higher education bill. Under its terms a student would lose federal aid if convicted of a crime involving the use of force, disruption of campus activities or seizure of college property, or if the student willfully refused to obey lawful college regulations. Funds could be cut off only after a hearing and a finding by school officials that the offense was "of a serious nature and contributed to the disruption of the administration of such institutions." Colleges had wide discretion to impose the penalty or not, and the Office of Education had no way to enforce the rule that initial applications for scholarships be turned down if the student had been convicted of a crime involving campus disruption.[63]

Limiting Selective Service Power

Efforts to curtail Selective Service reclassification policies continued in 1968. Since the Justice Department had failed to change Hershey's ruling, the National Student Association filed suit in federal court to restrain enforcement of his October directive. In March a District Court in Washington dismissed the suit, holding that the Director's letter had no legal effect whatsoever, was not binding on draft boards, and was merely an expression of Hershey's personal opinion. The court declared that individuals who believed their draft status was being changed illegally had other administrative and judicial remedies. A year later the Court of Appeals reversed this decision and declared Hershey's letter illegal since it could have a chilling effect on free speech. It put registrants in the position of facing reclassification if they made "a wrong guess as to the legality of a particular protest activity or of a failure to forsee the course an initially legal demonstration may take." Protesters could be reclassified only after conviction for violation of a statute, which the courts have found to be consistent with the First Amendment. To do otherwise might "deter not merely validly proscribed conduct but any protest activity which a registrant could plausibly expect his draft board to think unprotected or illegal."

The Court of Appeals declined, however, to issue an injunction to block application of Hershey's policy by local boards because of the practical problems of enforcing such an order and out of a belief that board members would not act contrary to law as judicially declared. Moreover, the Court upheld the Selective Service System's authority to reclassify registrants who violated delinquency regulations related to their own status by destroying or abandoning their draft cards. In effect, the Court sustained the position of the Justice Department and offered little comfort to those who hoped the courts would rule out reclassification for turning in draft cards.[64]

A number of other suits supported by the A.C.L.U. challenged such reclassification on the grounds that turning in a draft card was a symbolic public protest against United States military action in Vietnam. Prospects for these suits dimmed in May, 1968, when the Supreme Court upheld the validity of the draft card burning statute and refused to apply the symbolic speech doctrine. Chief Justice Warren's opinion held "that when 'speech' and 'non-speech' elements are combined in the same course of conduct, a sufficiently important governmental interest in regulating the non-speech element can justify incidental limitations on First Amendment freedoms." Citing the many functions performed by Selective Service certificates, the Court sustained Congress' "legitimate and substantial interest in preventing their wanton and unrestrined destruction and assuring their continued availability." The Chief Justice refused under settled principles to examine the motives of Congress in adopting the measure. The draft card burner was convicted for the "noncommunicative impact of his conduct, and for nothing else."[65] In view of the Supreme Court's decision, there was little doubt that federal courts would reject First Amendment challenges to draft board action as long as it was limited to the noncommunicative aspects of violating Selective Service regulations.

Civil liberties lawyers turned now to the argument that reclassification was barred by statute rather than by the constitution. The Supreme Court agreed to decide whether a divinity student, whose deferment was categorically mandated by statute, could be subjected to immediate induction for turning in his draft card. In an unusual step Solicitor General Griswold did not object to the Court's reviewing the case, despite the Selective Service System's contrary position. The Solicitor General even went so far as to block an attempt by Director Hershey to submit a memorandum asking the Court to decline to review the lower court's refusal to enjoin the divinity student's induction. The Justice Department agreed with Selective Service lawyers' argument that under the 1967 act courts could not intervene until a registrant had either been inducted or prosecuted for failing to appear for induction; but the Solicitor General felt the issue was ripe for Supreme Court adjudication. More significantly, Griswold refused to defend the use of Selective Service delinquency proceedings to deprive registrants of statutory exemptions because of conduct unrelated to merits of granting the exemption. Even if a divinity student burned his draft card, he should not be reclassified. The only question was what the appropriate remedy for this abuse of discretion should be.[66]

In December, 1968, the Court held that Congress did not intend to prevent court review and injunctive relief prior to induction of registrants entitled to exemptions granted by statute. Justice Douglas' opinion called the draft board's withdrawal of the divinity student's exemption for turning in his draft card "blatantly lawless." Since no special hearing was required to determine if a person qualified for such a statutory exemption, judicial review before induction was justified to prevent unnecessary harshness in the operation of the draft law. Congress had not defined delinquency, nor did it provide any standards for its definition. There was "no suggestion in the legislative history that, when Congress has granted an exemption and a registrant meets its terms and conditions, a Board can nonetheless withhold it from him for activities or conduct not material to the grant or withdrawal of the exemption. So to hold would make the Boards free-wheeling agencies meeting out their brand of justice in a vindictive manner." In a concurring opinion Justice Harlan suggested that if the registrant was unable to secure pre-induction judicial review in this case, it would raise serious constitutional problems.[67]

The Supreme Court made clear in a companion case that pre-induction injunctive relief was not available to persons denied conscientious objector classifications, since there was no doubt of draft boards' statutory authority to take such action. The Court believed this was "precisely the kind of 'litigious interruptions of procedures to provide necessary military manpower'. . .which Congress sought to prevent. . . .We find no constitutional objection to Congress' thus requiring that assertion of a conscientious objector's claims. . .be deferred until after induction, if that is the course he chooses, whereupon habeas corpus would be an available remedy, or until defense of the criminal prosecution which would follow should he press his objections to his classification to the point of refusing to submit to induction."[68] Several months later the Court ruled that a registrant who failed to appeal his classification within Selective Service channels could still challenge the validity of draft board action as a defense to such a criminal prosecution, at least when he claimed a statutory exemption.[69]

None of these decisions in 1968-69 addressed the crucial question of whether ordinary college deferments were statutory exemptions, like the exemption for divinity students, or were more like conscientious objector classifications which draft boards had the discretion to grant or deny after examining each individual case. Since Director Hershey's first instructions on the subject in 1965, draft boards had ordered the immediate induction of literally thousands of students who turned in their draft cards or otherwise violated delinquency regulations in protest against the war. Federal courts across the country were filled with cases in which students sued to block reclassification or appealed convictions for refusing to submit to induction after reclassification. Other students who did not raise the issue as a defense to prosecution or lost an appeal were in federal prisons. These were the consequences of the Justice Department's failure in 1967 to assert strongly the position that, since Congress had made undergraduate deferments mandatory, the Selective Service System could not reclassify college students. The Supreme Court also bore responsibility since in June, 1968, it declined to hear the appeal of a student who was convicted for refusing induction after his draft board removed his student deferment because he destroyed his draft card.

Perhaps the divinity student's case and the conscientious objector's case logically had to precede an undergraduate's case in order that the Court might be fully prepared, in terms of legal doctrine and an understanding of the practical issues, to upset the Selective Service System's main weapon against the war resistance movement. The Court did so in January, 1970, after Solicitor General Griswold, who remained in office under the Nixon Administration, declined to sign the Justice Department's brief defending reclassification of college students.[70]

The Chicago Convention Demonstrations

Within the executive branch 1968 saw development of more extensive and systematic intelligence gathering operations, with the Justice Department and Army Intelligence refining their parallel networks after the march on the Pentagon. One former intelligence officer has reported that the Army maintained files on the membership, ideology, programs, and practices of virtually every activist political group in the country.[71] Similar data were centralized in the Justice Department's new Interdivisional Intelligence and Information Unit. Within this framework the Department prepared for the national party conventions. Robert Kennedy's assassination, virtually assuring the Democratic nomination of Hubert Humphrey, brought antiwar groups back into action. According to J. Edgar Hoover, "Months before the Democratic National Convention was held, authorities were fully aware that it was the target of disruption and violence on the part of dissident groups and individuals from all over the country."[72] Faced with similar reports before the Pentagon march, Attorney General Clark had adopted a policy combining massive preparations for trouble with permission for the demonstrations to take place. Before the Chicago convention Clark probably had information indicating that some provocations of police would take place and that some revolutionaries would be present; but it is likely that he also realized, as the Walker report later put it, that "the vast majority of the demonstrators were intent on expressing by peaceful means their dissent either from society or from the administration's policies in Vietnam."[73]

The National Mobilization Committee and the Youth International Party (Yippies) planned demonstrations in Chicago during the convention, including a march to the convention hall and a "Festival of Life" in Lincoln Park. Mobilization coordinator Rennie Davis announced that the protests would be orderly and non-disruptive, while David Dellinger disavowed any intentions of Pentagon-like civil disobedience. On the other hand, Yippie leaders Abbie Hoffman and Jerry Rubin issued more provocative statements and often outrageous threats of haphazard disruptions designed to "trick the enemy into developing a policy of overkill." In an attempt to bring about an accommodation between Chicago Mayor Daley and protest leaders, Attorney General Clark sent Roger Wilkins, head of the Community Relations Service, and law enforcement expert

Wesley Pomeroy to Chicago. After talking at length with Rennie Davis, Wilkins was conviced he genuinely desired a peaceful demonstration. But the Justice Department representatives had no success in persuading Chicago officials that the best way to assure a peaceful convention was to offer the demonstrators an outlet for dissent. Deputy Attorney General Christopher met with the Mayor, who refused to compromise on arrangements for peaceful demonstrations. City officials would not grant permits to occupy parks and conduct marches which protest leaders believed were necessary to prevent disruption and possible violence.

When Mayor Daley urged President Johnson to pre-position federal troops near Chicago during the convention, Attorney General Clark advised against granting the request. Clark apparently suspected the threats were being disproportionately magnified and feared the presence of troops would have a negative effect by creating a climate of expectation that they would be used. Clark was overruled, however, when the President consulted military and White House staff advisors. The Attorney General also turned down F.B.I. requests to wiretap the communications of Mobilization Committee leaders. The subsequent events in Chicago have been described thoroughly in the report, *Rights in Conflict,* submitted by attorney Daniel Walker's Chicago Study Team to the National Commission on Violence.[74] They had a profound impact on the attitudes of the nation's law enforcement community. Although television reports portrayed the youthful protesters sympathetically, the convention week confrontations inspired widespread public antipathy toward the demonstrators and support for the police.

Concerned that the use of force by police against demonstrators, bystanders, and newsmen might set a pattern for police conduct elsewhere, the Attorney General directed the F.B.I. to gather objective accounts of what happened. (The Walker report relied on these statements taken by the F.B.I. as well as others collected by the Chicago Study Team staff.) In September a federal grand jury was convened to inquire into the disorders. Attorney General Clark advised the United States Attorney that the grand jury should focus on police brutality violations of the civil rights statute, but the presiding judge made sure the jury was empaneled to consider offenses under the new antiriot law as well. Meanwhile, Clark testified before the Violence Commission and leveled veiled criticism at Chicago authorities: "The clear offer of a fair and reasonable accommodation of requests to assemble and speak reduces the risk of violence. . . .It is the duty of leadership and law enforcement to control violence, not cause it. To seek ways of relieving tension, not to look for a fight." Before the Walker report was released in December, Department lawyers reviewed it and requested that sixteen pages describing some of the most flagrant examples of police brutality be deleted from the published version because the government was placing the information before the grand jury. The Department's request clearly indicated it planned to secure indictments against police under the civil rights statute rather than against demonstrators.[75]

Nevertheless, a foundation for federal antiriot prosecutions had been laid in September when Mayor Daley issued a lengthy report prepared by Chicago corporation counsel Raymond F. Simon with the aid of the police department and other city agencies. The report contended that demonstrators led by revolutionaries who came to Chicago from other cities provoked the forceful methods used by police. These "nationally known agitators" arrived with "the avowed purpose of a hostile confrontation with law enforcement." The five principal organizers identified were David Dellinger, Rennie Davis, and Tom Hayden of the Mobilization Committee, and Abbie Hoffman and Jerry Rubin of the Yippies. They had employed guerrilla or psychological warfare tactics to foment disruption. Immediately after the Mayor released his report, Chicago Congressman Roman Pucinski, a co-sponsor of the antiriot bill, asserted that the document provided ample evidence for indictments against planners of the demonstrations. Fearing such action, the Mobilization Committee filed suit to halt the grand jury investigation on the grounds that the antiriot act was unconstitutional, but the suit was dismissed.[76]

An officer of the Chicago police department's intelligence unit repeated the city's story in testimony before the Un-American Activities Committee. The officer quoted from what he described as the minutes of a meeting at which Tom Hayden said the protests "should have people organized who can fight the police, should be willing to get arrested." According to a confidential source, Rennie Davis said "the Loop [the Chicago business district] would go up" if Eugene McCarthy lost the nomination. The committee's hearings in December compiled all available information tending to show Mobilization leaders planned and incited the convention disorders, although Dellinger and Hayden appeared to testify that their intentions were nonviolent. "Violence follows these gentlemen just as night follows day," Congressman Richard Ichord exclaimed after the hearings ended.[77] Since the grand jury remained in session after January, 1969, the final decision on the antiriot prosecution rested with Ramsey Clark's successor.

The final test of Attorney General Clark's policy of restraint in the face of antiwar protests came at the time of the inauguration of President Nixon. Several groups that participated in the Chicago demonstrations, including the Mobilization committee and the Yippies, called for protests in Washington preceding the inauguration. The Justice Department arranged for permits allowing a march from the Washington Monument to the Capitol on Pennsylvania Avenue and the use of the Mall for meetings, despite objections from incoming Deputy Attorney General Richard Kleindienst. While Mobilization officials planned no physical disruption or confrontation, they qualified their assurances with the disclaimer, "We can't control everybody."

Once again intelligence sources provided information about demonstration plans. On January 18 Army intelligence reported over its unclassified teletype network that Mobilization Committee officials and GI's would lead a parade down Pennsylvania Avenue on the 19th. Upon reaching the steps of the Capital, some participants reportedly would burn draft cards. After the parade the marchers were invited to attend a counter-inaugural ball, located in a tent on the Mall, which would last all night. On Inauguration Day small groups planned to leave the tent and place themselves along the inaugural parade route, attempting to stand five or six deep to conceal persons carrying signs. Their objective was to get the maximum number of signs in view of the main TV cameras. When Nixon arrived, they would begin to chant and show their signs.[78]

These events occurred as predicted with only five arrests before the inaugural parade. When some of the demonstrators threw objects at the President's passing car, troops and police immediately moved to disperse the protesters who scattered through the business district. A special staff study for the Violence Commission later reviewed the inauguration protest and drew a favorable contrast between the way the Justice Department and Washington police prepared for the demonstrations and the manner in which Chicago authorities had acted in August. As the Walker report had been entitled "Rights in Conflict," so this report on the inauguration bore the title "Rights in Concord."[79] Incoming Nixon Administration executives were less pleased, however, with Ramsey Clark's willingness to grant permits to potentially disruptive groups.

The events of 1968 illustrated the scope and limits of the Attorney General's ability to maintain a climate favorable to civil liberties. While Clark had substantial control over management of demonstrations in Washington, he had no influence with local authorities in Chicago. Although he was unable to change Selective Service policy by action within the executive branch, the Solicitor General could do so gradually by refusing to defend General Hershey before the Supreme Court. Encouraging the Violence Commission to study the Chicago convention disorders, Clark hoped its report would curb growing public hostility toward dissenters. Nevertheless, he could not prevent Mayor Daley and the Un-American Activities Committee from laying a foundation for a federal antiriot prosecution. Clark's successes and failures demonstrated that a civil libertarian Attorney General with support from the courts had limited power without backing from the White House. He had even less influence on the decisions of his successor in a new Administration.

4. THE NIXON ADMINISTRATION
AND ANTIWAR DISSENT, 1969

At his first news conference after taking office, Attorney General John Mitchell announced he would recommend against granting parade permits to demonstrators like those who threw objects at the President's car during the inaugural parade. If these activists could be recognized as such, in advance, there would be no permit. Mitchell was expressing not only his own sense of propriety, but the sentiments of the electorate. An opinion poll reported that eighty-six percent of the public wanted the Nixon Administration to crack down on anti-Vietnam protesters.[80] One of the new Attorney General's first decisions was to bring the federal antiriot prosecution against convention protest leaders, for which Chicago officials and the Un-American Activities Committee had prepared the way. Assistant Attorney General Jerris Leonard went to Chicago in mid-February to supervise the drafting of indictments returned a month later against eight policemen for civil rights offenses and perjury and against eight demonstration participants for violating and conspiring to violate the antiriot law.

In addition to the five leaders identified in Mayor Daley's report, the indictments included two less important protest figures and Black Panther Party chairman Bobby Seale. The defendants allegedly traveled across state lines with intent to incite a riot by, among other things, encouraging people to come to Chicago for the demonstrations, maintaining an office to plan the protests, and arranging illegal marches. Since the conspiracy charge covered far more than specific acts of incitement, it posed questions similar to those raised in the pending appeal of the Spock case. If the defendants were convicted without proof that they committed particular illegal acts or made speeches inciting law violation, the A.C.L.U. believed there would be a chilling effect on the right to travel from one part of the country to another "to agitate, to stir people up, to try to bring about social change."[81]

Attorney General Mitchell threatened other antiriot prosecutions besides the Chicago case. When the National Governors Conference considered a resolution from California Governor Reagan urging a Justice Department investigation of campus disorders to determine if there was a nationwide plan or organization behind the current outbreaks, Mitchell disclosed that the Department was actively considering prosecutions arising from campus unrest. At the same time H.E.W. Secretary Robert Finch sent letters to college officials reminding them of their duty to enforce student aid bans, and the President asked Mitchell and Finch to look into reports that students arrested at San Francisco State College were recipients of federal aid.[82] As campus disorders spread during the spring, the Department adopted a dual policy of threatening federal prosecution and encouraging college and local officials to take a hard line against disruptions. In a Law Day address Mitchell declared, "We have substantial information confirming the widely accepted belief that several major university disturbances have been incited by members of a small core of professional militants who make it their tragic occupation to convert peaceable student dissatisfaction into violence and confrontation. . . .You can be sure that these violence-prone militants will be prosecuted to the full extent of our federal laws." Characterizing some student protesters as "new barbarians" and "ideological criminals," other executives urged prompt local prosecutions. The Department's advice was clear: "When people may be injured, when personal property may be destroyed, and when chaos begins, the university official only aids lawlessness by procrastination and negotiation."[83]

The Attorney General heeded Secretary Finch's advice, however, and opposed new Congressional proposals for cutting off aid to disrupted schools as likely to play into the hands of the militants. Testifying before a House education subcommittee, Mitchell added that he would prosecute only in an unusual case where local law enforcement could not act. The principal federal role was to investigate disorders and pass on any information thus gained to local police and school authorities. Investigations had already discovered that revolutionary student groups financed by outside sources were causing much of the trouble; among them were S.D.S. and the Black Student Union. "Their sole aim is to disrupt. Their leaders brag about being revolutionaries and anarchists. They state their purpose to be to close the schools. They openly and brazenly profess a desire to destroy the establishment." On the other hand, the Attorney General suggested that, since students should enjoy the fullest and most vigorous debate guaranteed by the First Amendment, it might be advisable for some universities "to permit even more dissent than the minimum guaranteed by the Constitution."[84]

While Mitchell took this milder positon before the education subcommittee, Assistant Attorney General Leonard told a closed appropriations hearing that the Department was formulating a task force to gather military-like intelligence for use in prosecuting national leaders of organizations promoting campus disorders. A month later the House Appropriations Committee reported the Attorney General had ordered a "strong program looking toward the vigorous prosecution of dissidents on college campuses" utilizing the antiriot law to the fullest extent. When the report was made public, Leonard denied that a special task force had been set up but admitted the Department did send teams to monitor all major disorders, including those on campus, "to keep informed on what is happening, in case there is a breakdown in local law enforcement."[85] As noted in Chapter Three, such a special task force was eventually created to deal primarily with the Black Panther Party.

During late May and June the Nixon Administration further moderated its stand on student unrest. Law enforcement agencies had reacted with massive force to the "People's Park" demonstrations at the Berkeley campus of the University of California. The death of one bystander and injuries to many others brought charges of widespread police abuses and led United States Attorney Cecil Poole to begin a grand jury investigation of civil rights violations by sheriff's deputies. Eight months later twelve deputies were indicated for shooting demonstrators and bystanders with shotguns with the intent of imposing summary punishment.[86] No other campus dis-trubance had so dramatically portrayed the dangers of official overreaction. Another moderating influence came from a group of young Republican Congressmen, representing a wide ideological spectrum, who toured colleges in May. After conferring with the President, they warned against repressive legislation which "would only serve to confirm the cry of the revolution-aries" and asserted that "the fundamental responsibility for order and conduct on the campus lies with the university community." Nevertheless, by September the Office of Education reported that about seventy colleges had cut off federal scholarships or loans from 350-400 students. Forty students lost their support following criminal convictions, while the remainder were penalized for violating college rules in the course of a serious disorder.[87]

Although it withdrew from its earlier commitment to prosecute campus activists, the Department kept pressure on S.D.S. J. Edgar Hoover described S.D.S. as representing "a threat to established law and order and to the stability of our society"; and the F.B.I. became openly involved in an attempt to counter its plans for summer activities in factories and among workers. William C. Sullivan, the Assistant Director of the F.B.I. for domestic intelligence, addressed a closed meeting of businessmen in New York called to plan strategy against an S.D.S. project to forge a worker-student alliance. The meeting followed a series of warnings about S.D.S. from the U.S. Chamber of Commerce headquarters in Washington. Sullivan had spoken before the Chamber of Commerce convention in April, furnishing copies of an S.D.S. "work-in" manual. The Chamber's newsletter warned that infiltrators masquerading as short-haired summer employees would invade industry "bent on disrupting plant operations and propagandizing." A.F.L.-C.I.O. President George Meany issued a similar warning.[88] The message transmitted from the F.B.I. through business and labor executives not only exposed S.D.S. activities, but implied that employers and unions should check closely the political views of summer job applicants.

Electronic Surveillance of "Dangerous Groups"

The most controversial issue raised by the Department in the summer of 1969 involved its electronic surveillance of groups believed dangerous to national security. While the Chicago conspiracy indictment was being prepared, the Supreme Court ruled that whenever conversations of a criminal defendant were overheard by illegal electronic surveillance, all transcripts and records had to be turned over to the defendant so that his lawyer might object to the introduction of evidence secured through leads provided by illegal surveillance. The Alderman decision bore directly on the Chicago case, since in December the Department had disclosed in a separate case that one potential defendant, Jerry Rubin, had been overheard as the result of electronic surveillance directed against others in the interests of national security. Criminal Division head Will Wilson temporarily delayed the Chicago indictment for fear the Department might be forced to reveal records of national security surveillance. Prosecution went ahead only after Wilson realized the Supreme Court had not ruled on the question of whether national security surveillance was illegal. Only if a trial judge found surveillance illegal was he required to order disclosure of the records to defense counsel for use during the trial.[89]

These issues were first raised in May when lawyers for Muhammed Ali, whose draft conviction had been appealed on Alderman grounds, asked a federal District Court to order production of electronic surveillance records. The government replied by offering to submit logs of four wiretaps to the defense, but not the log of a fifth which involved foreign intelligence information. The offer of logs, which recorded only the bare facts and not the full contents of the conversations, did not satisy Ali's counsel, who demanded the full transcripts and information about who had access to surveillance data. In particular, the defense alleged the Department circulated such data to government officials in memoranda known as "air-tels."

With respect to the fifth wiretap, the government offered to let the judge examine the log in private. Asserting that the

President had the power to order wiretapping to obtain information "necessary for the conduct of international affairs and for the protection of national defense secrets and installations," Attorney General Mitchell stated it would prejudice the national interest to disclose the particular facts concerning this surveillance. The government also asked that the defense be ordered not to reveal the contents of the four other logs because the unauthorized dissemination of the facts relating to these surveillances would prejudice the national interest and might prejudice the interest of third parties.[90]

After hearing arguments, the District Judge ruled that the four logs had been obtained illegally and could be made public by the defense. He agreed with the government, however, that the fifth should be sealed since revealing its contents possibly would endanger national security. While the judge did not order production of transcripts or "air-tels" (government attorneys said the original transcripts had been destroyed), he did permit defense counsel to question F.B.I. agents and clerks who supervised the four illegal wiretaps. If the defense could show that evidence used to convict Ali was connected to the wiretaps, his conviction would be reversed. The government argued that Ali had not been the target of the taps, but that some of his conversations were overheard during surveillance of other persons. A month later after open hearings on the four taps and his private examination of the fifth, the District Judge decided wiretap information had not been used to convict Ali. He chose not to rule on whether the Attorney General's authorization of a wiretap for the purpose of gathering foreign intelligence information violates the Fourth Amendment, since the fifth tap was irrelevant to the evidence presented at Ali's trial.[91]

Meanwhile, in the Chicago conspiracy case defense counsel filed a motion for production of all records of illegal electronic surveillance of any of the defendants. In reply the government admitted that five defendants—Rubin, Dellinger, Hayden, Davis, and Seale—had been overheard through wiretaps placed with the express approval of the then Attorney General (apparently Ramsey Clark). Attorney General Mitchell submitted an affidavit contending that even if this wiretapping might have violated existing Fourth Amendment standards, it should be exempt from disclosure because the President (acting through the Justice Department) had the constitutional power "to utilize electronic surveillance to gather intelligence information concerning those organizations which are committed to the use of illegal methods to bring about changes in our form of government and which may be seeking to foment violent disorders." Such surveillance should also be exempt from the Fourth Amendment requirement of prior judicial warrant since the question of its appropriateness in order to protect the nation against a dangerous organization was one that properly came within the competence of the executive and not the judicial branch. Thus Mitchell asked trial judge Julius Hoffman to seal the surveillance records during the course of the trial and examine them later in the secrecy of his chambers to determine whether they tainted any evidence presented by the government.[92]

Defense counsel believed the Alderman decision clearly mandated a pretrial hearing to decide the legality of the government's electronic surveillance, but Judge Hoffman followed the Attorney General's advice and refused to conduct such a hearing. Only if the jury found some or all of the defendants guilty would he consider the issue; and even then he would rule on the legality of the surveillance only if upon examining the records himself he found any prosecution evidence connected to the surveillance.[93] Throughout the trial, therefore, defense counsel had no way of knowing if the evidence might be challenged as tainted by illegal wiretapping or bugging, even though Judge Hoffman had not considered the merits of the Justice Department's theory of executive power.

The Attorney General's assertion of executive authority in the Chicago case went far beyond his narrower foreign intelligence surveillance claim in the Muhammed Ali case, which several Supreme Court Justices had already been willing to consider.[94] It immediately provoked a legal challenge by the A.C.L.U., representing the Chicago defendants and nine organizations. Filing a class action suit in Washington on behalf of all Americans who hold unpopular, controversial, and dissenting political positions, the A.C.L.U. asked a federal District Court to order an end to such surveillance because the absence of court review of the standards by which political groups were related to national security violated the First and Fourth Amendments. By announcing a policy of unfettered executive power to determine the possible danger presented to the nation by dissenting persons or groups, Attorney General Mitchell and F.B.I. Director Hoover had assumed judicial and regulatory authority over the protected activities of all dissenting Americans. Their policy of unfettered searches and seizures had created "a chill and pall on all those who would desire to associate with those persons and groups caught within the dragnet of the announced policy in violation of the associational rights protected by the First Amendment."[95]

The Spock Decision and the Chicago Trial

In addition to Judge Hoffman's ruling on national security surveillance records, the Chicago conspiracy trial received another indispensible sanction when the Court of Appeals in Boston decided the Spock case, reversing the convictions but sustaining the use of conspiracy doctrine. The two conspiracy prosecutions were similar in that both were addressed to what the Court of Appeals called "a bifarious undertaking, involving both legal and illegal conduct." Since their activities were "political within the shadow of the First Amendment," the Spock case defendants were granted certain protections before they could be convicted of conspiracy. In weighing the interests at stake, the Court said it would start "with the assumption that the defendants were not to be prevented from vigorous criticism of the Government's program merely because the natural consequences might be to interfere with it, or even to lead to unlawful action." As a result the Court placed one significant limit on traditional conspiracy law, ruling that a defendant's specific intentions could not be "ascertained by reference to the conduct or statements of another even though he has knowledge thereof." Instead, it was necessary to prove that each individual defendant personally agreed to employ the illegal means contemplated by the agreement—in this case counseling or aiding and abetting violation of the Selective Service act.

Nevertheless, the Court held that a defendant's adherence to the illegal aims of the conspiracy (and thus his guilt) could "be shown in one of three ways: by the individual defendant's prior or subsequent unambiguous statements; by the individual defendant's subsequent commission of the very illegal act contemplated by the agreement; or by the individual defendant's subsequent legal act if that act is 'clearly undertaken for the specific purpose of rendering effective the later illegal activity which is advocated.' " On considering the trial record, the Court found evidence that Rev. Coffin and Mitchell Goodman had the requisite specific intent, but Dr. Spock and Michael Ferber did not. The convictions of all four were reversed, however, because the trial judge had improperly instructed the jury. In reviewing the evidence against Rev. Coffin, the Court concluded that because he assisted in the collection of draft cards to be turned over the the Attorney General, his action could well have been found to be aiding and abetting nonpossession, and this was "the very type of resistance that the agreement might have been found to contemplate." Goodman could have been convicted without having committed such an act because his unambiguous remarks at the Washington demonstration clarified his specific intent.[96]

The Court's standard with respect to Goodman, therefore, permitted conspriacy prosecutions where the evidence was composed entirely of speech protected by the First Amendment. At no time did the Court find the "Call to Resist," which embodied the conspiracy's aims, or Goodman's own statements to be incitement to draft resistance. Yet as the Supreme Court had ruled in Brandenburg v. Ohio, the First Amendment did not allow the government "to forbid or proscribe advocacy of. . .law violation except where such advocacy is directed to inciting or producing imminent lawless action and is likely to incite or produce such action."[97] Dissenting Judge Frank M. Coffin identified the breadth of the Court of Appeals' standard: "To say that prior or subsequent unambiguous statements change the color of the litmus is to say that while one exercise of First Amendment rights is protected, two are not." The Court treated conspriacy to counsel draft law violations the same as conspiracy to aid and abet such violations, requiring only a showing of specific intent in both. But the two aims were very different—one was an exercise of free speech (unless found to be incitement), the other was not.

The Spock decision posed many other problems; but its primary effect was, as Judge Coffin pointed out, to let the government continue to use "the conspiracy weapon. . .again on another day in another court" against political advocacy. Because all the convictions were reversed on technical grounds, Rev. Coffin and Mitchell Goodman could not easily appeal the decision to the Supreme Court. The Justice Department also chose not to appeal, possibly fearing the Supreme Court would apply the Brandenburg rule and place more stringent limits on conspiracy prosecutions. Ultimately Attorney General Mitchell decided not to re-try Goodman and Rev. Coffin, even though the Court of Appeals said they might be convicted in a trial free of procedural error. The Court's decision was victory enough (although perhaps a defeat for Ramsey Clark), since it paved the way for the Chicago conspiracy trial to take place.

Before the trial began, an Ad Hoc Lawyers Committee charged that since the government would rely for its proof on constitutionally protected, but unpopular, speeches and demonstrations, it might intimidate "untold thousands who would wish to join the defendants in protest and cannot under threat of future prosecution."[98] Lasting from September, 1969, until February, 1970, the Chicago trial encompassed far more than the First Amendment issue. The binding of Bobby Seale in the courtroom when he tried to act as his own counsel, the dramatic conduct of judge, defendants, and lawyers, the heavy contempt penalties—these and many other incidents made it the most highly publicized trial in recent history. Seale's case was severed from the others before the end of the trial. The jury's verdict acquitting the remaining seven defendants on the conspiracy charge, but convicting the five leading figures (Dellinger, Hayden, Davis, Hoffman, and Rubin) for individually inciting to riot was as suprising as it was indecisive. Judge

Hoffman, whose rulings on evidence and testimony, courtroom conduct, and contempt sentences provoked widespread criticism, carefully followed the Spock opinion in instructing the jury and even interpreted the antiriot statue in line with the Brandenburg decision.[99] Because the defendants were acquitted of conspiracy, their appeals could not challenge the constitutionality of the government's conspiracy theory. Once again, the Justice Department was left free to bring another conspiracy prosecution in the future.

After the jury returned its verdict, Judge Hoffman examined the records of electronic surveillance against the convicted defendants and concluded they had no relevance to the evidence presented at the trial. He found it necessary, *finally*, to rule on the Attorney General's contention that electronic surveillance of dangerous groups without judicial warrant was a legitimate exercise of executive power and required an exception to normal Fourth Amendment requirements. The judge had already made such an exception to the Alderman procedures by refusing to let defense counsel examine the records. The Attorney General's argument would, therefore, be open to possible scrutiny on appeal. The District Court in Washington had postponed a hearing on the A.C.L.U.'s suit until after the Chicago case was concluded. Now civil liberties lawyers would try to revive that litigation as a more certain means of securing judicial review on both First and Fourth Amendment grounds of the Justice Department's electronic surveillance power.

The November March on Washington

Despite many dire predictions of intimidation, the Chicago trial did not diminish the energies of antiwar groups in the fall of 1969. President Nixon's assurances that he would end the Vietnam war had quieted criticism during the first half of the year, but confidence in his intentions began to diminish. The Vietnam Moratorium Committee, led by former McCarthy and Kennedy campaign workers, gained the protest initiative when it organized nationwide peaceful demonstrations on October

15. Moratorium leaders had no difficulty securing permits for a rally on the Washington Monument grounds and a candlelight procession around the White House, although Moratorium attorneys had to go into court to win permission for Dr. Spock to address a gathering at the National Institutes of Health. Several days before the October Moratorium President Nixon announced that Selective Service Director Hershey would be replaced. On the eve of the demonstrations, however, Vice President Agnew emerged from a meeting with the President to call on protest leaders to repudiate a message of support from North Vietnam. Reaching unexpected proportions across the country, the October 15 Moratorium was a moderate, broadly based, peaceful show of opposition to the war.[100]

The Moratorium focused public attention away from a violent march in Chicago the preceding week, organized by a faction of S.D.S. During the summer S.D.S. had split into three groups—members of the Progressive Labor Party and two other factions calling themselves Revolutionary Youth Movement I and II, who differed primarily over the use of violent protest. R.Y.M. I, soon to be known as the Weathermen, planned an appeal to alienated high school students by showing their willingness to fight, while R.Y.M. II contended that violent tactics would drive away potential supporters and lead to increased police repression.[101]

In October the Weathermen battled police in the streets of Chicago, with at least 250 arrested and one city official seriously injured. Although the intelligence unit of the Chicago police maintained constant surveillance of the group, the city granted permits for the rallies and parades that produced the disorders; and Daniel Walker, author of the report on police misconduct at the 1968 convention, praised law enforcement authorities for their restraint. F.B.I. agents investigated at least one incident where a police undercover informant, having been discovered by the Weathermen, was assaulted and beaten. When the disturbances subsided, the Justice Department announced that a special F.B.I. team would question witnesses for possible antiriot prosecutions. William Sullivan, the F.B.I.'s Assistant Director for domestic intelligence, declared that S.D.S. was moving toward "open advocacy of violent revolution" and that violent confrontations, bombings and arson could be expected to increase.[102]

Before the October Moratorium and the Weathermen's outburst, the New Mobilization Committee (successor to the National Mobilization Committee) had called for a march on Washington to be held Saturday, November 15. Its attorney Phillip J. Hirschkop began negotiations with Associate Deputy Attorney General John W. Dean on march permits in late October. After submitting a memorandum outlining the New Mobilization's plans for a march down Pennsylvania Avenue, Hirschkop revealed that Dean opposed this route since it would cause the White House to be virtually surrounded by demonstrators. Hirschkop was still optimistic that an agreement would be reached, even though Dean had repeatedly asked if violent groups like the Weathermen would take part. While he said it was impossible to predict the movement of individuals and groups, Hirschkop told Dean the Weathermen would not be included under the official New Mobilization umbrella and would be denied elaborate legal services planned for demonstrators in the event of arrest. [103]

Recognizing legitimate concern for protecting the White House, New Mobilization leaders were prepared to modify the Saturday parade route. On November 4, however, the process of negotiation was upset by a dramatic and apparently firm Department statement laying down its terms for the march permit. Following immediately upon President Nixon's November 3 address to the nation defending his "Vietnamization" policy, the Department's position seemed part of a larger attempt to discredit the forthcoming demonstration. Attorney General Mitchell declared on November 2 that some of the stated, known members of the New Mobilization coordinating committee were "active militants who want to destroy some of the processes and some of the institutions of our government." The next day Assistant F.B.I. Director Sullivan observed that the New Mobilization steering committee included "more Communist influence than you will find probably on any other committee of the New Left."[104] The Department's official statement said it had "reliable reports that a minority of those expected to come to Washington may be planning to foment violence or to stage confrontations which could cause personal and property damage not only to the peaceful participants of the planned demonstration but also to the citizens of the city. . . .It is the considered opinion of the Department that, should any serious violence erupt, coordinated and effective law enforcement would be impossible if a large mass of demonstrators were to be scattered along the Pennsylvania Avenue route, with the possibility of violence flowing into the downtown business and residential areas."

In view of this situation, the Department offered the use of the Mall to hold a demonstration and the use of Pennsylvania Avenue for a small symbolic parade on November 15. The New Mobilization was told it would be limited to a hundred persons for such a parade.[105]

Two days later Deputy Attorney General Kleindienst disclosed intelligence reports that pro-violent groups were seeking to infiltrate the mass march. Kleindienst refused as a matter of policy to identify any groups other than the Weathermen, except to say that persons who "had engaged in violence on scores of campuses will participate in the demonstration. If they engaged in violence there, we must assume that they may engage in violence here." Kleindienst added, "I don't understand the magic of marching down Pennsylvania Avenue." Asked what would happen if demonstrators tried to march on the avenue without a permit, he replied, "They will be violating the law. . .and we will use the minimum force necessary."[106]

New Mobilization leaders had been willing not only to avoid the White House, but to use just four lanes of the eight-lane avenue and to limit the number of parade participants to 60-70,000 while all other demonstrators followed the Mall route from the Capitol to the Washington Monument. The Department's refusal to accept such arrangements and its predictions of violence sparked serious criticism. Commenting that local police had confidence in their ability to keep the situation under control, the *Washington Post* charged the

Department with needless provocation. The A.C.L.U. called its action an infringement of First Amendment rights to peaceable assembly. Citing the Chicago convention disorders, New York Senator Charles Goodell predicted denial of a permit acceptable to the New Mobilization would "create a clear and serious danger that a large number of demonstrators will attempt to take that route anyway. If this occurs, the use of force will become inevitable and our national capital will be marred by violence and bloodshed."[107]

Anticipating this danger, former Attorney General Clark began organizing a lawyers' task force recruited from private law firms, government agencies, and Congressional offices to monitor the behavior of marchers and police. Clark believed the Department was ignoring all the standards for handling demonstrations developed out of the experience with the 1967 Pentagon protest and the 1968 Poor People's Campaign, as well as the lessons learned from the Chicago convention. The first rule was not to talk publicly about intelligence reports of potential violence, which often contained unverified rumors. In conducting permit negotiations, the lessons were to remain flexible and to keep talking until mutually acceptable terms could be found. If the government insisted on an adament position and broke off negotiations, the consequences could be another Chicago since the protesters would feel they had been denied their constitutional rights. Deputy Attorney General Kleindienst had broken these rules by publicizing intelligence reports, insisting he would not yield on use of the avenue, and letting negotiations break down.[108]

On Monday, November 10, District of Columbia Mayor Walter Washington intervened personally with President Nixon and White House domestic affairs assistant John Ehrlichman. In what was described as their first serious talk since the new Administration had taken office, the Mayor told Nixon of his concern that refusal to allow the Pennsylvania Avenue march might provoke a confrontation and that tensions were being built up by Kleindienst's statements about possible violence. Local police officials, including Chief Jerry Wilson, felt they could handle any demonstrations and any violence. "We're used to handling big crowds," one said later. "We're going to get them in here and get them out safely. They certainly have a perfect right to be here." During his conference with Mayor Washington, the President reportedly agreed with his concern about mounting tension and telephoned Attorney General Mitchell, who passed the word to Kleindienst that permission to use the avenue should be granted. The Mayor then met with Kleindienst to draft a joint statement released the next day, and the White House announced that President Nixon "feels very strongly that citizens have every right to express their point of view."[109]

The Kleindienst-Washington joint statement gave permission for the Pennsylvania Avenue parade on the terms offered by the New Mobilization, accepting its assurance that order would be maintained and expressing confidence "that the November 15th march can be conducted peacefully and without danger to citizens or property." The New Mobilization would provide 2,000 parade marshals to keep participants on the south side of the avenue and 500 marshals to keep crowds away from the government buildings along the route. The marshals would prevent any demonstrations during the course of the march. Participants would enter the avenue between 10:00 and 12:30, at which time the remaining marchers would move down the Mall to the Washington Monument.[110]

Why did the Justice Department so readily agree to change its position, rather than attempt to refute Mayor Washington? One reason may have been new intelligence indicating a reduced likelihood of violence during the march. This explanation is supported by analysis of an unclassified intelligence memorandum prepared after the Department's decision to bar the Pennsylvania Avenue parade. Based on information furnished by "reliable sources" to the Interdivisional Intelligence and Information Unit, the memo offered an assessment of the potential for violence, personal injuries, and possible deaths. It predicted that the intensity and extent of violence would be considerably beyond that experienced at the 1967 Pentagon march, the Democratic convention, or the Weathermen's recent Chicago demonstration. Among the specific intelligence reports it cited were the following:

"October 14th—Student for a Democratic Society leaders are planning to 'take the town apart, piece by piece,' on November 15th.

"October 24th—Meetings have been held in New York, Washington and Chicago by the violent Weathermen faction of the Students for a Democratic Society. They intend to turn the November 15th demonstrations into another Chicago disturbance by blocking street traffic, breaking store windows, running against pedestrian traffic and harassing businesses in the downtown areas.

October 27th—Abbie Hoffman and Jerry Rubin, on trial for the Conspiracy Eight stated that an attempt will be made at the November 15th demonstration to break into the Department of Justice, using Molotov cocktails and also to blow up the Vietnamese Embassy.

November 4th—James Lafferty a leader in the Detroit Coalition to End the War Now announced to a meeting that a split had developed at a Steering Committee meeting of the New Mobilization Committee between the New Mobilization Committee itself and the Vietnam Moratorium Committee. The Vietnam Moratorium Committee felt that too many radicals were becoming involved and were concerned with a radical takeover of the November 15th demonstration."[111]

These intelligence reports conveyed three basic points: that moderate Moratorium leaders were not cooperating with the New Mobilization, that Hoffman and Rubin envisioned assaults on the Justice Department building and the South Vietnamese Embassy, and that the Weathermen planned equally violent street disorders. By November 10 when Mayor Washington went to the White House, however, it was becoming clear that the first point was no longer accurate and that the others were less relevant to the main Pennsylvania Avenue march.

After President Nixon's November 3 speech, the Moratorium leaders committed their manpower and logistic skills to help plan and control the march. Twenty-five people with extensive experience in crowd management came to Washington to form a combined task force to organize parade marshals. Meanwhile, a coalition of radical groups unaffiliated with the Mobilization, including all S.D.S. factions, announced plans for a rally at DuPont Circle and a march to the South Vietnamese Embassy on Friday night before the main parade. In addition, Hoffman and Rubin said their group would protest at the Justice Department on Saturday evening after the mass rally at the Washington Monument was over.[112] Since neither of these separate demonstrations would be affected by denial of the Pennsylvania Avenue permit, the Department's logic in opposing use of the avenue became less persuasive. If violence were to occur, it was most likely at these other locations. Nevertheless, had not the Mayor intervened, Deputy Attorney General Kleindienst would probably have persisted in his refusal to allow more than symbolic use of the avenue.

On Saturday, November 15, the main march and rally of over 250,000 people (the police estimate) was entirely peaceful, as police let parade marshals maintain order. On Friday night and again on Saturday evening, as anticipated, fringe groups provoked police into using tear gas to break up crowds near the South Vietnamese Embassy and at the Justice Department. Incidents of violence were relatively minor. Several score police were hit by bricks and bottles Friday night, but no one was seriously injured. As many as seventy-five stores in the business district lost windows, and the Justice Department suffered seventeen broken windows. Only 114 persons were arrested, all but four on charges of disorderly conduct. A Defense Department spokesman reported no serious injuries and no major damages to property. Attributing the trouble to a small band of people who wanted to discredit the march, Mayor Washington praised the leaders of the main demonstration for their efforts at keeping it peaceful.[113]

Attorney General Mitchell refused to admit intelligence predictions had been wrong and credited police and the threat of troops with preventing greater eruptions of violence. He asserted the protests "were marred by such extensive physical injury, property damage and street confrontations that I do not believe that—over all—the gatherings here can be characterized as peaceful." Accusing the New Mobilization of aiding the violence through a combination of inaction and affirmative action, Mitchell charged its leaders with failing to disassociate themselves from the Friday night and Saturday evening demonstrations. Speakers at the Washington Monument rally were permitted to incite the crowd to move on the Justice Department. Two days later Deputy Attorney General Kleindienst disclosed that some members of the New Mobilization steering committee were under investigation for possible antiriot law violations. Specifically mentioning David Dellinger as having a background and history of violence, Kleindienst charged that his speech at the Monument rally had incited the violent demonstration at the Department building. A New Mobilization spokesman replied, "The Justice Department was unable to limit our demonstration beforehand and now seems intent on diminishing its effect after the fact."[114]

In a controversial television interview several days laters, Mrs. John Mitchell recalled her husband's comment "that looking out of the Justice Department, it looked like the Russian revolution going on." She continued, "I don't think the average Americans realize how desperate it is when a group of demonstrators, not peaceful demonstrators, but the very liberal Communists, move into Washington. This place could become a complete fortress. You could have every building in Washington burned down. It could be a great, great catastrophe." The Attorney General qualified his wife's statement only to the extent of substituting "violence-prone militants" for "liberal Communists."[115] Most observers found Martha Mitchell's remarks a comic sidelight to the November events, but they revealed an attitude shared more deeply in the Department's intelligence structure.

Besides specific reports of plans for violence, the intelligence memo quoted earlier contained a lengthy general background section on the history of the antiwar movement and described the past activities and associations of prominent members of the New Mobilization steering committee. The analysis began with a warning against coming "to the conclusion that this is a

'Communist plot,' " and against drawing "any conclusions with respect to the goodness or badness of the particular philosophy which these individual may hold." Nevertheless, it suggested at the outset that the "prorevolutionary proclivity of the individuals coupled with their activities leads one to the conclusion that the Hanoi government has had important input into the concept of these activities."

The history started with developments up to the 1967 march on the Pentagon, including information probably used by President Johnson at that time in briefing Congressional leaders:

"The thread linking together persons and incidents associated with the Vietnam war moratorium movement can be traced back to a visit by David Dellinger, a member of the Steering Committee of the New Mobilization Committee, in 1966 with Ho Chi Minh in Hanoi. This meeting may well have been the beginning of considerable behind-the-scenes coordination of the anti-war movement.

"On May 20-22, 1967, at a meeting in Washington, D.C., the Spring Mobilization Committee became the National Mobilization Committee to End the War in Vietnam and agreed on the date of October 20-22, 1967, for the Pentagon demonstration. This date was fixed through the insistence of Arnold Johnson, a national officer of the Communist Party and George Novack and Harry Ring of the Socialist Workers Party. Dellinger again met in Hanoi for a series of meetings, lasting from May 26, 1967, until June 13th.

"There then followed the World Conference on Vietnam in Stockholm on July 6-9, 1967, which coordinated a series of simultaneous anti-war demonstrations throughout the world, including the Pentagon activity scheduled for October. In August, 1967, Dellinger helped organize a similar conference in Bratislava, Czechoslovakia from September 5-13. Following the meeting, seven of the United States delegates flew to Hanoi.

"In late summer, 1967, VIETPEACE in Hanoi asked the World Council of Peace to propose that October 21, 1967, be designated an international day of protest 'against wars of aggresssion' and 'American Imperialism' in Vietnam.

"The Pentagon demonstrations and violence in October followed."

After citing "the approval of Hanoi and the National Liberation Front" for the 1969 Washington demonstration, the memo explained how preparations were similar to those in 1967.

"Another Stockholm conference was held on October 11-12, 1969, with a primary purpose of expanding the New Mobilization Committee's 'Fall Offensive' into an international movement. Representing the United States were Roland Young and Irving Sarnoff, East Coast and West Coast organizers, respectively, of the New Mobilization Committee. Three other New Mobilization Committee co-chairmen were invited but were unable to attend. They were David Dellinger, Stewart Mecham and Cora Weiss.

"The United States delegates told the meeting that the crucial task of the New Mobilization Committee over the next six to eight months was to create a variety of highly visible pressures on the Nixon administration. They characterized the Committee as the broadest-based coalition of anti-war forces in the history of the country, which includes the Communist Party, the Socialist Workers Party, the World International League for Peace and Freedom, and the Vietnam Moratorium Committee.

"Suggested activity for post-November 15th was also discussed and this would include a petition campaign calling for total, unconditional, amd immediate withdrawal of United States troops from Vietnam."

Since none of this information disclosed any intentions of violent protest, the most crucial data were the biographies of members of the New Mobilization steering committee. The

memo observed that sixteen committee members "also participated in the Pentagon demonstration in October, 1967, or the
planning for it." Twelve were chosen as a selected, but
representative number for detailed description of their previous
activities. Six of these were identified as either being members
of the Communist Party or having associated with the Communist Party, while the others had had contacts with officials of
Communist governments. One had been arrested during demonstrations at San Francisco State College in 1968. Another was
arrested for resisting arrest, aggravated assault, and disorderly
conduct at the Chicago convention. David Dellinger and Rennie
Davis were on trial in Chicago. Arthur Waskow was said to
advocate "creative disorder—the use of illegal or nearly illegal
methods to force revolutionary change in society." Sidney Peck
had reportedly "advocated the destruction of the nation's six
largest indiction centers and other disruptive tactics designed to
adversely affect the war effort." John Wilson had "requested a
moment of silence in memory of Che Guevara" at the Pentagon
in 1967. The memorandum concluded that the potential for
violent demonstrations in Washington was "extremely high" in
part because of these "past violence associated activities" of the
New Mobilization leadership.

In its overall summary the memo reasserted that there was a
"thread" linking possible behind-the-scenes coordination of the
antiwar movement back to Dellinger's 1966 visit to Hanoi.
While a "conspiracy" in a legal sense was not the question of
the moment, there was a "close and significant relationship
between activities and people." The participants were dedicated
to a like objective, "whether for the limited purpose of ending
the war or broader and deeper purposes."[116]

What broader and deeper purposes did the authors of this
intelligence memorandum have in mind? An overall evaluation
of their report can only lead to the conclusion that the Justice
Department was now operating on the assumption that the
antiwar movement was, indeed, in the nature of a Communist
plot, despite earlier disclaimers to the contrary. Nixon Administration executives may even have brought this assumption with
them when they took office. During the 1968 election

campaign, Vice Presidential candidate Spiro Agnew, who was assigned to express the Nixon camp's views on dissent, told reporters he had no doubt that among Vietnam war protesters there was "a conspiracy of the type which is legally punishable in this country—a conspiracy to overthrow the government by force."[117] Whether or not Agnew's views were shared fully by the President or the Attorney General, emphasis on this theory within the Department's intelligence structure would continue to limit its perceptions of antiwar protest.

The investigation of New Mobilization Committee leaders for possible antiriot law violations did not result in any prosecutions during the following months. Participants in the Weathermen's October rampage in Chicago were, however, indicted for federal antiriot offenses in 1970 despite extensive local prosecutions. By the end of 1969 the government had real fears of bombings and threats to bomb public buildings in many major cities. The Justice Department might stay its hand, as it did in the spring of 1969 when it drew back from prosecuting campus agitators under the influence of young Republican Congressmen who feared such action would only serve to intensify youthful disenchantment. The White House might intervene at the urging of outsiders like Mayor Washington to reverse a Departmental decision. Pressures like these seemed necessary, nonetheless, to contain the repressive impulses that had gained momentum over five years of a divisive military commitment in Southeast Asia.

5. THE JUSTICE DEPARTMENT
AND ANTIWAR DISSENT

The evolution of protest against the Vietnam war from teach-ins and peaceful marches to civil disobedience and provocative demonstrations strained the capacity of the legal system to protect free speech. One measure of its success was continued vigorous criticism of national policy. Neither federal prosecutions and surveillance nor General Hershey's draft policies retarded the antiwar movement's growth; indeed, they may have encouraged stronger protests against threatened repression. This suggests that another standard should be used to evaluate the Justice Department's response to dissent. Rather than discouraging criticism, its actions may create the conditions for radical groups to win greater support and for emotional outbursts to replace rational argument.

Leaving aside moral and constitutional rationales for First Amendment rights, the course of Department policy can be examined according to two contrasting interpretations of the *self-interest* of the Administration in office. A civil libertarian program designed to avoid the appearance of repression might be advantageous since it would take ammunition away from the radicals and avoid disorderly confrontations. More repressive measures, on the other hand, might discourage dissent and win popular support from that segment of the public that was hostile to protest activity. During the late 1960's these divergent estimates of political advantage contended for influence over federal law enforcement.

Ramsey Clark's opposition to General Hershey, his reluctance to prosecute advocates of draft resistance, his negotiation of acceptable march permits, his approach to the Chicago convention—all represented a consistent attempt to disarm the extreme left and to avoid confrontations. If Clark had prevailed, his policies might have not only countered those who wished to capitalize on charges of repression, but also prevented clashes between demonstrators and police that gave the uncommitted public an impression that the Administration could not maintain order. Chicago confirmed the logic of Clark's position, since the violence there fatally attached the Democratic Party to an image of upheaval. When he rejected Clark's advice in dealing with General Hershey and Mayor Daley, President Johnson disregarded the possibility that his Administration would take some of the blame for the consequent growth of radicalism.

Officials like Daley and Hershey, as well as many Congressmen, did not see the government's self-interest in Ramsey Clark's terms. They apparently acted on the assumptions that dissent could be reduced by strong counter-measures and that such steps would win popular approval despite confrontations. Perhaps they failed to anticipate the way their image would alienate greater numbers of young people. Even if they recognized the persistence of antiwar sentiment and the dangers of polarization, they did not risk their political futures because their constituencies were firmly behind them. By shifting the blame for disorders onto the protesters, they might gain still more support. In contrast to Attorney General Clark, they could disregard the possibility that unrest would undermine public confidence in the national Administration's ability to maintain order since their own independent positions seemed secure.

During 1969 Attorney General Mitchell appeared to vacillate between these two conceptions of the Administration's interests. Like Mayor Daley and General Hershey, he sometimes acted as if repressive policies—the Chicago conspiracy prosecution, the assertion of sweeping electronic surveillance powers, the handling of the March on Washington—would discourage radical dissent and satisfy the electorate. In November he risked serious confrontation and magnified the disorders in order to blame unrest on the protesters. On other occasions, however, Mitchell seemed to understand that overreaction to campus disruptions would just recruit more student radicals. President Nixon's reversal of the Department's stand on march permits in November indicated that the White House saw risks to the President's prestige in being associated with a violent confrontation like the one at the Chicago convention. While opinion polls said the public wanted the government to act firmly against radicals and protesters, public opinion was a misleading guide for national policy-makers. If Attorney General Mitchell chose to take measures that appeared increasingly repressive, the electorate might ultimately blame the Nixon Administration for the resulting turmoil.

The protection of civil liberties should be more than just a matter for political calculation. In the volatile setting of the late 1960's, however, constitutional principles alone could not prevent repression if they conflicted with the political interests of the President. The White House and the Attorney General occasionally recognized that they would not benefit from constant confrontations, but they still were tempted to use antiwar dissent as a scapegoat. Justice Department policy often depended less on legal principles than on the Attorney General and the President's estimates of their political advantage at a time when repression provoked unrest and a popular majority wanted both firmness and order. Given the extent of antiwar feeling, the government could not silence dissent. Instead, its refusal to adopt a consistently civil libertarian policy drove some of its critics to the extreme left and provoked chaotic confrontations for which the electorate would hold the Administration partly responsible.

5

DOMESTIC

INTELLIGENCE SURVEILLANCE

The Justice Department's most significant response to black militancy and antiwar dissent during the 1960's was the development of an extensive domestic intelligence surveillance program. While most Department policies are made public in court and in statements to Congress or the press, the nature of its intelligence operations has been kept largely secret. The Attorney General has never defined the scope and limits of intelligence surveillance over domestic political groups. This is not a new problem. In an address to a conference of United States Attorneys in 1940, Attorney General Robert Jackson warned that the concept subversive activities was "dangerous to civil liberties because the prosecutor has no definite standards to determine what constitute a 'subversive activity,' such as we have for murder or larceny."[1] At the time Jackson spoke the F.B.I. had already been undertaking political surveillance since 1936, when President Roosevelt directed it to gather intelligence "concerning subversive activities being conducted in the United States by Communists, Fascists and representatives or advocates of other organizations or groups advocating the overthrow or replacement of the Government of the United States by illegal methods."[2]

During the 1960's the Justice Department supplemented the F.B.I.'s activities by creating its own computerized Inter-divisional Intelligence and Information Unit, originally designed to anticipate civil disorders. When Ramsey Clark and the Kerner commission encouraged state and local authorities to set up or expand intelligence programs to cope with civil unrest, they provided additional sources of information for the Department. In recent years the military intelligence divisions and the Secret Service also greatly enlarged their political data collection. Along with other federal law enforcement agencies including those in the Treasury Department, they share their reports with the Justice Department. As one informed critic has noted, "Few Americans—including most members of Congress—know any-thing about the activities of the *domestic* intelligence com-munity. Many do not realize that the growth of formal and informal ties among law enforcement, intelligence, and security agencies has made it necessary to think in such terms."[3]

There are few administrative, legislative, or judicial guidelines for these intelligence operations. In order to develop rules to govern surveillance of political groups, several aspects of the problem should be explored. First, what kind of information is gathered about whom? Are there some persons or groups about whom law enforcement agencies have no legitimate reason to collect certain types of intelligence? Second, what techniques of intelligence gathering are appropriate and permissible? Should electronic surveillance, the use of undercover agents, or other methods be circumscribed because they invade privacy or have a chilling effect on the exercise of free speech? Third, what uses are made of intelligence data after they are collected? Are reports confined within a single agency, are they shared among many different levels, or do they become part of a single comprehensive dossier? Finally, which agency collects what information? Unfortunately, few definitive answers can be given on the basis of the public record of federal, state, and local activity.

Before the mid-1960's these questions would have applied almost solely to the F.B.I. In September, 1939, President Roosevelt asked all law enforcement officers in the United

States to turn over to the nearest F.B.I. field office any information they obtained relating to subversive activities. The President explained that this investigative task should be conducted in a comprehensive manner on a national basis, because the information had to be "carefully sifted and correlated in order to avoid confusion and irresponsibility."[4] Attorney General Jackson repeated to a conference of state law enforcement officials in 1940 that intelligence surveillance should be placed under the direction of J. Edgar Hoover, "whose pre-eminince in this field has given the country confidence that the task will be thoroughly done." Jackson told state officials of his concern that there not be competition in this field of investigation. "It is highly important that there be centralized control of activities of this kind so that your agents and ours do not become involved in a competitive race for premature disclosure."[5] Until the 1960's, therefore, few local police agencies devoted significant resources to intelligence.

With the development of a national intelligence community including states and cities besides several federal agencies, the risks of abuse have become greater. Some involve the use of electronic surveillance, which the Supreme Court has held to be an unconstitutional invasion of privacy unless limited by appropriate procedural safeguards. Covert infiltration poses dangers because undercover agents or informants may produce unreliable information or act as agents provocateurs. Other examples of potential abuse were suggested in New Jersey, where the N.A.A.C.P. and A.C.L.U. challenged the constitutionality of a system instituted by the state Attorney General. Local police were asked to prepare special reports on groups and persons involved not only in civil disturbances, but in rallies, marches, and other forms of peaceful protest. The report forms instructed police to collect exhaustive information on political activists, including the names and addresses of friends and employers, financial and credit status, habits and traits, places frequented, and past activities. State police collected these reports in central dossiers for each individual and organization.

In August, 1969, a state court ruled that maintenance of these files violated the First Amendment since it tended to restrict those who would advocate, within the protected areas, social and political change. The court did not believe the state had adequately shown how the personal information gathered in the dossiers would be helpful in preventing civil disorders; and the police report forms were "so broad and sweeping that any gathering or event could qualify for a write-up." While the court's ruling applied only to the specific questionnaires distributed by the state Attorney General, officials feared it might be interpreted as making other intelligence gathering methods unconstitutional.[6]

The New Jersey Supreme Court reversed the lower court's decision in 1970, sending the case back for further hearings to determine whether the Attorney General's program was, in fact, "intended or has been read by local police officials to call for any action which invades a constitutionally protected area." The appellate court advised that the hearings should go beyond the specific questionnaire and consider the entire range of intelligence activities. Among the questions to be considered at the hearings were the following: Are some items on the questionnaire "wholly unrelated to the police obligation with respect to anyone involved in any type of incident?" Is there any evidence to indicate "that a mere rally, protest, demonstration or march of a pacifist group will precipitate a police dossier of everyone who attends, including therein his butcher's and banker's opinion of his credit?" Is there any proof that the dossiers result in a citizen being "harried amid his family, friends, and business associates?" The court envisioned the possibility of judicial intervention if specific abuses occurred. Its standard for limiting police intelligence was whether "the police are gathering information which they believe to be relevant to the police function, detectional or preventive."[7]

The New Jersey Supreme Court's opinion claimed that the police function legitimately extended beyond gathering "such information as will be used to charge persons with specifically defined criminal conduct. . . .The police have a preventive role; its intelligence may not be confined to past criminal events, and even there the police may not be limited to information which constitutes the basis of the criminal charge itself." The Justice

Department makes a similar distinction between gathering "evidence which can be used in legal proceedings" and collecting "intelligence data."[8] What criteria, therefore, determine whether a politically active individual or group will become the subject of federal intelligence reports and dossiers?

The first measure relates to the concept "subversive activities." In 1940 Attorney General Jackson said the F.B.I. engaged in "steady surveillance over individuals and groups within the United States who are so sympathetic with the systems or designs of foreign dictators as to make them a likely source of federal law violation. This includes Nazi, Fascist and Communist groups and societies. It does not include and will not include surveillance over legitimate business or labor activities or religious movements."[9] In recent years the F.B.I. has continued to rely on President Roosevelt's September, 1939, statement as the basis of its responsibility for "detecting the labyrinth of domestic and foreign enemies of the United States." J. Edgar Hoover has emphasized repeatedly that the "legitimate activities" of political organizations are not investigated by the F.B.I., which is "concerned only with the Communist penetration involved."[10] It is not clear, however, whether other groups like the Black Panthers and S.D.S. have joined the Communist Party as domestic enemies. If so, then the F.B.I. may believe itself justified in investigating still more organizations that may be associated with S.D.S. or the Panthers.

The most comprehensive description of the characteristics of subversive organizations is probably that contained in Executive Order 10450 prescribing procedures for the federal employee security program. Originally adopted by President Truman in 1947, it was retained by President Eisenhower in 1953. One of the elements of an employee's or applicant's history concerning which information is to be elicited by investigation is "membership in, or affiliation or sympathetic association with, any foreign or domestic organization, association, movement, group or combination of persons which is totalitarian, Fascist, Communist, or subversive, or which has adopted, or shows, a policy of advocating or approving the commission of acts of force or violence to deny other persons their rights under the Constitution of the United States, or which seeks to alter the form of government of the United States by unconstitutional means."[11] These are also the criteria for the Attorney General's list of subversive organizations. While the Attorney General's list has not been revised since the 1950's, a Congressional report implies that the list does not represent or limit the scope of the Attorney General's "discretion with respect to what advice he shall give the President respecting subversive organizations."[12] In other words, not all groups fitting the criteria of Executive Order 10450 and requiring intelligence surveillance need appear on the list.

One other document further extends the F.B.I.'s intelligence sphere beyond groups found to be subversive. In 1942 an Interdepartmental Committee on Investigations set up by Attorney General Biddle grouped organizations "roughly in three classes: (1) those regarded as subversive. . .(2) those not regarded as subversive. . .but with respect to which the evidence of subversive infiltration was such as clearly to require that they be included within the scope of the investigation, and (3) those not regarded as subversive. . .and consequently outside the scope of the investigation."[13] The interdepartmental committee's report and Executive Order 10450 offer the only public guidelines available for defining the objects of F.B.I. domestic political intelligence.

During the 1960's the Department's intelligence work expanded with creation of the Civil Disturbance Group and its Interdivisional Intelligence and Information Unit. The problems of civil disorders and large-scale protest demonstrations were vastly different from the subversive activities which were the concerns of intelligence in the 1940's and 1950's. Although no new standards have been made public, one legal basis for federal intelligence to anticipate civil disorders is the statute giving the President discretionary power to use the military to put down domestic violence. According to the law, "Whenever there is an insurrection in any State against its government, the President may, upon the request of its legislature or of its governor if the legislature cannot be convened. . .use such of the armed forces as he considers necessary to suppress the insurrection." The President is also empowered to suppress domestic violence or unlawful assemblages when, in his judgment, a state is unable to enforce the law.[14] After the Detroit riots federal intelligence could be justified whenever necessary to assist the President in exercising his authority.

Perhaps equally important in defining the scope of intelligence in the late 1960's was the role assumed by the Department in advising local authorities how to cope with domestic unrest. Thus federal data collection could match the breadth of local police powers for the maintenance of public order. The New Jersey Supreme Court attempted to define the legitimate purposes of police intelligence:

"There have been serious disorders involving heavy losses of life and property. The police function is pervasive. It is not limited to the detection of past criminal events. Of at least equal importance is the responsibility to prevent crime. . . .In the current scene, the preventive role requires an awareness of group tensions and preparations to head off disasters as well as to deal with them if they appear. To that end the police must know what forces exist, what groups or organizations could be enmeshed in public disorders. This is not to ask the police to decide which are 'good' and which are 'bad.' In terms of civil disorders, their respective virtues are irrelevant, for a group is of equal concern to the police whether it is potentially the victim or the aggressor. The police interest is in the explosive possibilities and not in the merits of colliding philosophies. And it must be evident that a riot or the threat of one may best be ended with the aid of private citizens who because of their connections with the discordant groups can persuade them from a course of violence. Hence a police force would fail in its obligation if it did not know who could be called upon to help put out the burning fuse or fire."

The court cited affidavits from the state police Central Security Unit, an assistant to the Governor, and the director of the state Division on Civil Rights to explain current uses of police intelligence reports.[15]

Given the broad conception of law enforcement functions and the similarly wide latitude given the F.B.I. in collecting data about subversive or subversive-infiltrated groups, there seems no limit to the politically active organizations or persons who may come within the ambit of intelligence reports. As J. Edgar Hoover has stated, the F.B.I. must investigate groups covering "the entire spectrum of the social and labor movement in the country."[16] There are, however, major distinctions among individuals and groups according to the surveillance methods used and the types of information gathered about them. Much of the controversy over intelligence focuses on these questions.

In terms of surveillance techniques, the two most questionable methods are electronic surveillance and covert infiltration. Other modes of intelligence collection are less objectionable. Law enforcement agents may rely on newspaper articles and publications; they may attend public meetings as observers; they may receive unsolicited offers of information from private citizens; they may develop open, regular channels of communication with community leaders and organization officials. None of these sources is secret; any or all of them may provide enough information to serve law enforcement needs. Serious questions may be raised, however, about the propriety of interviews of employers, school officials, or associates who may be asked to reveal the subject's opinions or personal characteristics without his knowledge. If the purpose of the interview is not related to a specific law violation or perhaps a job application, such interviews may invade privacy without proper justification. Their potential for indirect intimidation is greater if the questions create an impression that the subject is viewed with disfavor by the law enforcement agency. Similarly, police may legitimately attend a public meeting; but their obtrusive presence at a peaceful gathering with cameras to film the proceedings can easily deter the vigorous expression of opinion. Even the most innocuous modes of inquiry may have a chilling effect on free speech if carried out indiscriminately and without careful supervision.

Electronic surveillance for regular criminal law enforcement has been sanctioned by the Supreme Court and the Omnibus Crime Control Act of 1968 with safeguards requiring a judicial warrant (except for the 1968 Act's "emergency" provision). While state and local police are thereby barred from using electronic devices solely to gather intelligence, the F.B.I. has been permitted to do so since 1940. In a confidential memorandum to Attorney General Jackson, President Roosevelt authorized wiretapping for "grave matters involving the defense of the nation." The President stated,

> "It is, of course, well known that certain other nations have been engaged in the organization of propaganda of so-called 'fifth columns' in other countries and in preparation for sabotage as well as actual sabotage.
>
> "It is too late to do anything about it after sabotage, assassination and 'fifth column' activities are completed.
>
> "You are, therefore, authorized and directed in such cases as you may approve, after investigation of the need in each case, to authorize the necessary investigating agents that they are at liberty to secure information by listening devices directed to the conversations or other communications of persons suspected of subversive activities against the Government of the United States, including suspected spies. You are requested furthermore to limit these investigations so conducted to a minimum and to limit them insofar as possible to aliens."[17]

This authorization was repeated by President Johnson in 1965 for "investigations directly related to the protection of the national security."

Title III of the 1968 act acknowledged two separate bases for the President's power to authorize electronic surveillance. First, it exempted the President from any limits on his "constitutional power. . .to protect the Nation against actual or potential attack or other hostile acts of a foreign power, to obtain foreign intelligence information deemed essential to the security of the United States, or to protect national security information against foreign intelligence activities." Second, the act allowed the President to take "such measures as he deems necessary to protect the United States against the overthrow of the Government by force or other unlawful means, or against any other clear and present danger to the structure or existence of the government."[18] President Johnson had requested only the first of these exceptions from the act's procedural requirements. During Congressional debate on Title III, an amendment was proposed to restrict the exemption to foreign threats to the national security. The Justict Department under Ramsey Clark recommended that the amendment be adopted. "The concept of a *domestic* threat to the national security is vague and undefined," the Department explained. "Use of electronic surveillance in such cases may be easily abused."[19]

Attorney General Mitchell asserted the Department's authority to wiretap for domestic intelligence purposes in 1969. But it is not clear to what extent his policy departed in practice from that of his predecessors. The records produced in the Muhammed Ali case revealed that both Dr. Martin Luther King and Black Muslim leader Elijah Muhammed had their telephones tapped prior to President Johnson's order in July, 1965. In testimony at the Ali hearing, moreover, F.B.I. agents disclosed that Elijah's conversations were monitored at least until May, 1966, and that Dr. King may have remained under electronic surveillance until his death in 1968. Although no testimony was allowed on the reasons for the wiretaps, Associate F.B.I. Director Clyde A. Tolson later said the wiretap on Dr. King "was strictly in the field of internal security."[20]

Testimony by an F.B.I. agent that Dr. King's wiretap continued into 1966 and possibly until his death conflicted with J. Edgar Hoover's subsequent statement that the tap was discontinued on April 30, 1965. Former Attorney General Clark recalled, "Mr. Hoover repeatedly requested me to authorize F.B.I. wiretaps on Dr. King while I was Attorney General. The last of these requests, none of which was granted, came two days before the murder of Dr. King." Clark's predecessor Nicholas Katzenbach confirmed that he and Attorney General Kennedy had approved the wiretap in 1963-65 in an attempt to dispel Hoover's belief that Dr. King was too closely associated with Communists.[21] Whatever the duration of the wiretap, Katzenbach, Kennedy, and Hoover clearly defined internal security broadly enough to encompass electronic surveillance of Dr. King and Elijah Muhammed.

Ramsey Clark denied authorizing electronic surveillance of either man while he headed the Department. But the records sealed in the Chicago case apparently covered wiretaps placed during Clark's term of office, although not directed specifically at the defendant's pre-convention activities. The Department has also admitted wiretapping conversations of Rap Brown prior to his federal prosecution in 1967. In neither of these instances was it clear whether the wiretaps were approved for domestic security or foreign intelligence purposes.[22]

The main contrast between John Mitchell's policy and that of his predecessors involved his decision to assert publicly and ask judicial approval for an undefined surveillance power extending beyond foreign threats to include domestic groups. Unlike the Johnson Administration which sought legislative sanction for its foreign intelligence surveillance, Mitchell claimed executive power independent of Congressional authority. Title III of the crime bill was irrelevant because of the President's inherent powers. "There is a great symbolic difference," Professor Yale Kamisar has observed, "between quietly tapping in violation of the law and achieving the imprimatur of the courts. If they are sneaking in, future Attorneys General can cut it to a minimum, just as Ramsey Clark did pursuant to Johnson's order in 1965. But if it becomes legitimized it will be next to impossible to reverse the trend in calmer days."[23]

The Supreme Court must ultimately decide the validity of Attorney General Mitchell's claims of executive power. Its decision should consider the context in which President Roosevelt's 1940 directive was issued. Its origins lie in the apprehensions of the 1930's and 1940's that certain "fifth column" political groups, because of their relationship to powerful foreign governments, threatened national security. Basically, there seemed to be no difference between foreign and domestic political intelligence during those years. The Smith Act's related prohibition against advocacy of violent overthrow of the government must also be read in this context. As the Commission on Government Security stated in 1957, "From its inception this act was intended to combat and resist the organization of Fascist and Communist groups owing allegiance to foreign governments whose operations and activities were clearly contrary and dangerous to the Government of the United States."[24] The Supreme Court probably acted on this premise in 1951 when it upheld the Smith Act conviction of Communist Party leaders. The Presidential powers acknowledged in Title III should, therefore, be limited to groups that pose a danger only by virtue of the support they receive from hostile nations. Electronic surveillance of allegedly dangerous domestic groups and their leaders should be subject to the judicial warrant requirement and other procedural safeguards.

Even if the Supreme Court made such a decision, however, unlimited wiretapping and bugging might continue to be used against domestic groups on the grounds that most radicals have contacts with Communists at home or overseas. Should the Justice Department make extensive use of this loophole, the courts would have to consider the First Amendment issue directly. Selection of unpopular groups for electronic surveillance, without sufficient probable cause to secure a judicial warrant, has a chilling effect on the exercise of free speech. The invasion of privacy is less important than the interference with freedom to associate freely to pursue legal political goals. Unless the Attorney General narrowly circumscribes the scope of national security surveillance, he may invite more stringent judicial restrictions on executive authority.

While electronic surveillance presently requires the Attorney General's specific approval in each case when it is done by federal agents, state and local police face no such limit. The breadth of offenses for which Title III allows states to use wiretaps, combined with Attorney General Mitchell's policy of encouraging local police to develop the technical capacity for electronic surveillance, make it more likely that police may use such devices for gathering political intelligence. They are deterred only by the prospect of having to reveal their activities if the subjects of surveillance are prosecuted. Even that limit would no longer exist if Congress succeeded in reversing the Alderman decision. Each state and city should, therefore, develop administrative standards that assure strict compliance with the probable cause requirements of Title III. Since the Justice Department is assigned to enforce the Congressional ban on unauthorized electronic surveillance, it has a clear duty to persuade local police to adopt proper safeguards against abuse.

Unlike electronic surveillance, covert penetration has not received the same degree of publicity or executive attention. The leading Supreme Court decision, Hoffa v. United States, ruled that neither Fourth Amendment restrictions on search and seizure nor the Fifth Amendment privilege against self-incrimination place any limits on the use of paid informants. It cited Judge Learned Hand's opinion upholding the Smith Act conviction of Communist Party leaders in 1949: "Courts have countenanced the use of informers from time immemorial; in cases of conspiracy or in other cases where the crime consists of preparing for another crime, it is usually necessary to rely upon them or upon accomplices because the criminals will almost certainly proceed covertly."[25] The Supreme Court admitted in Hoffa that an informer might have motives to lie, but it did not follow that this testimony should be inadmissible. "The established safeguards of the Anglo-American legal system leave the veracity of a witness to be tested by cross-examination, and the credibility of his testimony to be determined by a properly instructed jury." Only Chief Justice Warren and Justice Douglas, in dissent, called for restrictions on deliberately planted informants as breaches of privacy and affronts to the quality and fairness of federal law enforcement.[26]

The constitutional issues may be explored further if the courts consider the problems of privacy for political associations that are posed if informants are planted solely to gather intelligence rather than to report evidence of criminal law violations. There are virtually no public guidelines for this type of surveillance.

Sociologist Morris Janowitz has stated that "only official surveillance and covert penetration supplies an effective technique" for controlling conspiratorial political organizations. But he warns, "It bodes ill when it is necessary to rely on covert operators. The control of secret operations is at best difficult. The task becomes even more complex and troublesome when these surveillance agencies develop the conception, as they often do, that to collect information is not enough. They begin to believe that they must act as active agents of control, particularly in spreading distrust within these organizations."[27] It would be a tragic paradox if officials' perceptions were distorted by the activities of their own undercover informants. The F.B.I.'s solution during the 1950's was to rely on many sources:

> "In the interests of democratic justice and to insure the immediate detection of Communist 'plants,' the information furnished by confidential informants is checked and rechecked to the fullest extent possible. The F.B.I.'s confidential informants are unknown to each other. On occasion, two or more of them may submit information concerning the same Communist function, thereby providing a direct means of verifying reliability. Investigations conducted on the basis of data which informants furnish also serve as a check upon their reliability. Any informant who supplies inaccurate information or whose reliability otherwise is subject to question is dropped by the F.B.I.[28]

While policies like these, if still in effect, help insure accurate reporting, they may not cover the possible role of undercover operators as agents provocateurs who might participate in or even encourage illegal plans, as did New York police agents who joined the Black Liberation Front and the Revolutionary Action Movement.

When Attorney General Clark and the Kerner commission encouraged local intelligence activities, no one addressed openly a basic question about the use to which these intelligence programs would be put. Would they serve only to help in preventing or planning for potential disorders, as the New Jersey Supreme Court described, or might they provide a basis for legal assaults on political groups? The latter option was consistent with the way the President's crime commission envisioned strategic intelligence against organized crime. If dangerous political groups were substituted for organized crime in the crime commission's report, it would have read as follows: Strategic intelligence is the information regarding the capabilities, intentions, and vulnerabilities of dangerous political groups. Prosecution based merely upon individual violations that come to the attention of law enforcement may result in someone's incarceration, but the organization simply places someone else in the vacated position. A body of strategic intelligence would enable agencies to predict what directions dangerous political groups might take. Law enforcement and regulatory agencies could then develop plans to destroy the organizational framework and coherence of the groups.[29]

Attorney General Jackson once called this "the most dangerous power of the prosecutor: that he will pick people that he thinks he should get, rather than pick cases that need to be prosecuted. . . .In such cases, it is not a question of discovering the commission of a crime and then looking for the man who has committed it, it is a question of picking the man and then searching the law books, or putting investigators to work, to pin some offense on him. It is in this realm—in which the prosecutor picks some person he dislikes or desires to embarrass, or selects some group of unpopular persons and then looks for an offense, that the greatest danger of abuse of prosecuting power lies. It is here that. . .the real crime becomes that of being unpopular with the predominant or governing group, being attached to the wrong political views, or being personally obnoxious to or in the way of the prosecutor himself." Jackson believed that law enforcement agencies should have, as nearly as possible, a detached and impartial view of all groups in the community.[30]

The greatest risk of domestic intelligence activity is, therefore, that it will encourage or facilitate strategic repression of political organizations. As police harassment of the Black Panther Party indicated, highly publicized prosecutions like the Spock and Chicago cases are not the only instrument for suppression. The potential uses of intelligence to curtail protest demonstrations or even strike at their leadership was shown by the events surrounding the November, 1969, march on Washington. With computers storing all forms of data and teletype networks distributing them across the country, the details about an individual or group's lawful political activity can be retrieved so easily that the distinction between legal and illegal conduct may be lost. For years the F.B.I. has asserted that its reports are highly confidential and that access to them is strictly limited. One important practical bar to widespread circulation of these reports was the sheer physical problem of making copies and summaries by hand. Computers, teletypes, and duplicating facilities remove that barrier and thus threaten the traditional secrecy that kept intelligence reports in the hands of only those few top executives whose knowledge of their contents was absolutely necessary.

In view of these potential dangers, what is the most promising route for bringing under control the unbridled discretion that has been vested in domestic intelligence agencies? Professor Kenneth Culp Davis has suggested one answer. While neither judges nor legislators may have the expertise to do more than establish a broad framework for administrative discretion, they can and should compel executive officials themselves "to develop and to make known the needed confinement of discretionary power through standards, principles, and rules."[31] The Justice Department should take the lead in preparing careful guidelines for federal intelligence operations and in persuading states and cities to follow similar, if not more stringent, standards. If the Attorney General fails to do so, then Congress and the courts must require that he come up with rules that address all the potential abuses of intelligence gathering.

The Department's record of disclosure to Congress has thus far been poor. The Office of Management Support in the Administrative Division says that it provides technical assistance to the Criminal and Internal Security Divisions in their efforts "to develop, implement and expand intelligence data systems." While the Office recognizes "the need for effective quality reviews of output. . .to assure accuracy, proper format, and correct distribution of output reports and tabulations," there is no indication of how this is achieved. The only mention of the Civil Disturbance Group in the Department's 1970 appropriations hearings appeared in the Criminal Division's report. The Assistant Attorney General assigned two staff assistants "to the Attorney General's Interdivisional Information Center which is responsible for gathering facts from sources within and without the Department relating to activities which are or may be related to planning for or participating in civil disturbances." A substantial amount of the Internal Security Division's work was concerned "with the activities of some of the New Left groups and black militant organizations." There was no explanation of how these separate agencies coordinated their intelligence analysis with each other or with the F.B.I.

J. Edgar Hoover's report was equally enlightening. The F.B.I. maintained "wide coverage" of subversive groups, organizations, and movements "to follow on their activities and changing tactics." Hoover merely hinted at the nature of his Bureau's operations: "In spite of the proliferation of these organizations, our informant coverage at all levels has been of great value and assistance in enabling us to keep abreast of our investigative responsibilities. Through our coverage, information is continually developed concerning matters within the jurisdiction of other agencies. This information is promptly referred to them and better enables these other agencies to meet their individual responsibilities." Elsewhere, Hoover described the expansion of the F.B.I.'s activity in recent years: "Civil rights work, as well as that required to keep abreast of racial disturbances, collect racial intelligence and disseminate it to interested civil authorities, and follow the activities of militant and hate groups, called for the participation of an average of 1,974 F.B.I. agents each month during the fiscal year 1969. This compares with a monthly average of 1,678 in 1968 and 1,246 in 1967. A substantial requirement upon our investigative resources for this kind of work can be expected for as long as racial struggles persist in our Nation."[32] If their 1970 appropriations testimony is any indication, neither the Department nor the F.B.I. has given Congress an adequate picture of its intelligence activity.

While no detailed set of rules can be drafted without full knowledge of intelligence operations, several general requirements may be laid down. Each agency must have clear legislative authorization for its intelligence program so that there is a basis for periodic review to insure that the lawmakers' intentions are being carried out. Congress especially should not only replace vague Presidential directives with a statutory framework, but also devote committee resources to regular inquiry into domestic intelligence activity. This means probing more deeply into the work of agencies like the F.B.I., the Secret Service, and military intelligence divisions. Having assumed a coordinating role among domestic intelligence agencies, the Justice Department should act as the administrative arm of Congress in controlling the details of intelligence operations. The Attorney General can no longer make decisions case-by-case, as he does when he approves electronic surveillance. Instead, he needs to regulate patterns of behavior with a series of procedures that assign responsibility clearly.

These procedures should address all the potential abuses of intelligence gathering, both its invasions of privacy and its chilling effects on free speech. There must be standards to determine (1) which federal agencies are authorized to engage in intelligence activity, (2) what kinds of information they are and are not to collect, (3) what individuals or groups they may and may not place under surveillance, (4) what techniques of surveillance are proper and improper under specified conditions, and (5) who has access to intelligence reports and who is barred from seeing them. The Attorney General's general guidelines for the entire executive branch and his advice to state and local governments should be made public, while detailed rules and operating procedures should be made known to Congress.

Both Congress and the Justice Department have to make another fundamental decision. Do they wish to authorize the maintenance of comprehensive centralized dossiers on certain persons and groups, gathering all available information about them into a single, readily available, and computerized source? Because of its authoritarian implications, this policy should be the subject of open public debate if it is to be adopted. There is a possibility that it may emerge silently, after a series of unpublicized steps, without full understanding of its potential danger to political liberty. In the absence of a Congressional policy decision in favor of a national intelligence bank, the Justice Department ought to make certain that intelligence activity is completely decentralized. Legitimate data collection is properly fragmented among a variety of agencies; and no agency should exceed the scope of its limited authority.

In summary, increased domestic intelligence surveillance during the late 1960's has imposed a special obligation on Congress and the Justice Department. Since the Attorney General used his influence to inspire these programs, he now must control and when possible dismantle the vast apparatus for domestic political surveillance. While the Department's Interdivisional Intelligence Unit has obtained more sources of information, federal agencies and local police have gained greater opportunities to harass unpopular groups. As created under Ramsey Clark's leadership and expanded by John Mitchell, a domestic intelligence program seemed the necessary response to civil disorder and radical protest. While both Attorneys General may have hoped to limit the scope and uses of intelligence operations, their policy was not accompanied by assurance against misuse or abuse of that power: "Evil men are rarely given power; they take it over from better men to whom it had been entrusted."[33] There can be no doubt that a shapeless and all-embracing domestic intelligence structure can serve as a dangerous instrument of political intimidation and coercion in the hands of those so inclined.

6

CONCLUSION: FEDERAL JUSTICE—

ADVANTAGES AND RISKS

Greater centralization of law enforcement policy-making has made the Justice Department a crucial agency for preserving the integrity of legal processes and the vitality of political liberty. In the years ahead the decisions of the Attorney General and his subordinates will affect the character of criminal justice at all levels. They already play a major role in determining whether police and prosecutors, legislators, lawyers, and judges work together or become divided by political conflicts that sap their energies. The Attorney General's attitudes also help set the terms for public debate over how best to reconcile values of effectiveness and fairness in the administration of justice. With the capacity to monitor all forms of political activity, the Justice Department is now one of the most powerful domestic agencies of the national government.

Why did the Department assume such an influential role in the legal system? The narrative of the way its policies toward criminal justice and domestic unrest evolved over a decade suggests several reasons. Traditionally, law enforcement authority has been dispersed among cities, states, and a variety of federal agencies. State and local financial resources were too limited, however, to support the development of modern police techniques, prison and probation reforms, judicial reorganization, or the employment of more highly qualified personnel. Modernization was possible only with a massive infusion of federal funds. In addition, the uneven application of federal constitutional principles in the states, combined with pervasive discrimination against racial minorities and the poor, required the imposition of national standards by the Supreme Court. When the court's rulings aroused controversy, the Attorney General was pulled into the debate over the impact of decisions like Escobedo and Miranda. The inadequacy of local resources and the Warren Court's initiatives made criminal justice a national issue by 1965.

Urban riots, black militancy, and antiwar dissent in the late 1960's expanded law enforcement concerns beyond ordinary crime to include a new range of problems. When local police responded to civil unrest and protest demonstrations with heavy-handed and ill-prepared measures that inflamed rather than contained disorders, strong federal leadership was demanded to promote more reasonable methods of control. After the dispatch of federal troops to Detroit and the march on the Pentagon in 1967, Department executives believed extensive domestic intelligence operations were required to predict disorders and cope with them effectively. The reports of the President's crime commission and the Kerner commisison further emphasized the need for national law enforcement policies. All these pressures culminated in Congressional enactment of the Crime Control Act and the antiriot law in 1968, providing partial legislative sanction for the Justice Department's greater powers.

In light of the Department's expanding activity, what are the possible consequences of more centralized law enforcement policy-making, both for its own operations and for the entire legal system? Chapter Five examined the problems created by domestic intelligence surveillance, but it is necessary to look more broadly at the Department's other roles. There are important advantages and perhaps more significant disadvantages to the nationalization of criminal justice.

As a national agency the Justice Department may be more likely than states or cities to respect procedural fairness and individual rights. Seeing the legal system as a whole, the Attorney General has a breadth of view that tends to lead him away from particularistic impulses. From his perspective, as from the Supreme Court's, it is easier to see the law as the embodiment of the highest ideals in the Anglo-American constitutional tradition. Federal executives are closely associated with leaders of the legal profession and consult bar groups like the A.B.A. and the American Law Institute. Organized defenders of civil rights and liberties can focus their limited resources on the Attorney General with greater hopes of influencing a single federal decision than a variety of state or local policies. Paying better salaries, attracting more talented lawyers who handle a rich variety of cases which forces them to take more considerations and precedents into account, the Justice Department has higher prestige than any other law enforcement agency.

Thus a system of federal rather than local justice might be an effective remedy for overcoming ingrained regional prejudices and limiting the abuse of discretion by local officials. The scope of national authority could lead to the development of clear rules that would be conducive to an atmosphere of liberty and procedural due process. The Department of Justice is potentially more likely to respect and espouse the values of legality— impartiality, consistency, and generality of application. Observing what Lon L. Fuller calls "the internal morality of law," it can insure that there are rules, that they are made known, and that they are observed in practice by those charged with their administration.[1] While independent state jurisdictions will remain, the Department's powers over the distribution of federal money could enforce higher standards of performance; and its authority to investigate violations of due process under the civil rights statutes could be used to influence police practices.

As long as ordinary criminal law enforcement remained in the hands of local officials, the Department would rely primarily on its leadership role, setting an example and using techniques of persuasion. Its sponsorship of commissions and conferences brings expert professional advice to the attention of cities and states, while the Attorney General's own words and deeds provide a model for others to emulate. His legislative proposals to Congress may influence states to adopt similar measures. Since its local representatives, the United States Attorneys and F.B.I. field offices, maintain regular contacts with state prosecutors and local police, the Department can encourage better law enforcement through these day-to-day working relationships. Most important of all, the Attorney General's access to the national news media gives him the chance to inform the public about criminal justice problems with balance and detachment from local issues. All these channels of influence can be used to insure more consistent respect for standards of fairness and equality of treatment.

The more functions it takes on, the more likely the Department is to reconcile different points of view. Because it includes both a Criminal Division and a Civil Rights Division, an F.B.I. and a Community Relations Service, the Attorney General is forced to consider a variety of opinions from his own subordinates. Even his political calculations as an agent of the President or in dealing with Congress create a healthy tension among competing interpretations of the Administration's interests. No Attorney General is likely to impose a single, monolithic policy on the Department. In sum, the potential advantages of greater Justice Department influence result from its own institutional character as a national agency with high prestige and broad perspective, from its opportunity to establish general rules and bring about their uniform application, and from its leadership role as a source of practical guidance for other law enforcement agencies.

Despite these apparent benefits, there are considerable risks in concentrating power in the hands of a federal department. Perhaps the best way to explain the disadvantages of increased centralization is by looking at the political forces which resulted in the Attorney General's policies during the 1960's. Among the most influential were pressures from the White House, from electoral politics, and from Congressional perceptions of public opinion. These forces not only insured that no uniform policy would dominate the Department, but they also made it frequently impossible for the Attorney General to have any coherent impact on the problems of criminal justice. Constantly conflicting impulses virtually disintegrated federal policy, thus negating the theoretical advantages of having national standards applied uniformly and of providing useful advice to local law enforcement agencies.

Presidential electoral politics probably affected the Department more decisively than any other factor. During the year before an election the Attorney General was the object of vigorous attack from the opposition party. In 1964 this encouraged Robert Kennedy to commit the Administration to a national crime control program as an answer to Senator Goldwater's charges. Four years later Richard Nixon's use of the law and order issue helped polarize Congress along party lines, reducing Ramsey Clark's influence over crime legislation. The consequences of campaign commitments were even more pronounced, most visibly in 1969 when the Nixon Administration had to carry out its pledges to take a firm stand against radicals and to oppose the Warren Court's decisions. While some of these measures would have been taken anyway, electoral politics made them more necessary.

Many Congressmen and local officials found it easier to win popular support by blaming black militants and antiwar protesters for disorders. Increasing reported crime rates did not fully account for rising hostility to the courts. Instead, when political candidates focused on the Supreme Court as a convenient target, they shifted public attention away from fundamental problems of inadequate resources and out-dated techniques for law enforcement. The causes of crime and unrest were complex; but an effective appeal to the electorate seemed to require clear, simple answers. Thus the climate of election campaigns set the frame of reference for both public and official perceptions of law enforcement issues, limiting the Justice Department's options and pulling it in dfferent directions. Congressional sensitivity to opportunities for partisan advantage and for ways to satisfy constituency opinion prevented the Department from securing legislation it wanted and imposed new burdens under laws like the antiriot act.

Practically nothing upset the coherence and stability of Department policy more than the transition from one Administration to the next. Except for the F.B.I. and the Internal Security Division, every agency within the Department saw a change in its executive leadership as new men, unfamiliar with past operations and experience, took over direction of their programs. New United States Attorneys were appointed in every part of the country. Even where a holdover like Cecil Poole remained in office for a time, his authority over sensitive cases was sharply limited. The instability of the transition period increased the possibility for decisions, such as the Chicago conspiracy prosecution and creation of the Panther task force, which later proved to have far-reaching unanticipated consequences. The Department had difficulty maintaining uniform rules and exercising constructive influence when its policies were subject to major revision after a new President took office. Yet such changes were inherent in a structure of national government that gives the President the power to replace most top executives. Transition problems would have been worse if the Department was a cohesive organization whose new executives had the power to change all its policies. Instead, revisions were made gradually, step by step, largely in response to events and seldom with comprehensive goals in mind.

Electoral politics and transition were not the only sources of instability. Because of pressures from Congress or other executive agencies, the Attorney General occasionally took symbolic actions that were inconsistent with basic policies in order to reduce criticism. The Spock case was one example, for it did not inaugurate a program of criminal prosecution against other leaders of the draft resistance movement. If he did prepare a set of program objectives as a guide to better integrated policymaking in less controversial areas, other aspects of the Attorney General's program could not be so readily planned. A President with a deep aversion to wiretapping, a Congressional committee determined to change the law, a Supreme Court majority devoted to innovation—all constrained his ability to pursue his goals systematically. In short, Justice Department policy was often unpredictable, not because the Attorney General wanted it that way, but because political pressures created an environment of uncertainty.

The Department's instability in the face of conflicting demands is one of its most serious disadvantages as a source of national leadership. It is probably unreasonable to expect that the Attorney General, standing at the center of national politics and constantly buffeted by criticism, can provide effective direction for law enforcement throughout the country as long as law and order remains one of the most controversial public issues. Instead of looking to it for solutions to the problems of criminal justice, the public and the legal community must recognize that the Department should play only a limited role in the process of developing and implementing law enforcement policy. As a source of federal financial aid to state and local criminal justice systems, it is indispensable. Its technical assistance to local police, apart from intelligence surveillance programs, poses few difficulties.[2] But the maintenance of public order must continue to be primarily the responsibility of cities and states. Where federal and local functions may overlap, the distinction between their separate spheres should remain; and federal statutes need not be extended to cover offenses under state law without a compelling national interest. While at times the Department has encouraged professional law enforcement administration, better police-community relations, and adherence to due process of law, the best safeguard against the volatility of American national politics is the independence of local criminal justice from total federal domination.

If the Justice Department fully satisfied its highest aspirations to professional detachment, adopted and followed uniform rules, and offered consistent policy guidance and leadership, its growing influence might be valuable for the legal system. The narrative of Department actions in the preceding chapters indicates, however, that it falls considerably short of these standards. Neither the Attorney General's own decisions nor his attempts to influence others brought coherence to law enforcement policy. Change and instability, reform and counter-reform persisted as the pattern of federal policy development. The dramatic conflicts of the 1960's between the

Court and Congress, between police and radicals, between Ramsey Clark and John Mitchell, magnified the Department's position far beyond its proper role as one institution among many in the legal system.

The nationalization of criminal justice risks not only unstable leadership, but also a shift in the balance between the Supreme Court and Congress. Criticism of the Court has often in the past led new Justices to pause or even retreat after a period of assertion of judicial power. More recently, however, Congress has gone beyond criticism and has attempted to overrule Court decisions by statute. If Congress continues exercising its authority under the Fourteenth Amendment to establish rules for criminal due process, the chances for temporary emotions or partisan politics to determine constitutional standards will increase. Preoccupied with reforming the administration of criminal justice across the country, Nicholas Katzenbach failed to defend the Supreme Court effectively. John Mitchell's willingness to see legislative reversal of its rulings contributed further to the Court's decline. The outcome could be the substitution of Congressional for judicial power rather than a return to state responsibility for criminal due process.

Finally, the dangers in its efforts to monitor and control political activity outweigh the Justice Department's contributions to crime control. Few men have thought more deeply about this threat than Robert H. Jackson, whose experiences as Attorney General, as war crimes prosecutor, and as Supreme Court Justice led him to write in 1954, "I cannot say that our country could have no central police without becoming totalitarian, but I can say with great conviction that it cannot become totalitarian without a centralized national police. . . .All that is necessary is to have a national police competent to investigate all manner of offenses, and then, in the parlance of the street, it will have enough on enough people, even if it does not elect to prosecute them, so that it will find no opposition to its policies. Even those who are supposed to supervise it are likely to fear it. I believe that the safeguard of our liberty lies in limiting any national policing or investigative organization, first of all to a small number of strictly federal offenses, and secondly to nonpolitical ones. The fact that we may have confidence in the administration of a federal investigative agency under its existing head does not mean that it may not revert again to the days when the Department of Justice was headed by men to whom the investigative power was a weapon to be used for their own purposes."[3]

The answers to national problems of crime and disorder need not be found in greater federal law enforcement power. With financial assistance from Congress, each state and municipal criminal justice system can be revitalized, developing its own expertise and relying less on the Justice Department. As the land grant colleges in the nineteenth century supported modernization of American agriculture, so should a variety of similar educational and research programs in the administration of justice create the skills necessary for more effective police, prosecutors, courts, and corrections. Organized groups and lawyers concerned about the protection of civil liberties ought to concentrate their efforts on working with state and local law enforcement agencies. By improving the quality of these lower levels of the legal system, those who fear repression will provide the most practical barrier to the trend toward national control of criminal justice.

If political liberty is to be firmly established in the long run, the Justice Department must give up its functions under statutes that proscribe essentially political offenses. Laws like the Smith Act and the antiriot act, which give the F.B.I. jurisdiction to investigate advocacy instead of conduct, are the cruical targets for elimination. While the courts may limit their usefulness as a basis for prosecution, such laws remain the foundation for federal surveillance of political activity and for potential abuse in periods of high public emotion. Likewise, the doctrine of conspiracy should have no place in the enforcement of such laws because of its susceptibility to distortion into an instrument to serve the political interests of an Administration. The protection of national security requires measures to counter acts of espionage by foreign governments, not the suppression of competing ideologies or political movements. An opportunity was lost in the calmer years of the early 1960's to eliminate the remnants of McCarthyism; that chance should not be missed again if a period of confidence follows the present turmoil.

There is little prospect that the Justice Department will soon return to a more modest role in the legal system. The momentum of events in the 1960's will carry over for years to come. But the Department's current visibility should not disguise the alternatives available to more centralized law enforcement. Cities and states are equally capable of reasserting their primacy if given sufficient resources and skills. From the New Deal to the Great Society, progressive reform in American politics has envisioned a strong national government as the answer to domestic needs. Federal rather than state action was required to insure a stable economy, to promote public health, education, and welfare, and to combat racial discrimination. Of all the functions of government, however, criminal law enforcement is both the most necessary and the most dangerous. While the Supreme Court and the Attorney General encouraged reforms to improve the effectiveness and fairness of criminal justice, their leadership carried with it the risk of national domination. That risk challenges the legal system to preserve and invigorate its traditionally decentralized features as a defense against repression.

NOTES

1. Introduction: The Department of Justice

1. Jerome H. Skolnick, *The Politics of Protest* (New York: Ballantine Books, 1969), p. 278.

2. Homer Cummings and Carl McFarland, *Federal Justice: Chapters in the History of Justice and the Federal Executive* (New York: Macmillan, 1937), p. 495.

3. Ibid., p. 498.

4. Francis Biddle, *In Brief Authority* (Garden City: Doubleday, 1962), p. 254; Hearings before the Special Subcommittee to Investigate the Department of Justice, House Committee on the Judiciary, Part I, 82d Cong., 2nd Sess. (1952), p. 5.

5. Peters v. Hobby, 349 U.S. 331 (1955); Gutknecht v. United States, 90 Sup. Ct. 506 (1970).

6. James Eisenstein, "Counsel for the United States: An Empirical Analysis of the Office of the Office of United States Attorney," A Dissertation Presented to the Faculty of the Graduate School of Yale University (1968), p. IV-1.

7. 1954 Annual Report of the Attorney General of the United States (Washington: United States Department of Justice, 1954), p. 3; Investigation of the Department of Justice, Report to the House Committee on the Judiciary, H.R. 1079, 83d Cong., 1st Sess. (1953).

8. Eisenstein, op. cit., p. IV-19.

9. 1954 Annual Report, op. cit., p. 2; Investigation, op. cit., p. 132.

10. Robert H. Jackson, "The Federal Prosecutor," Journal of the American Judicature Society 24:18 (June, 1940).

11. "Clearance by Department of Justice of Certain F.B.I. Investigations," Memo for Peyton Ford, The Assistant to the Attorney General, 1948, in Department of Justice File 44-03-2. For a discussion of investigative clearance in civil rights cases, see John T. Elliff, "The United States Department of Justice and Individual Rights, 1937-1962," A Dissertation presented to the Faculty of the Graduate School of Harvard University (1968).

12. Alpheus T. Mason, *Harlan Fiske Stone: Pillar of the Law* (New York: Viking Press, 1956), p. 149; Max Freedman, *Roosevelt and Frankfurter: Their Correspondence,* 1928-1945 (Boston: Little, Brown, 1967), p. 129.

13. Biddle, op. cit., p. 259.

14. Nicholas deB. Katzenbach, "Introduction" to Richard Harris, *The Fear of Crime* (New York: Praeger, 1969), pp. 5-6.

2. Criminal Justice

1. National Commission on Law Observance and Enforcement, *Report on Lawlessness in Law Enforcement* (Washington: U.S. Government Printing Office, 1931); Roscoe Pound and Felix Frankfurter, *Criminal Justice in Cleveland* (The Cleveland Foundation, 1922).

2. Powell v. Alabama, 287 U.S. 45 (1932); Moore v. Dempsey, 261 U.S. 86 (1923); Brown v. Mississippi, 297 U.S. 278 (1936).

3. 18 U.S.C. 241 and 242; see Robert K. Carr, *Federal Protection of Civil Rights: Quest for a Sword* (Ithaca: Cornell University Press, 1947).

4. Screws v. United States, 325 U.S. 91 (1945).

5. Betts v. Brady, 316 U.S. 455 (1942).

6. E.g., Crooker v. California, 357 U.S. 433 (1958).

7. Wolf v. Colorado, 338 U.S. 25 (1949).

8. Mallory v. United States, 354 U.S. 449 (1957).

9. Walter F. Murphy, *Congress and the Court* (Chicago: University of Chicago Press, 1962).

10. See appendix to Elkins v. United States, 364 U.S. 206, 224 (1960).

11. Mapp v. Ohio, 367 U.S. 643, 652 (1961).

12. 367 U.S. 643, 659-660.

13. 367 U.S. 643, 680-681.

14. United States Commission on Civil Rights, *1961 Report: Justice,* Book 5 (Washington: U.S. Government Printing Office, 1961), pp. 109-111.

15. Olmstead v. United States, 227 U.S. 438 (1928).

16. Herbert Brownell, "The Public Security and Wiretapping," Cornell Law Quarterly, 39:195 (1954).

17. Nardone v. United States, 302 U.S. 379 (1937); Benanti v. United States, 355 U.S. 96 (1957).

18. Schwartz v. Texas, 344 U.S. 199 (1952).

19. *Crime and Justice in America*, 2nd Ed. (Washington: Congressional Quarterly Service, 1968), p. 45.

20. New York Times, February 2, 1962.

21. Washington Post, April 5, 1962; May 11, 1962.

22. Archibald Cox, *The Warren Court: Constitutional Decision as an Instrument of Reform* (Cambridge: Harvard University Press, 1968), p. 81.

23. Report of the Attorney General's Committee on Poverty and the Administration of Federal Criminal Justice (Washington, 1963), pp. 10-11.

24. 18 U.S.C.A. 3006A. See Robert F. Kennedy, "The Department of Justice and the Indigent Accused," Journal of the American Judicature Society, 47:182 (January, 1964).

25. Arnold S. Trebach, "New England Defender Systems," Journal of the American Judicature Society, 47:170 (January, 1964).

26. Gideon v. Wainwright, 372 U.S. 335 (1963).

27. Ronald Goldfarb, *Ransom: A Critique of the American Bail System* (New York: Harper & Row, 1965).

28. Daniel J. Freed and Patricia M. Wald, *Bail in the United States: 1964* (Washington: National Conference on Bail and Criminal Justice, May, 1964), p. 21.

29. Stack v. Boyle, 342 U.S. 1 (1951). See *The Bail Reform Act: An Analysis of Proposed Amendments and an Alternative* (Washington: American Enterprise Institute, 1969).

30. A. Kenneth Pye, "The Warren Court and Criminal Procedure," Michigan Law Review, 67:249 (1968).

31. Reynolds v Sims, 377 U.S. 533 (1964).

32. Adamson v. California, 332 U.S. 46 (1947).

33. Malloy v. Hogan, 378 U.S. 1, 10-11 (1964).

34. 378 U.S. 1, footnote 8.

35. 378 U.S. 1, 7-8.

36. Briefs for the A.C.L.U. as amicus curiae and for the State of Illinois in Livingston Hall, et al., *Modern Criminal Procedure,* 3rd Edition (St. Paul: West Publishing Co., 1969), pp. 484-489.

37. Escobedo v. Illinois, 378 U.S. 478, 488-490, 498-499 (1964).

38. Livingston Hall and Yale Kamisar, *Modern Criminal Procedure,* 2nd Edition (St. Paul: West Publishing Co., 1966), p. 392.

39. Hall, op. cit., p. 486.

40. 378 U.S. 478, 498-99.

41. New York Times, July 22, 1964.

42. "Standards for Criminal Justice," American Bar Association Journal, 51:246 (March, 1965).

43. Lewis F. Powell, Jr., "An Urgent Need: More Effective Criminal Justice," American Bar Association Journal 51:437 (May, 1965).

44. Robert F. Kennedy, *The Pursuit of Justice,* edited by Theodore J. Lowi (New York: Harper & Row, 1964), pp. 84-86.

45. Public Law 89-197, September 22, 1965.

46. J. Edward Lumbard, "New Standards for Criminal Justice," American Bar Association Journal 52:431 (May, 1966).

47. New York Times, May 14, 1965; August 1, 1965.

48. J. Skelly Wright, "Crime in the Streets and the New McCarthyism," New Republic (October 9, 1965), p. 10.

49. New York Times, December 3, 1964.

50. Herbert L. Packer, "Policing the Police: Nine Men Are Not Enough," New Republic (September 4, 1965), p. 17.

51. Paul M. Bator and James Vorenberg, "Arrest, Detention, Interrogation and the Right to Counsel: Basic Problems and Possible Legislative Solutions," Columbia Law Review, 66:62 (1966).

52. The Bazelon-Katzenbach letters are reprinted in Kentucky Law Journal 54:486 (1966).

53. New York Times, November 20, 1965.

54. Yale Kamisar, "Has the Court Left the Attorney General Behind?" Kentucky Law Journal, 54:464 (1966).

55. Quoted in Yale Kamisar, "When the Cops Were Not 'Handcuffed,' " New York Times Magazine, November 7, 1965.

56. New York Times, May 22, 1965.

57. New York Times, May 18, 1966.

58. New York Times, January 1, 1966.

59. James Vorenberg, "The War on Crime," Boston Globe, July 31, 1966.

60. Exerpts from oral arguments in Hall, op. cit., p. 503.

61. Ibid., pp. 497, 500-501.

62. Miranda v. Arizona, 384 U.S. 436, 476, 469-470 (1966).

63. New York Times, October 2, 1966.

64. 384 U.S. 436, 474.

65. Medalie, et al., "Custodial Police Interrogation in Our Nation's Capital: The Attempt to Implement Miranda," Michigan Law Review, 66:1347 (1968).

66. President's Commission on Law Enforcement and Administration of Justice, *The Challenge of Crime in a Free Society* (Washington, U.S. Government Printing Office, 1967), p. 307.

67. Ibid., p. 94.

68. Washington Post, August 6, 1966; August 7, 1966.

69. New York Times, October 2, 1966; Walter V. Schaefer, *The Suspect and Society* (Evanston: Northwestern University Press, 1967).

70. New York Times, February 23, 1967.

71. Washington Post, October 19, 1966.

72. Washington Post, November 14, 1966.

73. Washington Post, January 1, 1967.

74. New York Times, February 7, 1967.

75. Silverman v. United States, 365 U.S. 505 (1961).

76. Alan Westin, *Privacy and Freedom* (New York: Atheneum, 1967), pp. 195-210.

77. New York Times, March 23, 1966.

78. Washington Post, October 7, 1966.

79. Washington Post, November 23, 1966.

80. President's Commission on Law Enforcement and Administration of Justice, *Task Force Report: Organized Crime* (Washington: U.S. Government Printing Office, 1967), p. 80.

81. New York Times, January 20, 1967.

82. *The Challenge of Crime,* op. cit., p. 203.

83. New York Times, March 6, 1967; March 11, 1967; March 16, 1967.

84. See David W. Abbott, et al., *Police, Politics and Race: The New York City Referendum on Civilian Review* (Cambridge: Joint Center for Urban Studies, 1969).

85. President's Commission on Law Enforcement and Administration of Justice, *Task Force Report: Crime and Its Impact* (Washington: U.S. Government Printing Office, 1967), pp. 85, 92-93.

86. Richard Harris, *The Fear of Crime* (New York: Praeger, 1969), pp. 38-39.

87. New York Times, March 29, 1967; Washington Post, March 29, 1967.

88. New York Times, May 1, 1967; Washington Post, April 27, 1967.

89. New York Times, May 14, 1967; May 19, 1967.

90. Richard Harris, *Justice: The Crisis of Law, Order, and Freedom in America* (New York: Dutton, 1970), pp. 16-25.

91. *The Challenge of Crime,* op. cit., Chapter 2.

92. Berger v. New York, 388 U.S. 41 (1967).

93. New York Times, July 7, 1967.

94. Washington Post, July 21, 1967; July 23, 1967.

95. New York Times, July 25, 1967.

96. Westin, op. cit., pp. 388-397.

97. Berger v. New York, 388 U.S. 41, 115-116 (1967).

98. Editorial, Washington Evening Star, July 12, 1967.

99. Wade v. United States, 388 U.S. 218 (1967).

100. New York Times, February 28, 1968; March 3, 1968.

101. Katz v. United States, 389 U.S. 347 (1967).

102. See Herman Schwartz, "The Legitimation of Electronic Eavesdropping: The Politics of 'Law and Order,'" Michigan Law Review, 67:455 (1969).

103. New York Times, March 14, 1968.

104. New York Times, May 9, 1968.

105. New York Times, April 27, 1968.

106. New York Times, May 18, 1968; May 22, 1968. See Harris, *The Fear of Crime,* op. cit.

107. New York Times, June 20, 1968.

108. Letter to the Editor, New York Times, June 16, 1968.

109. New York Times, September 20, 1968.

110. New York Times, January 15, 1969; February 12, 1969.

111. New York Times, July 15, 1969.

112. New York Times, December 16, 1968.

113. New York Times, August 21, 1969.

114. Schwartz, op. cit.

115. Washington Post, November 4, 1969.

116. New York Times, November 2, 1969.

117. Press Release, Department of Justice, August 13, 1969.

118. New York Times, November 10, 1968; November 17, 1968.

119. New York Times, February 16, 1969.

120. New York Times, March 1, 1969; Washington Post, May 1, 1969.

121. New York Times, April 18, 1969.

122. *Task Force Report: Organized Crime,* op. cit., p. 100.

123. Katzenbach v. Morgan, 384 U.S. 641, footnote 10 (1966). See Archibald Cox, "Constitutional Adjudication and the Promotion of Human Rights," Harvard Law Review, 80:91 (1966).

124. Schaefer, op. cit.

125. Washington Post, August 13, 1967; Julius Duscha, "Chief Justice Burger," New York Times Magazine, October 5, 1969.

126. Harris, Justice, op. cit., pp. 235-236.

127. New York Times, August 1, 1969; Washington Post, August 1, 1969.

128. Fred P. Graham, New York Times, August 3, 1969.

129. Washington Post, August 13, 1969.

130. Press Release, Department of Justice, October 6, 1969.

131. Press Release, Department of Justice, January 20, 1968.

132. Skolnick, op. cit., pp. 279-289; New York Times, May 18, 1969.

133. New York Times, January 30, 1969; Harry I. Subin of the Vera Institute, quoted in New York Times, February 17, 1968. See Goldfarb, op. cit., pp. 127-128.

134. Carlson v. Landon, 342 U.S. 524, 545-546 (1952). See *The Bail Reform Act,* op. cit.

135. New York Times, July 15, 1969; August 17, 1969; September 16, 1969.

136. 374 U.S. 23, 40 (1963).

137. New York Times, April 24, 1969.

138. Washington Post, August 26, 1969; August 19, 1969; Press Release, Department of Justice, June 3, 1969.

139. Washington Post, November 4, 1969.

140. New York Post, June 5, 1969; Press Release, Department of Justice, June 3, 1969.

141. Alderman v. United States, 394 U.S. 165 (1969).

142. Public Law 91-452, 91st Cong., October 15, 1970. See Nardone v. United States, 308 U.S. 338 (1939).

3. Black Militancy

1. 1964 Annual Report of the Attorney General (Washington: U.S. Department of Justice, 1964), p. 375.

2. New York Times, July 22, 1964; July 25, 1964.

3. New York Times, July 20, 1964; July 25, 1964; July 27, 1964; September 27, 1964; November 30, 1965.

4. New York Times, September 27, 1964.

5. Malcolm X (with Alex Haley), *Autobiography* (New York: Grove Press, 1965), pp. 419-420.

6. Washington Post, February 17, 1965; 1965 Annual Report, pp. 360, 363.

7. Epton v. New York, 390 U.S. 29 (1968).

8. Yates v. United States, 354 U.S. 298 (1957); Scales v. United States, 367 U.S. 203 (1961).

9. Epton v. New York, 390 U.S. 29, 33-34.

10. See Hirabayashi v. United States, 320 U.S. 81; Lanza v. New York, 370 U.S. 139.

11. 390 U.S. 29, 33-35.

12. 1965 Annual Report, pp. 358, 363.

13. Washington Post, June 6, 1969.

14. Robert Conot, *Rivers of Blood, Years of Darkness* (New York: Bantam, 1967), p. 429.

15. Stokely Carmichael and Charles V. Hamilton, *Black Power: The Politics of Liberation in America* (New York: Vintage, 1967), pp. 96-120.

16. New York Times, July 21, 1966; Washington Post, August 18, 1966; 1966 Annual Report, p. 395.

17. New York Times, July 31, 1966; Washington Post, August 10, 1966.

18. New York Times, September 10, 1966; Washington Post, October 4, 1966.

19. Washington Post, October 6, 1966; New York Times, October 6, 1966.

20. New York Times, May 17, 1967; *Revolution in Civil Rights,* 4th Edition (Washington: Congressional Quarterly Service, 1968), p. 13.

21. New York Times, June 23, 1967.

22. Washington Post, September 20, 1967.

23. New York Times, April 2, 1969.

24. New York Times, June 16, 1968; October 4, 1968.

25. 1967 Annual Report, p. 395; New York Times, June 1, 1967.

26. President's Commission on Law Enforcement and Administration of Justice, *The Challenge of Crime in a Free Society* (Washington: U.S. Government Printing Office, 1967), pp. 118-119.

27. President's Commission of Law Enforcement and Administration of Justice, *Task Force Report: The Police* (Washington: U.S. Government Printing Office, 1967), p. 193.

28. Gary Willis, *The Second Civil War* (New York: Signet, 1968), p. 39.

29. *Report of the National Advisory Commission on Civil Disorders* (New York: Bantam Books, 1968), p. 323; New York Times, July 26, 1967; *The Challenge of Crime,* op. cit.

30. Washington Evening Star, July 25, 1967; *Revolution in Civil Rights*, op. cit., p. 82.

31. *Report on Civil Disorders*, op. cit., pp. 534, 538.

32. New York Times, August 2, 1967; August 3, 1967.

33. New York Times, August 3, 1967; January 28, 1968.

34. New York Times, July 27, 1967.

35. New York Times, May 22, 1968.

36. New York Times, May 14, 1968; July 18, 1968; April 4, 1969.

37. New York Times, January 6, 1968.

38. Press Release, Department of Justice, January 20, 1968.

39. *Report on Civil Disorders*, op. cit., pp. 487, 490; New York Times, March 2, 1968.

40. Christopher H. Pyle, "CONUS Intelligence: The Army Watches Civilian Politics," Washington Monthly, January, 1970.

41. *Report on Civil Disorders*, op. cit., pp. 202-206.

42. Ibid., p. 397.

43. Ibid., pp. 323, 343, 524.

44. New York Times, February 8, 1968. The Justice Department's proposed antiriot bill included the following definitions: "(B) A riot is a public disturbance involving an assemblage of twenty or more persons, which by tumultuous and violent conduct creates grave danger of damage or injury to property or persons. (C) To incite or organize a riot shall mean urging or instigating other persons to riot, where such urging or instigating is done at a time and place and under such circumstances as to further the course of an existing riot or to create an imminent danger of a riot occurring, and shall not mean the mere advocacy of ideas or the mere expression of belief." Congressional Record, 90th Cong., 2nd Sess., Vol. 114, p. 14717.

45. Public Law 90-284, 90th Cong., 2nd Sess., April 11, 1968.

46. New York Times, March 6, 1968; March 7, 1968; *Revolution in Civil Rights*, op. cit., pp. 86-87.

46a. *Time,* May 3, 1971; Testimony of Robert Mardian before the Senate Subcommittee on Constitutional Rights, March 17, 1971.

47. Press Release, Department of Justice, May 2, 1968; New York Times, June 29, 1968; Jerome Skolnick, *The Politics of Protest* (New York: Ballantine, 1969). p. 146.

48. Pyle, op. cit., p. 8.

49. Ben W. Gilbert, et al., *Ten Blocks from the White House: Anatomy of the Washington Riots of 1968* (New York: Praeger, 1968), p. 66.

50. Press Release, Department of Justice, May 2, 1968.

51. Gilbert, op. cit., pp. 61, 64-65.

52. Ibid., pp. 10-11.

53. New York Times, February 3, 1968.

54. New York Times, February 11, 1968; March 4, 1968; March 30, 1968.

55. Press Release, Department of Justice, May 2, 1968.

56. 1968 Annual Report, p. 68.

57. New York Times, May 11, 1968; May 19, 1968.

58. New York Times, May 22, 1968; May 23, 1968; May 24, 1968; May 30, 1968.

59. New York Times, June 2, 1968; June 4, 1968; June 5, 1968.

60. New York Times, June 20, 1968.

61. New York Times, June 21, 1968.

62. Gilbert. op. cit., pp. 201-202.

63. Ibid., pp. 203-207; New York Times, June 25, 1968.

64. New York Times, November 3, 1969.

65. Thomas A. Johnson, New York Times, October 22, 1968; Skolnick, op. cit., p. 174.

66. Louis H. Masotti and Jerome R. Corsi, Civil Violence Research Center, Case Western Reserve University, *Shoot-Out in Cleveland: A Report Submitted to the National Commission on the Causes and Prevention of Violence* (New York, Bantam Books, 1969), p. 117; New York Times, July 26, 1968; July 28, 1968.

67. *Shoot-Out*, op. cit., pp. 26-36.

68. Ibid., pp. 121-126.

69. Gene Marine, *The Black Panthers* (New York: Signet, 1969), pp. 52-56; Skolnick, op. cit., p. 152.

70. Marine, op. cit., p. 133.

71. New York Times, September 10, 1968; Skolnick, op. cit., p. 172.

72. Robert Scheer, "Introduction" to Eldridge Cleaver, *Post-Prison Writings and Speeches* (New York: Vintage, 1969), pp. xviii-xxi.

73. Marine, op. cit., pp. 179-186.

74. New York Times, September 5, 1968; September 11, 1968.

75. New York Times, December 11, 1968; January 21, 1969.

76. New York Times, July 16, 1969.

77. New York Times, March 8, 1968.

78. New York Times, September 16, 1968; September 29, 1968; September 30, 1968.

79. Urban America, Inc., and the Urban Coalition, *One Year Later: An Assessment of the Nation's Response to the Crisis Described by the National Advisory Commission on Civil Disorders* (New York: Praeger, 1969), pp. 115-117.

80. Morris Janowitz, "Patterns of Collective Racial Violence," in Hugh Davis Graham and Ted Robert Gurr, *Violence in America: Historical and Comparative Perspectives* (New York: Signet, 1969), pp. 412-414.

81. New York Times, November 22, 1968.

82. Marine, op. cit., pp. 192-193; Washington Post, June 25, 1969; Wall Street Journal, August 29, 1969.

83. Marine, op. cit., p. 179.

84. Jason Epstein, "The Trial of Bobby Seale," in *Trials of the Resistance* (New York: Vintage, 1970), p. 193.

85. New York Times, December 21, 1969.

86. Washington Post, July 30, 1969.

87. New York Times, August 10, 1969; August 24, 1969.

88. Washington Post, October 23, 1969.

89. 18 U.S.C. 242. See John Hersey, *The Algiers Motel Incident* (New York: Bantam, 1968).

90. Washington Post, October 31, 1969.

91. Memorandum from Director, F.B.I., to Assistant Attorney General Burke Marshall, December 22, 1961, in Department of Justice File No. 144-012.

92. Washington Post, October 29. 1969.

93. Brandenburg v. Ohio, 395 U.S. 444, 447-448 (1969).

94. Watts v. United States, 394 U.S. 705 (1969).

95. New York Times, April 3, 1969.

96. New York Times, April 5, 1969.

97. New York Times, December 14, 1969. See "Department of Justice Appropriations for 1970," Hearings before a Subcommittee of the Committee on Appropriations, House of Representatives, 91st Cong., 1st Sess. (1969).

98. New York Times, April 12, 1969; April 16, 1969.

99. Cited in Murray Kempton and David Shimkin, *Panther 21* (New York: Committee to Defend the Panther 21, 1970).

100. New York Times, April 2, 1969; April 3, 1969.

101. Janowitz, op. cit.

102. New York Times, May 23, 1969.

103. Washington Post, June 25, 1969.

104. Press Release, American Civil Liberties Union, New York, December 24, 1969.

105. New York Times, June 6, 1969.

106. New York Times, August 28, 1969; September 13, 1969; December 2, 1969.

107. New York Times, August 21, 1969; December 14, 1969; Wall Street Journal, August 29, 1969. In 1970 the Department stated, "A special group comprised of five attorneys and a secretary has been created within the General Crimes Section [of the Criminal Division] to keep as currently informed as possible on the activities of militant organizations with a view to criminal prosecutions being instituted wherever the activities of an organization are deemed to constitute a violation of Federal law. Section personnel in this group have conducted grand jury proceedings in California, Pennsylvania, Chicago and Connecticut." Department of Justice Appropriations for 1971, Hearings before a Subcommittee of the Committee on Appropriations, House of Representatives, 91st Cong., 2nd Sess. (1970), p. 379.

108. Washington Post, June 25, 1969.

109. Washington Post, January 14, 1970.

110. Morton Kondracke, Chicago Sun-Times, March 9, 1970.

111. Washington Post, December 2, 1969.
112. New York Times, December 6, 1969.
113. New York Post, December 29, 1969.
114. New York Times, December 4, 1969.
115. Washington Post, January 14, 1970.
116. Epstein, op. cit.
117. Washington Post, February 9, 1970.
118. New York Times, December 5, 1969; December 6, 1969; December 9, 1969; December 10, 1969; Washington Post, December 9, 1969; December 12, 1969.
119. New York Times, December 11, 1969; December 13, 1969; December 16, 1969; December 18, 1969; December 21, 1969.
120. New York Times, December 11, 1969.
121. David Burnham, New York Times, December 14, 1969.
122. New York Post, December 29, 1969; Washington Post, February 9, 1970.
123. Press Release, American Civil Liberties Union, New York, December 24, 1969.
124. Washington Post, January 14, 1970; January 15, 1970.
125. New York Times, December 14, 1969.
126. New York Times, January 26, 1970; February 3, 1970.
127. New York Times, February 11, 1970; February 14, 1970.
128. New York Times, February 5, 1970; February 6, 1970.
129. Washington Post, January 14, 1970; February 9, 1970.

4. Antiwar Dissent

1. Letter from F.B.I. Director Hoover to field offices, September 5, 1936, quoted in Don Whitehead, *The FBI Story* (New York: Pocket Books, 1958), p. 190.
2. 1964 Annual Report of the Attorney General (Washington: U.S. Department of Justice, 1964), pp. 373-376.
3. Jerome Skolnick, *The Politics of Protest* (New York: Ballantine, 1969), Chapter II.
4. New York Times, March 10, 1967.
5. Quoted by James Ridgeway, "Patriots on the Campus," New Republic, March 25, 1967.
6. New York Times, January 7, 1966.
7. See United States v. O'Brien, 391 U.S. 367 (1968).
8. New York Times, October 18, 1965; October 19, 1965.
9. United States v. Seeger, 380 U.S. 163 (1965).
10. Abner Brodie and Harold P. Southerland, "Conscience, The Constitution, and the Supreme Court: The Riddle of *U.S. v Seeger*," Wisconsin Law Review (Spring, 1966), p. 306.

11. New York Times, October 16, 1965; October 17, 1965.

12. New York Times, October 18, 1965; October 19, 1965.

13. New York Times, December 1, 1965; February 8, 1966; February 23, 1966.

14. New York Times, October 19, 1965; October 28, 1965; November 19, 1965; Decmber 23, 1965.

15. New York Times, January 12, 1966.

16. New York Times, December 15, 1965.

17. New York Times, January 7, 1966.

18. 1965 Annual Report, p. 73; 1966 Annual Report, p. 87.

19. New York Times, May 23, 1966.

20. New York Times, April 19, 1966; May 5, 1966.

21. 1966 Annual Report, pp. 279, 282.

22. New York Times, June 4, 1966; July 25, 1966; Washington Post, August 16, 1966.

23. Washington Post, August 18, 1966; Walter Goodman, *The Committee: The Extraordinary Career of the House Committee on Un-American Activities* (Baltimore: Penguin Books, 1969), pp. 476-479.

24. New York Times, August 24, 1966; Washington Post, September 23, 1966.

25. Washington Post, January 18, 1967; New Republic, January 28, 1967.

26. Hartzel v. United States, 322 U.S. 680, 684-685 (1944).

27. Washington Post, November 1, 1966; New York Times, November 3, 1966.

28. 1966 Annual Report, p 389.

29. New York Times, December 22, 1966.

30. Washington Post, January 31, 1967; New York Times, January 31, 1967. See Estep v. United States, 327 U.S. 114 (1946).

31. Wolff v. Selective Service Local Bd. No. 16, 372 F.2d 817 (2 Cir. 1967).

32. O'Brien v. United States, 376 F.2d 538 (1st Cir. 1967); New York Times, April 11, 1967.

33. National Advisory Commission on Selective Service, *In Pursuit of Equality: Who Serves When Not All Serves?* (Washington: U.S. Government Printing Office, 1967), pp. 31-36.

34. Townsend Hoopes, *The Limits of Intervention* (New York: McKay, 1969), p. 51.

35. New York Times, April 1, 1967; New Republic, April 29, 1967; September 16, 1967.

36. Washington Post, April 16, 1967; April 27, 1967; New York Times, April 17, 1967.

37. New York Times, March 7, 1967; James Reston, New York Times, May 5, 1967.

38. Washington Post, April 13, 1967; Civilian Advisory Panel on Military Manpower Procurement, Report to the Committee on Armed Services, House of Representatives, 90th Cong., 1st Sess., February 28, 1967.

39. New York Times, May 6, 1967.

40. Washington Post, August 6, 1967; New York Times, May 7, 1967.

41. Washington Post, May 30, 1967; New York Times, June 21, 1967; Public Law 90-40, 90th Cong., 1st Sess.

42. Washington Post, May 9, 1967; June 15, 1967; New York Times, May 11, 1967.

43. Press Release, American Civil Liberties Union, New York, June, 1967.

44. "A Call to Resist Illegitimate Authority," in Hugo Adam Bedau, ed., *Civil Disobedience: Theory and Practice* (New York: Pegasus, 1969), pp. 162-164.

45. James Ridgeway, "The National Conference of New Politics," New Republic, September 16, 1967.

46. New York Times, November 22, 1967.

47. New York Times, October 18, 1967; November 22, 1967; November 14, 1969.

48. New York Times, November 14, 1967.

49. Norman Mailer, "The Armies of the Night," Harper's, March, 1968, pp. 74, 77.

50. New York Times, January 7, 1969.

51. New York Times, November 3, 1967; November 8, 1967; Charles W. Schiesser and Daniel H. Benson, "The Legality of Reclassification of Selective Service Registrants," American Bar Association Journal 53:149 (February, 1967).

52. New York Times, November 10, 1967; November 11, 1967.

53. New York Times, December 10, 1967; 1967 Annuarl Report, p. 70.

54. New York Times, December 11, 1967; New York Post, December 12, 1967.

55. Jessica Mitford, *The Trial of Dr. Spock* (New York: Vintage, 1970), p. 56; New York Times, January 6, 1968.

56. New York Times, November 23, 1967.

57. New York Times, November 29, 1967.

58. New York Times, December 1, 1967.

59. Francis Biddle, *In Brief Authority* (Garden City: Doubleday, 1962), pp. 151-152.

60. Mitford, op. cit., Foreword.

61. Hoopes, op. cit., p. 224.

62. Press Release, Department of Justice, May 24, 1968.

63. New York Times, May 10, 1968; September 19, 1968.

64. New York Times, June 7, 1969.

65. United States v. O'Brien, 391 U.S. 367 (1968).

270   CRIME, DISSENT, AND THE ATTORNEY GENERAL

66. New York Times, May 19, 1968.

67. Oestereich v. Selective Service System, 393 U.S. 233 (1968).

68. Clark v. Gabriel, 393 U.S. 256 (1968).

69. McKart v. United States, 395 U.S. 185 (1969).

70. Gutknecht v. United States, 90 Sup. Ct. 506 (1970); Washington Post, October 23, 1969; November 21, 1969.

71. Christopher H. Pyle, "CONUS Intelligence: The Army Watches Civilian Politics," Washington Monthly, January, 1970.

72. New York Times, September 22, 1968.

73. Daniel Walker, *Rights in Conflict: A Report Submitted to the National Commission on the Causes and Prevention of Violence* (New York: Signet Books, 1968), pp. xxi-xxii.

74. Ibid., p. 67. See Richard Harris, *Justice: The Crisis of Law, Order, and Freedom in America* (New York: Dutton, 1970), pp. 66-67. and Tom Hayden, "The Trial," Ramparts, July, 1970, p. 27.

75. New York Times, September 19, 1968; December 5, 1968; December 10, 1968.

76. New York Times, September 8, 1968; November 2, 1968.

77. New York Times, December 5, 1968; December 7, 1968; Tom Hayden, *Rebellion and Repression: Testimony before. . .the House Un-American Activities Committee* (New York: Meridian, 1969).

78. U.S. Army Intelligence Command Daily Intelligence Summary No. 9018, January 18, 1969; New York Times, January 19, 1968.

79. Joseph R. Sahid, *Rights in Concord: A Special Staff Study by the Task Force on Law and Law Enforcement*, National Commission on the Causes and Prevention of Violence (Washington: U.S. Government Printing Office, 1969).

80. New York Times, January 22, 1969; New York Post, January 7, 1969.

81. New York Times, September 28, 1969.

82. New York Times, February 16, 1969; February 28, 1969; Washington Post, March 15, 1969.

83. Press Release, Department of Justice, May 1, 1969; Washington Post, May 2, 1969.

84. Washington Post, May 21, 1969; New York Times, May 21, 1969.

85. New York Times, June 14, 1969; Washington Post, June 14, 1969. The General Crimes Section of the Criminal Division reported in 1970: "The year 1969 was the first full year that the Federal antiriot statutes were in effect and Section attorneys reviewed investigation reports of approximately 2,000 possible violations. Section attorneys supervised investigations of possible violations of the antiriot laws on college campuses such as Voorhees College, Brandeis University, Colorado University, Cornell University, Massachusetts Institute of Technology, Howard University and San Francisco State College, during the year." Department of Justice Appropriation for 1971, Hearings before a Subcommittee of the Committee on Appropriations, House of Representatives, 91st Cong., 2nd Sess. (1970), p. 384.

86. Washington Post, February 2, 1970.

87. Washington Post, June 19, 1969; New York Post, September 30, 1969.

88. Washington Post, May 21, 1969; May 23, 1969; New York Times, June 24, 1969.

89. Alderman v. United States, 394 U.S. 165 (1969); Giordano v. United States, 394 U.S. 310 (1969), Justice Stewart, concurring; Washington Post, March 15, 1969.

90. Washington Post, May 31, 1969; New York Times, June 7, 1969.

91. Washington Post, June 5, 1969; June 6, 1969; New York Times, June 5, 1969, July 15, 1969.

92. New York Times, June 14, 1969; Washington Post, June 14, 1969.

93. New York Times, July 22, 1969.

94. Alderman v. United States, 394 U.S. 165, Justices Harlan and Fortas, dissenting in part.

95. New York Times, June 27, 1969.

96. Spock v. United States, ——— F.2d ——— (1st Cir. 1969).

97. Brandenburg v. Ohio, 395 U.S. 444, 447 (1969).

98. Peter Babcock, et al., eds., *The Conspiracy* (New York: Dell, 1969), p. 40.

99. Mark L. Levine, et al., eds., *The Tales of Hoffman* (New York: Bantam, 1970), pp. 257-259.

100. New York Times, October 11, 1969; Washington Post, October 15, 1969.

101. Jonathan Black, "The Expectation of Rising Revolutions," Village Voice, October 16, 1969.

102. Washington Post, October 13, 1969; October 14, 1969; New York Times, October 12, 1969; October 20, 1969.

103. Washington Post, October 31, 1969.

104. New York Times, November 3, 1969; Washington Post, November 4, 1969.

105. Press Release, Department of Justice, November 4, 1969; New York Times, November 5, 1969.

106. Press Release, Department of Justice, November 6, 1969; Washington Post, November 7, 1969; New York Times, November 7, 1969.

107. Washington Post, November 8, 1969; New York Times, November 9, 1969.

108. Frank Mankiewicz and Tom Braden, Washington Post, November 11, 1969; New York Times, November 14, 1969.

109. New York Times, November 11, 1969; November 13, 1969; November 17, 1969; Washington Post, November 11, 1969.

110. Press Release, Department of Justice, November 11, 1969.

111. Copy of memorandum provided by Warren Hoge, White House correspondent of the New York Post, and quoted in part in New York Post, Novebmer 20, 1969. According to Hoge, those who assessed it included Attorney General Mitchell, Deputy Attorney General Kleindienst, Lt. Gen. W. J. McCaffrey, commanding general of the Pentagon's riot-control agency, and F.B.I. and Secret Service Officials.

112. Washington Post, November 13, 1969; New York Times, November 13, 1969.

113. New York Times, November 17, 1969; November 18, 1969; Washington Post, November 17, 1969; November 22, 1969.

114. New York Times, November 19, 1969; Washington Post, November 19, 1969.

115. New York Times, November 22, 1969.

116. Memorandum provided by Warren Hoge, op. cit.

117. New York Times, September 12, 1968.

5. Domestic Intelligence Surveillance

1. Robert H. Jackson, "The Federal Prosecutor," Journal of the American Judicature Society 24:18 (June, 1940).

2. Don Whitehead, *The FBI Story* (New York: Pocket Books, 1958), p. 190.

3. Christopher Pyle, "CONUS Intelligence: The Army Watches Civilian Policits," Washington Monthly, January, 1970, p. 15. See Pyle, "CONUS Revisited: The Army Covers Up," Washington Monthly, July, 1970, p. 58.

4. J. Edgar Hoover, Letter to All Law Enforcement Officials, September 6, 1939.

5. Federal-State Conference on Law Enforcement Problems of National Defense, Proceedings (Washington: Department of Justice, 1940), pp. 3,4,9.

6. Anderson v. Sills, 106 N.J.Super. 545 (Ch.Div. 1969); New York Times, August 27, 1969; September 13, 1969.

7. Anderson v. Sills, Supreme Court of New Jersey, A-79 September Term 1969 (June 1, 1970).

8. 1968 Annual Report of the Attorney General (Washington: Department of Justice, 1968), p. 29.

9. Federal-State Conference, op. cit., p. 6.

10. 1967 Annual Report, pp. 388, 392.

11. Executive Order 10450, 18 Fed. Reg. 2489 (1953). See also Executive Order 9835, 12 Fed. Reg. 1935 (1947).

12. *Report of the Commission on Government Security* (Washington: U.S. Government Printing Office, 1957), p. 654.

13. Interdepartmental Committee on Investigations Pursuant of Public No. 135, Report to the Attorney General (Washington: Department of Justice, June 30, 1942).

14. Chapter 10, United States Code, Sections 331, 332, 333.

15. Anderson v. Sills, Supreme Court of New Jersey, A-79 September Term 1969 (June 1, 1970).

16. 1964 Annual Report, p. 375.

17. New York Times, June 19, 1967.

18. Chapter 18, United States Code, Section 2511.

19. Congressional Record, 90th Cong., 2nd Sess., Vol. 114, p. 14717.

20. New York Times, June 7, 1969; June 19, 1969.

21. New York Times, June 20, 1969; June 21, 1969; Washington Post, June 21, 1969. See also Victor S. Navasky, "The Government and Martin Luther King." *The Atlantic*, November, 1970, pp. 43-52.

22. Washington Post, September 24, 1969.

23. New York Times, June 22, 1969.

24. Commission on Government Security, op. cit., p. 8.

25. Dennis v. United States, 183 F.2d 201,224 (1950).

26. Hoffa v. United States, 385 U.S. 293 (1966).

27. Morris Janowitz, "Patterns of Collective Racial Violence," in Hugh H. Graham and Ted R. Gurr, eds., *Violence in America* (New York: Signet, 1969), p. 414.

28. 1955 Annual Report, p. 93. The F.B.I. included this rare description of its operating procedures in its 1955 report largely in response to criticism that arose when one of its former informants in the Communist Party, Harvey Matusow, claimed he had given false information.

29. President's Commission on Law Enforcement and Administration of Justice, *The Challenge of Crime in a Free Society* (Washington: U.S. Government Printing Office, 1967), p. 199.

30. Jackson, "The Federal Prosecutor," op. cit.

31. Kenneth Culp Davis, *Discretionary Justice: A Preliminary Inquiry* (Baton Rouge: Louisiana State University Press, 1969), p. 59.

32. Department of Justice Appropriations for 1971, Hearings before a Subcommittee of the Committee on Appropriations, House of Representatives, 91st Cong., 2nd Sess. (1970), pp. 274, 405, 464, 754, 780.

33. Screws v. United States, 325 U.S. 91 (1945), dissenting opinion of Justices Roberts, Frankfurter, and Jackson.

6. Conclusion: Federal Justice—Advantages and Risks

1. Lon L. Fuller, *The Morality of Law* (New Haven: Yale University Press, 1964), p. 232.

2. For a contrasting view, see Joseph C. Goulden, "The Cops Hit the Jackpot: Tooling Up For Repression," *The Nation*, November 23, 1970, pp. 520-533.

3. Robert H. Jackson, *The Supreme Court in the American System of Government* (New York: Harper Torchbook, 1963), pp. 70-71.

INDEX

Alcohol and Tobacco Tax Division (Treasury Department): 9, 139-140, 145.

Alderman v. United States: 76-78, 104, 205.

Ali, Muhammed: 205-207, 236.

American Bar Association: 25, 47, 62, 68; criminal justice project: 34-35, 58.

American Civil Liberties Union: 95, 177, 201; on legislation: 23, 75-76, litigation: 20, 30-32, 43, 46, 168, 207-208, 211, 229, 249; Black Panther report: 138, 144-146.

American Law Institute: 34, 39-41, 44, 249.

Antiriot Act of 1968: 93-94, 99, 107-110, 127, 202-203, 223; Chicago conspiracy case: 142, 198-199, 201, 206-207, 210-211, 255.

Army intelligence: 105-106, 112, 179-180, 195-196, 199-200.

Attorney General: 1-2, 5-6, 79, 247-248, 250-253.

Attorney General's Committee on Poverty and the Administration of Federal Criminal Justice: 21, 24-26.

Attorney General's list: 164-165, 231-232.

Bail reform: 25-26, 74.

Berger v. New York: 52, 57-58.

Biddle, Francis: 5-6, 154, 187, 232.

Black Liberation Front: 88, 91, 95-96, 137, 240.

Black Panther Party: 85, 123-133, 135-152, 242.

Blakey, G. Robert: 52, 57-58, 68.

Brandenburg v. Ohio: 133-134, 150, 209.

Brown, H. Rap: 102-104, 126, 151, 237.

Brownell, Herbert: 4-5, 7-8.

Burger, Warren E.: 70-71, 76, 81.

Carmichael, Stokely: 92-94, 102, 104-105, 112-113, 153, 167.

Celler, Emanuel: 62, 94, 99, 168.

Chicago, Illinois: 112, 212, 143-144; 1968 convention: 130, 196-199.

Christopher, Warren: 101, 111-112, 115, 183, 197.

Civil Rights Division: 16, 131-132, 144, 148, 151, 203, 250.

Clark, Ramsey: 5, 9, 12, 48-49, 144; on criminal justice: 41, 53, 55-56, 62-64, 73, 80; on electronic surveillance: 52, 55-58, 60-61, 64, 67, 80, 197, 206, 236-237; on protest: 163, 166, 176-177, 179, 181-189, 196-200, 215, 224-225; on urban violence: 84-85, 99-100, 104-105, 108-111, 113, 117-120, 126, 149-151.

Clark, Tom C.: 5, 12, 19.

Cleveland, Ohio, "shoot-out": 120-122.

Coffin, Rev. William Sloane: 178, 180-181, 186, 209-210.

Commission on Civil Rights: 20-21, 32, 144.

Communist Party: 84-85, 102, 154, 157, 159-160, 165, 168, 185-187, 220-222, 227, 231.

Community Relations Service: 115-116, 122, 131, 148, 151, 196, 250.

Congressional Committees—Appropriations: 242-244; Armed Services: 157-159, 174-176; Internal Security (Un-American Activities): 92-93, 165-166, 173, 199; Judiciary (House): 53, 62, 93-94, 176-177; Judiciary (Senate): 54, 57, 59, 60-61, 75-77, 109-110.

Criminal Division: 139, 149-151, 175, 243, 250.

Dellinger, David: 173, 178-179, 186, 196, 206, 219-222.

274